Early Puerto Rican Cinema and Nation Building

Bucknell Studies in Latin American Literature and Theory

Series editor: Aníbal González, Yale University

Dealing with far-reaching questions of history and modernity, language and selfhood, and power and ethics, Latin American literature sheds light on the many-faceted nature of Latin American life, as well as on the human condition as a whole. This highly successful series has published some of the best recent criticism on Latin American literature. Acknowledging the historical links and cultural affinities between Latin American and Iberian literatures, the series productively combines scholarship with theory and welcomes consideration of Spanish and Portuguese texts and topics, while also providing a space of convergence for scholars working in Romance studies, comparative literature, cultural studies, and literary theory.

Selected Titles in the Series

Rebecca E. Biron, *Elena Garro and Mexico's Modern Dreams*
Persephone Brahman, *From Amazons to Zombies: Monsters in Latin America*
Jason Cortés, *Macho Ethics: Masculinity and Self-Representation in Latino-Caribbean Narrative*
Tara Daly, *Beyond Human: Vital Materialisms in the Andean Avant-Gardes*
Earl E. Fitz, *Machado de Assis and Female Characterization: The Novels*
Earl E. Fitz, *Machado de Assis and Narrative Theory: Language, Imitation, Art, and Verisimilitude in the Last Six Novels*
Naida García-Crespo, *Early Puerto Rican Cinema and Nation Building: National Sentiments, Transnational Realities, 1897–1940*
Thomas S. Harrington, *Public Intellectuals and Nation Building in the Iberian Peninsula, 1900–1925: The Alchemy of Identity*
David Kelman, *Counterfeit Politics: Secret Plots and Conspiracy Narratives in the Americas*
Brendan Lanctot, *Beyond Civilization and Barbarism: Culture and Politics in Postrevolutionary Argentina*
Adriana Méndez Rodenas, *Transatlantic Travels in Nineteenth-Century Latin America: European Women Pilgrims*
Andrew R. Reynolds, *The Spanish American Crónica Modernista, Temporality, and Material Culture*
Elisa Sampson Vera Tudela, *Ricardo Palma's Tradiciones: Illuminating Gender and Nation*
Mary Beth Tierney-Tello, *Mining Memory: Reimagining Self and Nation through Narratives of Childhood in Peru*

Early Puerto Rican Cinema and Nation Building

National Sentiments, Transnational Realities, 1897–1940

NAIDA GARCÍA-CRESPO

Bucknell University | University Press

Lewisburg, Pennsylvania

Cataloging-in-Publication Data available from the Library of Congress

Library of Congress Cataloging in Publication Control Number: 2019012861

A British Cataloging-in-Publication record for this book is available from the British Library.

♾ The paper used in this publication meets the requirements of the American National Standard for Information Sciences—Permanence of Paper for Printed Library Materials, ANSI Z39.48-1992.

www.bucknell.edu/UniversityPress

Distributed worldwide by Rutgers University Press

Manufactured in the United States of America

For my parents, Radamés García Badillo
and Kathleen E. Crespo Kebler

Contents

Early Puerto Rican Cinema and Nation Building

Introduction

A common saying in Puerto Rico categorizes the island as "the oldest colony in the world."[1] Although the validity of this assertion is questionable, Puerto Rico is certainly a very old colony; settled by the Spanish "explorers" (conquistadores) in 1493, and conceded to the United States in 1898, Puerto Rico has never been an independent state. Still, most Puerto Ricans consider themselves members of a separate national entity that securely possesses its own autonomous culture. It is thus culture, and not necessarily political status, that serves as the basis for the concretization of a national Puerto Rican identity.

Puerto Ricans' belief in a unified and independent culture transcends and compensates for any perceived limitation to the identity-construction process stemming from the island's lack of political autonomy. In other words, the constant stream of self-identified Puerto Rican cultural products serves as the rallying point for identity, rather than the nationality inscribed on a legal document like a passport. Still, the fact that in the Puerto Rican case nation and state do not correspond to each other affects the way that Puerto Ricans rhetorically construct themselves as a people. Cinema, as a popular cultural production, can help us navigate and understand the problematic negotiations that arise from the interplay between nation and state in the process of nation building. Discourses surrounding cinema and its categorization as a national product for international consumption point to the nuanced ways through which day-to-day activities and the public sphere construct our identities as national and transnational subjects. Even so, cinema is never a mirror of social reality; rather, like other forms and systems of cultural production, films arise within specific historical contexts and translate a given set of economic and political circumstances and aesthetic practices into a necessarily ideologically inflected text.

In this book I concentrate primarily on the birth of the cinema industry in Puerto Rico and its relationship to the political transition from Spanish to U.S. command; thus, the period I examine extends from 1897 to 1940. I argue that the creation of a separate national identity reached its apex under the first half-century of the American occupation (1898–1952), and that the nascent cinema industry engaged and recorded these nation-building tensions. An ambiguous and somewhat contradictory discourse about sociopolitical inclusion and exclusion with regard to the United States and Spain marked the initial years of U.S. colonization. Under this tension-ridden climate, constructing a national identity meant that would-be citizens struggled to form a nation without having access to or even the possibility of creating a state. Further complications have arisen due to the interweaving of political discourses of nationhood with specific issues of political status in relation to the United States, with contributors to the discussion sometimes assuming that the existence of a national sentiment means a desire for a state or suggesting that the lack of state necessarily entails an incomplete and deformed nation. At this point cinema, as a cultural production, can at least tentatively help us demarcate the contested boundaries between state and nation even if at times they overlap or their borders blur.

For decades, only a few scholars, among them Juan Ortíz Jiménez, José Artemio Torres, and Joaquín "Kino" García, have investigated the early history of cinema in Puerto Rico, and in the process have had to struggle with research obstacles, like the absence of films.[2] The limited scholarship has meant that this important part of Puerto Rican cultural history remains understudied and thus beset with uncertainties and assumptions. However, despite the limitations due to the absence of primary film sources, I conducted a comprehensive study of these cultural productions by looking beyond the films themselves and engaging with the great amount of peripheral materials that are present in Puerto Rican archives and with transnational resources, even if challenging to locate. Through this project, I explore how historical records of the missing films and their reception can retroactively signal an address to viewers and thus point to the audience's identities and issues surrounding the making of the films and their categorization as national products.

Because, as I mentioned earlier, film exhibition came to Puerto Rico, as elsewhere, in the last decade of the nineteenth century, a historical period that coincides with the events of the Spanish-American-Cuban-Filipino War and the transference of colonial government from Spain to the United States, most contemporary discussions addressing early Puerto Rican film history tend to take expressly political turns.[3] That is to say, debates about the introduction of film exhibition and filmmaking to Puerto Rico have focused more on political concerns regarding the colonial relationship of the island to the United States—in both legal and economic terms—than on what exactly makes a national Puerto Rican cinema (with the exception of Kino García's work).[4] The lack of discussion regarding the meaning of a national cinema means that "Puerto Rican cinema" has remained a very elusive term. Scholars have yet to engage in prolonged discussion of what confusedly they refer to when they talk about national Puerto Rican films and their history, with most scholars who write on the subject treating the concept as self-evident and uncontroversial.

Established Frames and Images of Puerto Rican Cinema

In contrast to the comparatively few historians of cinema, numerous Puerto Rican filmmakers and film critics have repeatedly emphasized the need to understand and work toward a national cinema that serves as a cultural ambassador for the island. Director Marcos Zurinaga has written, for example, that "we [Puerto Rican filmmakers] have been influenced by other cultures, but we need to step out of our borders and bring our culture to other countries, value what we are and feel comfortable in our own skin."[5] The statement, while expressing affirmative national cultural politics, begs the question of who exactly are "we" and whether all Puerto Ricans have the same "skin." In other words, if we accept the idea of filmmaking as a form of diplomatic engagement, precisely what image or construction of Puerto Rican identity already is or should be disseminated across the world?

The cultural ambassador model for cinema is problematic because it tends to assume a singular and stable Puerto Rican culture that every Puerto

Rican can clearly recognize and understand as his or her own. The false supposition of a homogeneous culture, in the face of the realities of Puerto Rican racial, cultural, and even geographic diversity, has the perhaps inadvertent effect of delegitimizing many Puerto Rican experiences. As Carlos Pabón has controversially stated, "[T]he neonationalist discourse reduces our nationality to an ethnic (Hispanic) or linguistic (Spanish) essence. It is a discourse that postulates a homogeneous and hispanofilic nationality in a national imaginary that erases the others, eliminates differences and excludes the great majority of Puerto Ricans."[6] In fact, multiple and sometimes even contradictory identities constitute the Puerto Rican nation. The multicultural character of Puerto Rico reveals not only racial and political diversity but also the importance of transnational and cross-cultural exchanges in the making of what we understand today as the Puerto Rican nation. Leaving aside the diverse experiences lived inside the territory of Puerto Rico, we must also consider that Puerto Rico extends well beyond its geographical borders to include diasporic Puerto Rican communities all over the world, but most notably in the United States. Thus, it is impossible to claim that there is a universal and uncontested understanding of what the Puerto Rican nation is—and ought to be.

The vision promulgated to date of a singular, uncontested Puerto Rican cinema exhibits a similar degree of disregard for the lived historical reality of those who might consider themselves Puerto Rican. Nonetheless, I find more troubling than the assumption of a homogeneous identity implied in the cultural ambassador model—which too strictly delineates the parameters of a legitimate national cinema—some scholars' further restriction of "truly" Puerto Rican cinema to productions made in Puerto Rico by Puerto Ricans and for the most part with Puerto Rican capital.[7] This very nationalist rhetoric ignores and denies the influence of global cinemas, like Hollywood, on audiences and filmmakers, and, further, deprives the very substantial numbers of Puerto Ricans living in the United States of any role in the ongoing formation of a national culture, including a so-called national cinema. The homogeneous nationalist model also occludes and invalidates the experiences of other ethnic-cultural communities, like Dominicans, that form such an integral part of the multicultural Puerto Rican society.[8]

Despite this problematic—because arguably xenophobic—definition of Puerto Rican identity and, by extension, of Puerto Rican cinema, the reality is that the unwritten rules of belonging fall quickly at the first opportunity for a "positive appropriation." Thus, Jennifer López (born in New York of Puerto Rican parents), Benicio del Toro (born in Puerto Rico but working in the U.S. industry), and to some even Joaquin Phoenix (born of American missionary parents in Puerto Rico but raised in the United States), can count as belonging to our national cinema in the popular imagination.[9] The degree of a given person's "Puerto Ricanness" inheres, it would seem, in assessment of accomplishment or disgrace. Therefore, singer Marc Anthony (born in New York City) qualifies as a Puerto Rican cultural ambassador, while the acts of José Padilla (sentenced for terrorism in 2007) cannot shame Puerto Rico, for, after all, he never really lived in the island. The ambiguity of Puerto Ricanness, and its relatively easy appropriation or denial, appears to be linked to popular national pride, which clings to and consumes any positive achievement with a trace of Puerto Ricanness. Yet there are also limits to who and what can be appropriated into the national imaginary. For example, most Puerto Rican cinema scholars appear to agree that films produced in or depicting Puerto Rico but that are otherwise "fully American" (that is, when the producer, the director, and the actors were all born or live in the United States) cannot be considered a part of the national cinema "canon."

Notwithstanding such rejection of U.S. capital and producers as possible components of the Puerto Rican cinema industry, one cannot deny the links between the two nations, not only due to the great power of globalization of U.S. culture but also because Puerto Rico, as the 2016 Supreme Court decision in *Puerto Rico v. Sanchez Valle* ratified, is politically subsumed under the United States and therefore compulsorily linked to it. Consequently, the regular disavowal within political and cultural discourses of the international, equated to foreign, means that the division of "us vs. them," in relation to Puerto Rican cinema, applies for the most part only to involvements with the United States. This dichotomy suggests, paradoxically, that precisely its not being American defines Puerto Rican cinema. Therefore, one might point to the practice of filmmakers and film historians defending Puerto Rican productions against the "U.S. threat" while not expressing the same reservations about or sharp delineations against influences—and even capital—from other countries of the world.

Conceptions of the Puerto Rican Nation

Although I have referred to producers and products as Puerto Rican, an internationally recognized Puerto Rican citizenship does not really exist (with Puerto Ricans being internationally recognized as American citizens).[10] Puerto Rican nationality thus tends to be defined mostly in geographical and cultural terms. In the case of industrial development, Puerto Rico also holds a nebulous position inside the U.S. federation. The federal government allows the island certain state liberties in the regulation of local tax laws and industrial incentives, while at the same time significantly controlling Puerto Rican commerce by holding the power to veto any local law and, more concretely, by regulating local ports and consequently the island's capacity to import and export goods.[11] Hence Puerto Rico's perceived cultural independence does not extend to other areas of the island's sociopolitical life. Although Puerto Ricans understand their cultural industries as national industries, in reality U.S. laws regulate them, meaning that Puerto Rican cultural productions resemble more (and face similar challenges to those of) independent U.S. productions rather than those of other national industries.

Despite the limitations of colonial regulations on national productivity and dissemination, the concepts of national culture and national industries can grow as unifying calls against a reality conceived as oppressive. Organizing around an imagined idea of belonging can have potentially beneficial effects in certain contexts, as in dealing with issues of civil rights and liberties. However, as Pheng Chea eloquently states, traditional conceptions of nationalism can also be very oppressive because such conceptions presume a homogenizing national rhetoric into which anyone who would belong must fit, "mak[ing] the enemy indistinguishable from the self."[12] Although I recognize the construct's destructive potential, I still hold that a nation's inhabitants may so vividly imagine and strongly feel its powerful collectivity that they cannot disavow their emotional connection to the nation. Still, to avoid the potential threat of alienation embedded in nationalism, we must conceive the nation as a constant negotiation of a plurality of discourses related to the local and the global; the past, present, and future; and the public and the private. By admitting variation into the conception of the nation, we can open up the space for a discussion of national culture that allows for the existence of multi- and transnationalisms as core components of the nation.

Additionally, because I hold that international relations are extremely important but nuanced power dynamics that affect the construction of the national, throughout this work I employ the terms "global" and "transnational" to convey two different aspects of international exchange. I use the term "global" to refer to products, practices, and trends deployed and consumed in similar ways in different locations. Specifically, I understand global trends as emanating from a metropolitan location with little attention to local social contexts (i.e., the negotiations based on power structures associated with the term "globalization"). Contrastingly, I understand the term "transnational" to mean the dissemination of products and ideas through local networks that transcend national borders. That is, for the purpose of this book, transnational exchanges are rhizomatic, nonhierarchical relations across different local and international subjects.[13]

Cinema's position as both a national and an international product make it particularly important to demarcate the differences between global and transnational networks. Addressing issues of the transnational, specifically in the context of film production, Chris Berry has argued that "the specificity of 'transnational cinema' can be grasped by distinguishing the earlier international order of nation states from the current transnational order of globalization, and that the primary characteristic of 'transnational cinema' can be best understood by examining it as the cinema of this emergent order."[14] However, as I will show throughout this study, Berry's definition, which focuses on contemporary concerns, does not account for the multiple and varied border crossings, appropriations, and settlements that happen in the context of colonization (or other forms of power imbalance), where nation and state do not necessarily correspond. In these long-standing colonial situations, the exchanges between metropolis and colony necessarily affect how the populations of both locales conceive themselves and each other, and their respective cultures. Thus, many of the integration processes associated with globalization took place in colonial spaces even before conceptions of the nation surfaced globally. Hence (post)colonial nations do not necessarily fit into the two world orders that Berry cogently describes.

Certainly transnationalism has dominated as a practice in film production and distribution from its beginning, even though extensive targeted debates about the concept have arisen relatively recently in film studies.[15] In a 2010 article inaugurating the journal *Transnational Cinema*, Will Higbee and Song Hwee Lim define a transnational approach to film studies as one that "does not ghettoize transnational film-making in interstitial and marginal spaces but rather interrogates how these film-making activities negotiate with the national on all levels." They further suggest that "in examining all forms of cross-border film-making activities, [a transnational approach] is also always attentive to questions of postcoloniality, politics and power, and how these may, in turn, uncover new forms of neocolonialist practices in the guise of popular genres or auteurist aesthetics."[16] Higbee and Lim's definition recognizes that the transnational and the national are necessarily linked through the range of cultural and economic relationships that have long defined filmmaking. Similarly, I contend that colonial nationalism, like filmmaking, borrows, appropriates, and redefines international discourses into a new and unique product. For example, as I demonstrate later in chapter 2, an early cinema distributor like the Frenchman Eduardo Hervet, through the distribution and exhibition of actualities that connected film audiences to a global market and archive of representation, influenced the way that multiple nations, from Puerto Rico to Brazil, constructed their industries and their national narratives. Therefore, throughout this project, I seek to demonstrate that at least in colonial contexts, the national and the transnational become so intricately connected in the process of constructing a national culture that delineation between the two becomes impossible.

An Alternative Approach to the Study of Puerto Rican National Cinema

If we understand the nation—because of its inherent plurality of subjects—as constantly changing, we must also acknowledge the impossibility of delineating cultural productions and producers in accordance with some predetermined "national essence." As a response to the challenges of defining the national, as I previously mentioned, I deploy the term "national cinema" in this study in a way that takes into consideration more than geographic and legal definitions of the nation. I specifically understand national cinema as a *transnational web* of discourses about film that shape the way self-identified nationals construct themselves and their culture. Because the nation necessarily exists in an international context, a national cinema is also a form of cultural negotiation between the local and the global, and hence it emanates from the transnational.

Despite our desires to understand our nation as unique and self-determined, definitions of the self ironically rely on others' perceptions of us. Therefore, outside discourses also play a role as significant as the ones that originate from inside the nation. Consequently, my understanding of national cinema draws on Andrew Higson's well-known declaration that "national cinema should be drawn at the site of consumption as much as at the site of productions of films" to claim "foreign" or transnational productions that enter into a dialogue with the Puerto Rican nation as part of that nation's cinema.[17]

Although Puerto Rican national cinema is not particularly unusual, the island's position as a stateless nation means that the European model of the nation, as Eric Hobsbawm explains it, where the creation of the state precedes national consciousness, does not pertain.[18] Of course there are many other national models that do not rely on the state as the generating agent of the nation (with the most famous example being Benedict Anderson's *Imagined Communities*), but in many ways traditional understandings of national cinema have relied on the idea of the state as an integral factor in the existence of a national cinema industry. However, when the nation at hand suffers from the threat or reality of colonialism, national cultural productions (which may receive little political and financial state support) take up symbolic meaning as spaces enabling conscious or unwitting resistance. Moreover, cultural productions acquire even greater value for the process of nation building in the absence of the legally and compulsory unification enforced by the state. Thus, members of a nation that can offer no legal citizenship may hypervalue cultural productions as a way to cement the "imagined community."

Although Hollywood certainly influences most (if not all) national cinemas, in Puerto Rico, the response to U.S. cinema plays an even more pronounced role in defining the forms that the island's cinema has taken. Since the U.S. influence extends well beyond the proliferation of products to include the power to manage legal and economic regulations and policies in Puerto Rico, the United States represents not only the threat of a force controlling the globalized market but also the undeniable colonizing state. In this climate of economic, legal, and cultural colonization, outside representations of the Puerto Rican nation (like those encountered in cultural productions from "Hollywood") become integral parts of the national discourse. I therefore regard it as necessary to discuss a select group of U.S.-made films that represent the island (through plot, characters, or even setting) and that have been appropriated into the nation's cinema history, alongside the discourses about cinema generated inside the geographical confines of Puerto Rico.

Still, my assertion that the United States plays an unquestionable role in the creation of filmic discourses in Puerto Rico does not extend to imply that all Puerto Rican cultural productions seek to engage in a charged discussion about the island's political status. Rather, I point to how the United States as both film producer and political symbol has transformed into the negative against which the conceived "national community" constructs a unified Puerto Rican identity ("we are what we are not"). As political philosopher Wayne Norman argues, "nationalism sometimes precedes national-self-determination-seeking because . . . the national self has to be created, nurtured, shaped, and motivated. People who previously thought of themselves as having various sorts of identities . . . have to be convinced, perhaps over generations, that their primary identity is as a member of this particular nation."[19] In my study, I thus define Puerto Rican national cinema as the collection of film discourses that help us imagine and construct an independent (but not internationally isolated) Puerto Rican culture. Although I argue for this inclusive understanding of national cinema, I do not suggest that it is the only or "right" way to understand Puerto Rican cinema. I simply offer an alternative understanding to the way critics have traditionally discussed this national cinema as a way to engender new perspectives on the subject.

I should note that my approach is also novel in how I analyze primary texts because almost all of the presently identified early Puerto Rican film productions have disappeared, leaving only second-hand accounts of their existence. This lack of primary materials makes close readings of the film texts impossible and therefore requires a different methodological approach. Fortunately, the absence of primary materials does not mean that we cannot properly study or compile a compelling history of Puerto Rican cinema. Notwithstanding the absence of surviving early films on celluloid, I reconstruct from the ample records documenting the discourses surrounding film production and consumption (e.g., publicity and criticism as well as reports on the films' distribution and reception) the impact of cinema at a historical moment, including its effect on the processes of national identity formation.

I study early Puerto Rican cinema as having engaged in "conversations" with intellectual, economic, political, and historical trends to demonstrate the significance of artistic and film industrial rhetorical practices in the formation of the nation. Though Puerto Rican intellectuals have long considered other cultural productions like literature and journalism as integral to the formation of Puerto Rican identity, cinema has not received such recognition. Because of the relative silence surrounding Puerto Rican cinema history we need to uncover, rediscover, and decode the archive. I aim to address the "absent presences" in Puerto Rican cinema history by analyzing the important role elites have exerted in defining the nation and by bringing to light what has traditionally been kept invisible: the power struggle between elites, popular sectors, and the colonial power, which framed and molded Puerto Rican national identity.[20]

Consequently, to understand the complexities of the conception of the Puerto Rican nation, I address a range of films and filmmakers, mainly through analysis of promotional writing and critical works about films made both in and outside of Puerto Rico from 1897 to 1940 that signal (or conceal) in some significant way the island through, for example, connections of geography, theme, and/or production group. I look in particular at the discursive practices apparent in cinema-related materials and their engagement in the public conception and construction of the Puerto Rican nation. Because cinema mixes business with art, it allows for a survey of the integration of two very different rhetorical practices. Further, cinema offers the opportunity to study the conjunction of two distinct aspects of the construction of the nation often thought incongruous: the economic and the cultural.

This Study's Framework

I begin this book by providing a survey of crucial Puerto Rican economic, political, and cultural circumstances from the turn of the twentieth century through World War II. In order to provide this overview, chapter 1 focuses primarily on the transition from Spanish to American colonial rule, and that shift's contribution to shaping Puerto Rican identity and the conception of the nation. The second chapter presents my methodological approach. This chapter, which covers the period from 1897 to 1908, focuses on the first cinematic encounters in Puerto Rico. Here I explore how a more transnationally conscious approximation to the archives, as well as to film subjects, can help us elucidate previous historiographic absences. Chapter 2 also addresses the impact of outside discourses (particularly colonialist ones) on the process of nation building.

Following these introductory discussions I continue to analyze three major phases in early filmmaking in Puerto Rico that continue to influence the way local producers and critics undertake and understand cinema. The first phase, stretching roughly from 1910 to 1920, was defined by autonomous filmmakers trying to captivate local audiences by appealing to a national sense of duty (chapters 3 and 4). Rafael Colorado and later the Tropical Film Company, as well as critics discussing their works, made claims about the appeal of their productions based on local specificity at the same time that they appropriated global trends (like the genre of melodrama), and negotiated for products and audiences in outside markets. The chapters in this section discuss how filmmakers in the 1910s adopted a discursive position that highlighted nationalist elements in their works and that stressed the potential of films to carry abroad a particular (i.e., positive or civilized) representation of the island and its citizens. However, this nationalist rhetoric also occluded the many business and artistic relations that these filmmakers had in the United States and other Caribbean nations and that had helped to shape their vision of national culture.

The second phase (chapter 5), lasting most of the 1920s, involved a shift in the way that local agents approached the pre-production and production process, with a new focus on attracting foreign capital. During this period the island's cinema infrastructure advanced significantly with the development of a movie studio in San Juan, which attracted U.S.-based production companies like MacManus/Pathé and Famous Players-Lasky/Paramount to make films in Puerto Rico. In this chapter I argue that the involvement of American capital and talent in the development of Puerto Rican filmmaking posed a direct challenge to the previous conceptions of cinema made on the island as a "truthful" or authentic representative of Puerto Rican culture and identity. Nonetheless, local critics appropriated these U.S. productions and coproductions (which were replete with orientalist tropes) as Puerto Rican, transforming them into transnational works that could simultaneously speak to both local and U.S. desires and shape conceptions of the Caribbean and the tropics more generally.

In the third and last phase of early Puerto Rican filmmaking (chapter 6), lasting from the late 1920s to 1940, filmmakers reaffirmed the national through the use of transnational resources (including capital and artistic talent). Throughout this chapter I contend that the filmmakers working during this period embraced the transnational elements of filmmaking (such as production and distribution networks) as a means of advancing the island's cinema and making it sustainable. During the 1930s, the island's entrepreneurial filmmakers struggled with heavy costs and a small market. They sought both to please a local critical elite that craved everything national and to market their Spanish-language products as fulfilling an international need for films in local languages, thus having international appeal and the potential for global distribution in Hispanic markets in and outside the United States. Regardless of the level of success that these filmmakers had in defining and exporting the nation, their works stand as enlightening examples of the limitations of understanding national cinema and culture as strictly local and insulated phenomena.

This book addresses as its overarching subject the complex relations linking nation, state, and identity through a case study of Puerto Rico and its cinema. Focusing on a specific historical cinema as a form of cultural community building enables me to explore the problematic aspects of defining something or someone as "national." I argue, specifically, that this nation-building process is particularly difficult in a context where the population understands the national as being in danger of disappearing, given the lack of a state to protect it, especially in an international context. By closely examining how, in one historical instance, cultural productions made in the absence of a state have helped to form and maintain a national identity, I aim to address the historiographic paradox, even predicament, of the vital roles that both the state and the international arena play in the conception and experience of the national.

1

Contexts for a National Cinema

Cultural, Political, and Economic Movements in Puerto Rico (1860–1952)

The period that I study in this book represents a crucial moment in Puerto Rican political history: the transition from a Spanish to an American colonial government. This transition encompassed more than a geographic shift in the colonial metropolis; it signaled economic and cultural changes as well. The far-reaching cultural transformations were accompanied by discourses regarding the "nature" of the nation that to this day influence the way intellectuals approach Puerto Rican nationalism. As I will show in this chapter, intellectuals have constructed the Puerto Rican nation primarily around one key late nineteenth-century political event: the Spanish-American-Cuban-Filipino War and its aftermath. In turn, this political approach has marked the way scholars and critics interpret and categorize cultural productions, making the definition of "Puerto Ricanness" tightly tied to the concept of nation building.

The year 1898 represents a collective trauma of the Puerto Rican nation that it refuses to overcome. For, as Rubén Ríos Ávila contends, "coloniality is our [Puerto Ricans'] perverse love story, the master, the empire, the Other of our erotic tale," from whom we must symbolically divorce.[1] Although I agree with Ríos Ávila's analysis, I consider talking about the fraught political relationship as a fundamental way of healing the historical trauma. Nonetheless, such a healing process is complicated because it entails contextualizing and decoding the unresolved tension between the ever-present nation and the absent state. As Carlos Pabón has controversially indicated, intellectual elites have overexposed and commoditized so much the concept of nation in Puerto Rico that it has lost its meaning, and nationalism has become another product for sale.[2] Even though I do not fully agree with Pabón's assessment, I cannot deny that the Puerto Rican nation has gone through a process of commodification. However, I see these exaggerated outward expressions of nationalism as the day-to-day tools of Puerto Ricans for dealing with the ambiguity of having a nation without the presence (or even the possibility) of an autonomous state. So much academic discussion of the nation has relied on the term's presumed relationship to that of "state"—even if we constantly proclaim their difference—that we have forgotten what it is like to experience them as truly separate. With the following cultural–historical analysis I position the trauma of 1898 not as a residual trauma of coloniality per se but instead as the trauma of trying to understand the "insufferable ambiguity" (to use Pabón's term) of the nation that lacks a state. Furthermore, I argue that this national sociopolitical ambiguity has marked the way that Puerto Rican scholars define and defend the concept of an autonomous culture and of a national cinema more specifically.

Late Spanish Colonialism through 1898

Many Puerto Rican historians (e.g., Picó, Scarano, and Rosario) argue that we must understand 1898 in the international context of the widespread turmoil for political independence in the nineteenth-century Americas.[3] Following the outburst of the Latin American wars of independence (1808–1833), Spain increasingly relied economically on its Caribbean and Pacific colonies. As a consequence of the loss of territories, Spain increased taxes and established greater restrictions on areas still under its control, for example, limiting imports to the island colonies from places other than Spain in order to protect the peninsular market.[4] In the Caribbean, the dissatisfaction among both the Cuban and the Puerto Rican elites with the Spanish government grew to the point of revolutionary outburst in the fall of 1868. The Cuban "grito de Yara" (cry of Yara) in October of that year initiated what academics now refer to as the Ten Year War, the first of four wars that Cuba fought with Spain in the last half of the nineteenth century (which culminated with the Spanish-American-Cuban-Filipino War and the final independence of Cuba). Earlier that same fall, and in conjunction with the Cuban revolution, a small elite sector in Puerto Rico revolted against the colonial government in what the insurgents called "el grito de Lares" (the cry of Lares).[5] Although the Spanish government was not able to suppress the Cuban revolt completely, the 1868 revolt in Lares lasted only two days.

Even though the Lares revolt did not gain the support that its planners hoped for, the event became crucial in the discourse of Puerto Rican nationality formulated in later years. The failed attempt became in the Puerto Rican nationalist imaginary of later generations a mythical defining event, and its participants became heroes in the defense of a nascent Puerto Rican identity. For example, a leading figure in the Lares revolt, Eugenio María de Hostos, exerts ongoing influence over how twenty-first-century Puerto Rican intellectuals conceive the nation: as fundamentally Hispanic and geographically defined, despite decades of U.S. colonization and migration. Known as "el ciudadano de América" (the citizen of the Americas), Hostos believed that the Caribbean region (more specifically, Cuba, Puerto Rico, and the Dominican Republic) should form a political alliance—a Caribbean Confederation—to protect the interest of the "criollo" population against colonial powers like Spain. Hostos's "dream" of a free and united Hispanic Caribbean can still be found in pro-independence discourses that highlight the disadvantages of purportedly losing Caribbean camaraderie by becoming part of the United States.[6]

Moreover, part of the fascination with the cry of Lares in political and historical discourses comes from the perception that dissatisfaction among local elites increased after the failed battle. Even though the discontent of most landed elites did not come from any personal investment they had in the Lares revolt, the historical records—particularly newspaper columns—show that many were indeed unhappy with the colonial government.[7] In addition, historical records demonstrate that this dissatisfaction surfaced because instead of enacting social and economic reforms to guarantee the loyalty of its remaining colonies, Spain continued to ignore the complaints of the local landed sectors, which demanded more representation in their local governments and the peninsular one as well. When eventually, in 1894, Spain promised reform, the response came too late.

Prior to the 1868 revolutionary attempts in Puerto Rico and Cuba, the United States had in 1823 proclaimed the Monroe Doctrine, which threatened military retaliation if any European nation tried to interfere in North and South America. In 1895, Great Britain first tested the Doctrine's consequences in what historians now denote as the "Venezuelan Crisis," a conflict that set the stage for the United States to target Spain's New World claims.[8] Following the American Revolution, the U.S. expansionist drive had led to the Louisiana Purchase, the Annexation of Texas, the Oregon Treaty, the Mexican-American War, the Alaska Purchase, and, in 1893, the Hawaiian coup d'état that culminated in annexation in 1898. Given Cuba's proximity to the Florida Keys, the United States had particular interest in its political development; hence the island's political instability in the last half of the nineteenth century proved advantageous for its northern neighbor.

As is well known, the sinking of the USS *Maine* stationed in the Havana Harbor in 1897 served the United States as a historically contested justification to confront Spain, but violence in both Cuba and the Philippines had established the basis for the conflict long before that event. The Spanish-American-Cuban-Filipino War officially began in Cuba in the spring of 1898 and spread to Puerto Rico by the summer of that year. Although the acquisition of Puerto Rico does not seem to have been a main objective for the U.S. government, that outcome of the conflict was certainly well received, for Puerto Rico's geographic position provided a much-needed locale for storing coal and monitoring the entrance of ships into the Americas. In addition, already by 1890 the United States was the primary market for both Cuban and Puerto Rican sugar, even surpassing Spain.[9] With sugar cane as its main crop, Cuba soon became economically dependent on the U.S. market. If one also considers the mythical status that the United States held as a defender of "freedom" after its successful revolution, it should come as no surprise that the revolutionary elites in both Cuba and Puerto Rico sought U.S. support in resolving their problems with Spain. The local elites knew that they would find U.S. support for their revolutions because many American entrepreneurs had economic interests in the area; moreover, the newspaper coverage of the events suggests that the popular discourse propagated in the United States throughout the course of the Spanish-American-Cuban-Filipino War favored the delivery of Pan-American support.

Despite the idealized vision of the brotherhood between Cuba and Puerto Rico, historical facts show that their economic and political circumstances were extremely different by the turn of the century.[10] Although Puerto Rico also produced sugar, by the late nineteenth century, coffee was its most profitable crop.[11] A more expensive product than that consumed by most Americans at the time, Puerto Rican–produced coffee found its primary markets in European nations, where the Puerto Rican type of bean was in high demand. For the most part, while the coffee plantations in the mountains thrived, the sugar plantations along the Puerto Rican coast were unprofitable.[12] The two colonies also differed in that the powerful Cuban revolutionary movement met with skepticism in Puerto Rico regarding its effectiveness for politico-economic change. Furthermore, the strict press censorship Spain exercised in Puerto Rico kept most residents ignorant of the proceedings in Cuba.[13] Instead of armed conflict as occurred in Cuba, Puerto Rican political elites promoted a more peaceful approach to change, demanding a gradual governmental move toward autonomy, a strategy that by the end of the nineteenth century appeared to have brought results. However, despite the delayed Spanish action toward granting Puerto Rico autonomy, dissatisfaction with the colonial government persisted by the end of the nineteenth century, resulting in a low level of Puerto Rican "loyalty" toward Spain during the war.

Circumstances and Consequences of the U.S. Invasion

The neglectful practices of the Spanish administration throughout their colonization of Puerto Rico were a key factor enabling the American invasion to proceed rather "easily" as a "splendid little war," as U.S. ambassador John Hay described it. The campaign in Puerto Rico lasted only one month and resulted in few casualties, for as historian Fernando Picó argues, the natives met the American action for the most part with cunning indifference.[14] Even so, despite the war's short duration and few casualties, the events of 1898 have become in the Puerto Rican imaginary a wound that refuses to heal. At the same time, the imagination of later generations has transformed the loyalists who decided to fight for the Spanish colonial power into heroes of the nascent Puerto Rican nation. Nonetheless, this pro-Spain (as nationalist) position is filled with contradictions given that fighting in the war on the side of Spain would still have represented a pro-colonial stance. However, we must understand that the pro-Spain discourse of later generations actually relates to the larger trend in Puerto Rican nationalism toward hispanofilia. Hispanofilia evidently arose among Puerto Ricans subsequent to 1898 because the scars of that year are not really a product of the war itself but of the social changes that came as a result of the new colonial power's desire to culturally assimilate the Puerto Rican population. Elite intellectuals responded to the almost immediate forceful cultural assimilation with a withdrawal into the immediate past and hence linked resistance and Puerto Ricanness to Spanishness.

Because intellectuals throughout the years have continued to define Puerto Rican identity as fundamentally Spanish, later generations construed the absence of a bloody war as some sort of fault in the Puerto Rican character. For writers like René Marqués, the dearth of bellicosity became a sign of weakness and a signifier of lack and incompleteness in the process of nation building. Academics Luce and Mercedes López Baralt point out that "we Puerto Ricans remain nostalgic for heroism, for an honorable foundational myth on which to rest our retrospective historic gaze."[15] For those scholars there is no clearer evidence of this violent lack than the events that unfolded after the publication of Luis López Nieves's "Seva."[16] The story of the U.S. Army's massacre of the revolting town of Seva first appeared in the leftist newspaper *Claridad* in December 1983 without any reference to its fictional nature and was taken by many as an actual historical finding. Later the newspaper released a note clarifying the story's fictional nature, but still some nationalist groups proclaim its validity—if not in terms of historical facts then at least in the form of a mythical cultural imaginary. Nonetheless, the myth of violent resistance that the fictional Seva proposes relies heavily on an idea of loyalty toward another colonial metropolis, Spain. Author López Nieves's position also assumes that the only legitimate form of nation building is the one that results from great bloodshed, and that peaceful negotiations are a dishonest and incomplete form of nation building that would betray a nationalistic project.

Given its adherence to a Spanish-centered vision of history, Seva does not bespeak distinctly contemporary concerns about identity but rather in effect extends the hispanicist political–cultural tradition initiated by intellectuals like Luis Muñoz Rivera, Luis Lloréns Torres, and Nemesio Canales at the beginning of the twentieth century. However, although many turn-of-the-century intellectuals took this position, the defense of Spanishness neither encompassed the whole of the population nor represented a desire to resubmit to Spanish domination. Instead, the hypervalorization of Spain demonstrates the absence, to that point, of a strong, independent Puerto Rican identity and the rise of Puerto Ricanness as a response to Americanness. Fernando Picó contends that at the end of the century, unlike elites, common Puerto Ricans did not seem to care much about who ruled, for most were too sick and hungry to defend a colonial government that had done nothing for them and that now was asking them to defend a supposed (abusive) "mother country."[17]

In fact, at the beginning of the American colonial period in Puerto Rico, intellectual elites seemed optimistic regarding the new government.[18] But that optimism proved short lived because of social reforms that mostly benefited the absent state. After signing the 1898 Treaty of Paris, the United States, in opposition to the expectations of Puerto Rican capitalists, refused to freely open its market to Puerto Rican crops and continued to treat and tax Puerto Rican goods as foreign.[19] Another blow to the Puerto Rican economy that created political discontent came from the rapid change from the peso to the dollar with an exchange rate of sixty cents for every peso, which meant a significant devaluation of the country's riches. Finally, the U.S. government denied Puerto Ricans the opportunity to democratically elect their governor, reserving for the American president the right to choose this high official. As we can now appreciate, these policies deeply disappointed the Puerto Rican political leaders who had assumed that the United States would offer more economic and political freedoms than Spain. These shifts in response to the U.S. occupation bear great significance for present-day nationalist political figures and academics who tend to look at those who promoted an active relationship with the United States in subsequent years (like Luis Muñoz Marín) as shameful betrayers of the nation.[20]

Certainly, at the beginning of the twentieth century, the United States introduced extremely controversial social reforms that generated debate and resistance, particularly among the elite class, and that greatly influenced the construction of a Puerto Rican identity. One of the most notorious policies—and an issue to this day—was the implementation of English as the official language for both instruction and legal proceedings. Four hundred years of Spanish colonialism had made Spanish the native language of most of the Puerto Rican population. Thus, the quick implementation of English met with great resistance, not only because of its impracticality but also because only a very select group of people knew the language and benefited greatly from this advantage.[21] This particular colonial policy (the enforcement of the English language) illustrates the ramifications of the situation of nation and state not corresponding to each other (i.e., the disconnection between their needs). Of course Spanish colonialism had already forcefully implemented a language in 1493, but at that time notions of nationhood as we understand them today had not yet arisen, further complicating a retroactive understanding of the Spanish language and Puerto Rican nationalism.[22] That is, by the end of the nineteenth century, just when a distinct Puerto Rican national consciousness started to grow, the American invasion changed the course of that formation, muddling the creation of antagonisms, identifications, and definitions that were emerging in the process of nation building. Because the Spanish language was the one cultural practice shared by the entire Puerto Rican population across class lines, its use became one of the defining aspects of Puerto Rican identity from early in the U.S. occupation. The U.S. state's removal by fiat of this cornerstone of identity resulted inadvertently in the increased significance of the Spanish language (and "Spanishness" more generally) for Puerto Ricans.

In practice, although the law stated that instruction had to be delivered in English, very few teachers and students actually spoke the language in school, creating a disjunction between the English textbooks provided by the government and class discussions—and therefore diminishing the effectiveness of instruction.[23] However, the question of English- versus Spanish-language instruction bore importance beyond pedagogical concern; it brought into focus the possible role of the state in relation to national/identity matters. For example, to this day we can still hear some intellectuals proclaim that one of the greatest sign of resistance to U.S. colonialism is that Puerto Ricans, more than a hundred years after the U.S. occupation, still speak Spanish. What is more, in addition to pointing to the use of Spanish as an instance of resistance, some intellectuals heighten the significance of this position by looking to the past to show that "foundational patriots" made the same analysis years ago. For instance, Luis E. Agrait declares, "[T]wo years before his death, Luís Muñoz Rivera wrote that in Puerto Rico 'the Latin soul and the Castilian language will last as long as the waters of the Caribbean sea and the rocks of the Yunque mountain.' The Caribbean and the Yunque are still there . . . and the Latin soul and the Spanish language are still there as well."[24] As these lines reveal, the Spanish language serves as a reason for and defense of a Latinx identity that many interpret as threatened by the close relationship between Puerto Rico and the United States.

In 1993, when then governor Pedro Rosselló repealed the law that proclaimed Spanish as the official language of Puerto Rico and instituted English as a co-official language, protesters centered their claims on the importance of Spanish as a mark of identity, as can be evidenced in one of their most popular slogans, "¡viva la ñ, coño!"[25] Although Rosselló's new language law passed (making English a co-official language through the present), the language debate is still very much alive. Furthermore, the addition of English as an official language unleashed a new flood of defense for the Spanish language as evidenced in the Universidad del Sagrado Corazón's 1995 campaign "idioma defectuoso, pensamiento defectuoso," which aimed at substituting the proper Spanish for English phrases commonly used by Puerto Ricans.[26] However, while one can understand this purist position regarding language and language use as a reaction to a colonial status that persists without resolution, it also ignores the transnational reality of Puerto Rico, for millions of Puerto Ricans now live in the United States and use English as their primary language of communication.[27]

The forced implementation of English as the official language in the early twentieth century was not the only U.S. colonialist action following annexation that deeply affected Puerto Ricans' lives and their construction of a shared national identity. American capitalists interested in sugar also proceeded to restructure the island as a single-crop economy based on sugar cane.[28] By 1905 three major U.S. corporations took control of Puerto Rican sugar production: the South Porto Rico Sugar Company, the Fajardo Sugar Company, and the Central Aguirre Syndicate. These corporations represented absentee capital because their primary offices where outside the island, and the majority of their stockholders did not live in Puerto Rico.[29] Since by the end of the nineteenth century the coffee planters of the mountains were the most powerful landed "criollos," the shift away from coffee production not only stripped the locals of their political influence but also made their lands worthless under the new economy, given that sugar cane cannot be effectively cultivated in place of coffee in the mountainous terrain. César Ayala and Rafael Bernabe's research has shown that "between 1900 and 1910, sugar production grew 331 percent," meaning that under the American occupation sugar had effectively supplanted coffee as the most powerful industry on the island.[30]

As already mentioned, the introduction of U.S. capital precipitated the rise of sugar production in the form of four large plantations that covered most of the Puerto Rican territory: Central Aguirre (in Salinas), Central Guánica (the biggest in the country), Central Fajardo, and the conglomerate of the United Porto Rico Sugar Company (owning lands in Caguas, Juncos, Humacao, and Cayey). The significant increase in the number of sugar plantations accordingly changed the way most workers lived. Previously, workers would live inside the grounds of the coffee plantations (sometimes sugar plantations as well) and had a plot of land for personal farming, but U.S.-owned sugar plantations, to increase profit, relied instead on seasonal workers who did not (and could not) own or farm the small plot of land on which they lived.[31] Furthermore, because sugar is a seasonal crop, the time in which the sugar cane grew—known as "tiempo muerto" (dead time)—required no workers, leaving most of the population without a source of income between the twice-annual harvests.[32]

Initial U.S. Congressional Rule and the Formation of Puerto Rican Identity

By 1900 the United States had supplanted its military government of Puerto Rico with the introduction of the first organic law, the Foraker Act, which allowed for a civilian government appointed by the president of the United States. Despite its clear colonial nature, the Foraker Act also allowed for the creation of a local House of Representatives and the appointment of a Resident Commissioner to Washington, D.C., both elected by Puerto Rican men.[33] The Foraker Act also created and bestowed Puerto Rican citizenship on all those born in Puerto Rico. Although the creation of this citizenship might seem like a move toward autonomy, in effect this citizenship was devoid of any specified rights and was not internationally recognized, meaning that de facto Puerto Ricans possessed no citizenship.[34]

The most popular party in Puerto Rico at the time, the Partido Unión, favored the maintenance of the Puerto Rican citizenship (despite its clear flaws) over the acquisition of the American one. They argued against the imposition of an American citizenship because they believed that this citizenship would effectively reinforce Puerto Rico's status as a colony. However, the Partido Unión also fiercely criticized the Foraker Act because of its antidemocratic nature and called for its reform. Looking to cement U.S. claims over Puerto Rico, in March 1917 President Woodrow Wilson officialized the second organic law, the Jones Act. This law allowed for the extension (without consultation) of American citizenship to all Puerto Ricans. It also introduced the creation of a second legislative group, the Senate, elected by Puerto Rican men. Despite these changes, the law also stipulated that the president of the United States still held the power to assign a governor and could veto any law approved by the Puerto Rican government.

More important to this study, the Jones Act of 1917 established the basis for the problematic identity politics of Puerto Ricanness. This Act served as the first major instance of the inclusion/exclusion (nation/state) paradox that dominates Puerto Rican political discourses. On the one hand, the Jones Act allowed for an inclusion of Puerto Ricans in the international sphere by providing a much needed citizenship status—albeit one not chosen by Puerto Ricans themselves. On the other hand, it left the definition of that citizenship unresolvably ambiguous. Yes, Puerto Ricans were now considered Americans, but they did not have the right to choose the president of their newly assigned state. Further, the U.S. Congress did not extend the majority of states' rights to Puerto Rico; hence the U.S. federal government maintained control over fiscal and economic issues, as well as immigration and defense matters. In addition, the timing of the implementation of the act in March 1917 seems to indicate—as many have noted—that the U.S. government awarded Puerto Ricans American citizenship because the United States was about to enter World War I.[35]

Independent of their political leanings, most Puerto Rican historians today argue that the passing of the Jones Act had much to do with the need for wartime loyalty. What fuels this understanding is that in May 1917, just two months after the signing of the Jones Act by President Wilson, the Selective Service Act of 1917 (which had originally been envisioned as early as December 1916) extended conscription to the new Puerto Rican–American citizens. Historical discourses linking the two events have given rise to the conclusion that the U.S. government did not grant American citizenship due to any democratic conceptions of freedom and anticolonialist principles, but rather out of self-interest. Thus, in the 1910s, politicians in Puerto Rico saw American citizenship as a bittersweet achievement. On the one hand, some celebrated citizenship as it allowed Puerto Ricans increased movement both inside and outside the United States. Yet, since Puerto Rican–American citizens were denied representation in the federal government, the politicians by and large criticized the act of designating Puerto Ricans as Americans as an instance of hypocrisy (contradicting while ostensibly upholding the U.S. government's rhetoric of equality).

Juxtaposing the issues of citizenship with the economic and social reforms that the U.S. government implemented in the early twentieth century makes clear the extent to which Puerto Rican identity then stood at a crucial and problematic stage of development. I contend that this problematic national identity development resulted from the abrupt social changes occurring at the time, which yielded a sense of nation based on belonging or not belonging, both to the Spanish Empire and to the United States. Hence Puerto Rican identity did not emerge through the historically conventional colonial opposition to the metropolis but rather through a negotiation between opposition and alignment with two colonial powers, or what Arcadio Díaz Quiñones has called "el arte de bregar."[36] This peculiar identity process manifested itself in a divided alliance of cultural Hispanophilia and economic Americanophilia. In literary, political, and popular discourses of the period (and still to this day), we see simultaneous criticism and idealization of both the Spanish colonial past and the American colonial present. More specifically, these discourses encompass both a defense of Spanish culture and a desire for a privileged position in the U.S. markets.

The abrupt change of social circumstances early in the twentieth century that I have discussed so far soon invited extensive sociological analysis that aimed to understand the "nature" or "character" of the Puerto Rican subject, particularly in relation to turn-of-the-century political changes. One such study, Antonio S. Pedreira's *Insularismo*, one of the most influential works on Puerto Rican identity, first appeared in 1934. In this work, Pedreira argues that an identity crisis resulting from the mixing of races (Taíno, African, and Spanish) and an insular confinement that prevented interaction with other influential nations (particularly in Latin America) thwarted Puerto Rico's development. In addition, the author contends that the change in colonial government created a marked disjunction between the traditions of Spanish humanism and the practices of U.S. capitalism. As Luis Felipe Díaz explains, Pedreira considered the transformation of the academic and economic elite necessary to solve this crisis, through their "adoption of a Puerto Rican subjectivity that would be in synch with a past literary heritage, but which would also enable them to face the civilizing modernity about to come."[37] In Pedreira's view, in 1930, Puerto Rico had not yet achieved a sense of nationhood but was also somewhat contradictorily undergoing a crisis of identity. Like Arcadio Díaz Quiñones has more recently formulated, Pedreira's study considers the privileged year of 1898 as making "neither the testimony of the destruction, nor the redemption of a culture, but rather its possible transformation."[38] In other words, Pedreira argues that the radical politico-economic changes that the nation underwent at the time both defined and challenged what Puerto Rico could and should become.

However, while Pedreira's work still serves as a starting point in most discussions of Puerto Rican identity (e.g., René Marqués's *El puertorriqueño dócil* or José Luis González's *El país de cuatro pisos*), most current scholars understand his analysis as marked by racist and classist assumptions that nonetheless are still prevalent in Puerto Rico.[39] In his 1979 Marxist study of *Insularismo*, Juan Flores locates Pedreira's prejudices within the context of contemporary writers like José Vasconcelos and José Enrique Rodó. Flores argues that all these writers understood race as a decisive and essentialist factor, and furthermore, that—with the exception of Vasconcelos—they all considered indigenous and African races to be inferior to Europeans (particularly the Spanish).[40] In addition, Flores sees Pedreira as an aristocratic writer who had marked content for the masses; according to him, Pedreira's "ideal of the 'national culture' rested resolutely in the ideological supremacy of the local bourgeoisie, which frequently disdained the alleged polluting influence of the popular culture."[41] Flores's analysis of *Insularismo* reveals that, in Puerto Rico, the first conceptions of the national surfaced from an elitist and defensive definition of culture.

Puerto Rican Conceptions of the Nation from 1930 Onward

Pedreira's contemporary Pedro Albizu Campos, another important figure for Puerto Rican nationalism, emerged in the 1930s as the leading representative of the Nationalist Party. His turbulent relationship with U.S. authorities has earned him a high position in the "pantheon" of Puerto Rican patriot martyrs. Notwithstanding (and evidently prior to the development of) the anti-American politics for which he is popularly known, Albizu won a scholarship to the University of Vermont in 1912 and subsequently transferred to Harvard University, where in 1921, after returning from serving in the military during World War I, he earned a law degree. By the time Albizu returned to Puerto Rico in 1922, he had come to know and seemed to have been greatly influenced by Irish nationalists.[42] He officially entered Puerto Rican politics with the Partido Unión, which primarily espoused autonomy. After some disagreements around forming an alliance with the Socialist Party, he left the Partido Unión and joined the Nationalist Party. According to historians César Ayala and Rafael Bernabe, the leadership of the Nationalist Party did not initially approve of Albizu (who was biracial) due to racial prejudice, but in 1930 nonetheless elected him president of the Party.[43]

More than in any concrete action, the influence of Albizu Campos for Puerto Rican politics lies at the level of rhetoric. As Díaz Quiñones indicates, "the messianic aura of Albizu, at the same time radical and conservative, contributed to changing the way that Puerto Ricans think of themselves," for Albizu introduced the idea of sacrifice for the homeland—"la patria es valor y sacrificio"—and of self-determination through action, which was virtually absent from political rhetoric at the time.[44] If Albizu did not himself create the idea, he has certainly come to exemplify the concept of dichotomous delineation between being Puerto Rican and being American. Indeed, Albizu's designation of anyone who politically negotiates with the United States and does not declaim independence as a national traitor has for years been a central claim of the Nationalist Party and the Partido Independentista Puertorriqueño (PIP). To this day, avid defenders of the Puerto Rican nation recite Albizu's speech after the 1932 elections: "the supreme definition is on the table: either Yankees or Puerto Ricans. Traitors, construct your bleak legion under the evocative bars of the imprisonment in which you live; Patriots, enter the redemptive nationalism" ("Está sobre el tapete la suprema definición: o yanquis o puertorriqueños. Los traidores formen su legión desoladora bajo las franjas sugerentes del encarcelamiento en que viven; los patriotas ingresen en el nacionalismo redentor"). Such declarations stand in contrast to practice; for example, important members of the Nationalist Party like Juan Antonio Corretjer lived for years in the United States. The choice of residence of some of the nationalists throughout the past decades suggests that they did or do not base the dichotomy between Puerto Ricans and Americans on geographic essentialist visions but instead on a formulation of constructed identity politics. This group formulated national identity mainly around a defense of an idealized agrarian, Spanish, and Catholic past and in opposition to an industrialized, exploitative, and Protestant American present.

I must note, however, that Albizu attained his very significant popularity in part due to the violent events known as the "masacre de Rio Piedras" and the "masacre de Ponce" as well as due to the many years that he himself spent imprisoned in federal institutions.[45] Arguably, the colonial government's actions against the Nationalist Party, and particularly toward Albizu Campos, in retrospect broaden his appeal beyond any actual following during his lifetime. Because Albizu spent so much of his life imprisoned, his influence on politics remained mostly allusive and rhetorical; furthermore, his deep Catholicism coupled with a lifetime of violent censure worked to transform him into a martyr in the Puerto Rican imaginary. Therefore, even if most Puerto Ricans do not necessarily agree with his political vision, they still hold him in respect and praise his unfaltering commitment to an independent Puerto Rico. Díaz Quiñones accurately describes Albizu Campos as "perhaps the only saint produced by the Puerto Rican political culture of the twentieth century, with his martyrdom, canonization, liturgy, sacred texts, fanatics and heretics."[46]

Despite his conception of the Puerto Rican nation as necessarily sovereign, Albizu grounded his vision in a problematic idealization of the Spanish regime. Again, as in the case of Pedreira, the nationalist glorification of the Spanish past seems to surface in response to a repressive present, without any consideration for the actual economic realities for most Puerto Ricans under the Spanish colonial government. Thus, nationalists have reimagined and valorized economic units, like coffee plantations that distributed small plots of land to their workers, as signs of an egalitarian economic system, and looked at Catholicism as community-centered in opposition to individualistic Protestantism. Significantly, both Pedreira and Albizu Campos were born in the 1890s, which means that they did not live consciously (or at least not for a significant period) under the Spanish regime. Their idealization of a Spanish past they both understood as determining the Puerto Rican character likely arose from nostalgic discourses circulating in their youths, which created a romanticized memory of social and political circumstances which neither writer experienced.

FIG. 1.1 Promotion for *Los funerales de Muñoz Rivera* (1916)

Another exceedingly influential political figure, Luis Muñoz Marín, offers a great contrast to his contemporary Albizu Campos. Unlike Albizu Campos, Muñoz Marín came from a very well known and established family. His father, Luis Muñoz Rivera, was perhaps the biggest turn-of-the-century political figure, having come to prominence as one of the key politicians campaigning for autonomy during the final decades of the nineteenth century. In 1916, as the resident commissioner to Washington, D.C., Luis Muñoz Rivera sought more autonomy for the island, advocating for the repeal of the Foraker Act and the formation of a local civilian government. However, before the replacement of the Foraker Act by the Jones Act of 1917, Muñoz Rivera died. Muñoz Rivera's well-publicized and thoroughly discussed career and death influenced generations of politicians well beyond his contemporaries, and even served as the subject of two well-received local films in 1916 (discussed in chapters 3 and 4). Given Muñoz Rivera's great political importance, it should come as no surprise that his death left a void in the leadership of his Partido Unión, eventually filled by his son in the late 1920s.

Like his father, Luis Muñoz Marín became an exceedingly important (and arguably even the most influential) political figure in Puerto Rican history. Through his economic and cultural initiatives (including the creation of a government film division) Muñoz Marín helped to forge a conception of Puerto Rico as culturally independent but also economically and politically reliant on the United States that, to this day, shape the way that most Puerto Ricans understand the nation. Before his father's death, Luis Muñoz Marín was not a significant figure in the island's politics and, indeed, had spent a great deal of his youth in the United States. Prior to taking up political activity, Muñoz Marín had made himself known in artistic circles, where he had published literary works defending the rural agrarian worker (the *jíbaro*, further discussed in chapter 3) as the true representative of Puerto Rican culture. Politically, Muñoz Marín rose to prominence in conjunction with discourses in Puerto Rico formed around Franklin Delano Roosevelt's New Deal project and agrarian reform.[47]

Near the beginning of his political career Muñoz Marín defended the New Deal plan as a way to achieve more political independence for Puerto Rico. The Plan Chardón, which he helped draft, best exemplifies this part of Muñoz Marín's career. In its more liberal formulation, the Plan Chardón proposed the appropriation of lands from big farms to redistribute among smaller farmers or cooperatives.[48] It also proposed the creation of government-owned factories to relocate sugar workers left unemployed by the introduction of more efficient technologies on sugar plantations. However, under counterpressure from the wealthy landed sector, the government implemented only limited parts of the Plan Chardón, like the establishment of shoe, cement, and box factories. Notwithstanding its failure, later generations have (re)imagined the Plan Chardón as the solution to all of Puerto Rico's former and present problems. That is, the plan gained a mythical status for supposedly crystallizing a moment that had the potential of being a turning point toward Puerto Rico's economic independence from the United States.[49]

In fact, the Plan Chardón documents historical rhetoric far more persuasively than it signifies an achievable economic proposal of the past. Certainly the plan helps us understand the political stance of Luis Muñoz Marín and his political circle during the late 1930s, and why their discourse changed drastically in the following years. Subsequently its mythic function expanded, so that the very name of the proposition now points to the desire by contemporary Puerto Ricans to understand why the Puerto Rican national project feels so incomplete. That is, references to the Plan signal a desire to understand colonial frustration in terms of specific, concrete historical moments, like the invasion of 1898, the Plan Chardón of 1935, or the creation of the Estado Libre Asociado in 1952 (literally translates to the contradictory Free Associated State, but commonly referred to in English as Commonwealth).

The changes in Muñoz Marín's policy from a socialist, pro-independence stance to a more conservative commonwealth formulation reflect his negotiations with what he understood to be the sponsor of Puerto Rico's progress: the U.S. government.[50] Indeed, Muñoz Marín's principles throughout many years in leadership positions remained focused on the idea of progress, both economically and culturally. It is precisely such an obsession with "progress" and its link to "civilization" that has remained a constant in all political and many cultural discourses in Puerto Rico.

In fact, the idea that the island has remained economically underdeveloped, despite undertaking extensive industrialization, has remained a recurrent issue, from a historical perspective, in Puerto Rico's political rhetoric (regardless of party affiliation). Thus, while on the surface the populist slogan of the Partido Popular Democrático (PPD)—under which banner Muñoz Marín soldiered on politically for years—"Bread, Land and Liberty" appears to advocate for basic human rights rather than any particular economic project, the phrase actually served as an integral part of a general rhetoric of industrialization and development that remains pertinent today. That is, the way the PPD best saw to attain "bread, land, and liberty" was through the creation of modern infrastructure and the rapid modernization of economic production. Furthermore, as Ayala and Bernabe suggest, this particular strand of discourse about development stressed the importance of the United States for the proper and successful realization of this "market-propelled modernization."[51] The dependence on U.S. capital to advance and establish Puerto Rican industries even extended to cultural undertakings like the island's film industry, which currently relies on attracting foreign investment, particularly through tax credits, to endure.

Interestingly, whereas Muñoz Marín formulated his rhetoric of development during the harsh economic times of the Great Depression, a time when the policy would certainly have had wide appeal, succeeding generations have carried on the same discourse of "civilized" industrial development propelled by outside capital independent of actual economic contexts. For example, in 1976, Carlos Romero Barceló of the Partido Nuevo Progresista (PNP) ran for office under the slogan "la nueva vida (the new life)," which suggested the need for a rebirth of the island's economy.[52] In this case, the new developmental marketing strategy emphasized tourism. Further, in 2012, the governor, Luis Fortuño (also a member of the PNP), campaigned under the slogan "Puerto Rico no puede volver al pasado. Puerto Rico se merece mucho más. Vamos a seguir adelante . . . por Puerto Rico (Puerto Rico cannot return to the past. Puerto Rico deserves much more. Let us continue forward . . . for Puerto Rico)."[53] Clearly, Fortuño's message suggests an ongoing development progress, and that he saw the progress as dependent on never-ending modernization. At this juncture, politicians seem to believe that the best focal points for modernization are the pharmaceutical and biomedical industries. They—and all Puerto Ricans—are arguably indebted to Muñoz Marín for the enduring popularity of this long-standing, widely and repeatedly deployed modernizing discourse.

Despite Muñoz Marín's abandonment of the independence cause, he is also responsible for the popularity of a cultural nationalist discourse that highlights and promotes local iconography even if not political emancipation. Although Muñoz Marín renounced a *political* nationalist project, his administration actively promoted the creation and dissemination of Puerto Rican culture through such institutions as the Division of Community Education (DIVEDCO) and the Puerto Rican Culture Institute. Particularly important for this study, DIVEDCO served as the only government-sponsored producer of films in Puerto Rico. Throughout the period of 1949 to 1989 DIVEDCO became the biggest film producer on the island, transforming the perceived aim of local film from business to educational tool.[54] As this example suggests, after the U.S. Congress settled in 1947 that

Puerto Ricans could elect their own governor, Muñoz Marín (who was the first elected Puerto Rican governor, and served in the position for sixteen consecutive years) started a process of naturalization of culture that culminated in 1955's "operación serenidad" (operation serenity).

After his election as Puerto Rican governor in 1949, Muñoz Marín proceeded to systematically absorb the popular aspects of nationalist rhetoric, including the declarations of Albizu Campos, adapting them to a conception of economic development attached to the United States. In this way he cemented the idea of the possibility of a thriving nation even in the absence of a state. Furthermore, he upheld the developing discourse about the existence of a separate Puerto Rican identity radically different from that of the United States. Thus, the more than fifty years of political negotiations that culminated in the creation of the Estado Libre Asociado (ELA), sought to guarantee the survival of the nascent Puerto Rican nation, while structurally tying, both politically and economically, the island to the United States.

However, the solidification of the ELA "solution" seems to have had an unforeseen side effect. While Puerto Ricans may feel the nation as immanently present, the continuing absence of an engaged sovereign Puerto Rican state has also created the feeling of an incomplete nation-building project. Specifically, Puerto Rico's relation to the United States affects the way the island's population approaches identity formation, and how it constructs an independent national culture. On the island, concerns about colonialism remain in the foreground even as sales of products bearing national iconography (like the Puerto Rican flag) proceed apace, and politicians of all party affiliations constantly promote the idea of duty to the nation in their rhetoric.[55] It seems clear that tensions inherent in the paradoxical state of belonging while not belonging have found an escape valve in exaggerated outward expressions of nationalism, while the "trauma" of 1898 refuses to disappear from Puerto Rican academic discussions (including this one).

In the following chapters I trace how filmmaking—and discourses about and surrounding filmmaking and consumption—have articulated with facets of Puerto Rican nation building. Because, as I will argue, cinema in Puerto Rico, historically, linked the elite and popular demographic sectors, I examine film production and distribution on the island to understand how particular elite actors imagined and (re)produced the nation-building process to attract and reflect popular concerns. As I have shown in this chapter, the colonial metropolis has had a major influence on the construction of a Puerto Rican national identity; hence, in the next chapter, I begin my analysis of the cinematic imaginary of Puerto Rican identity by considering the connections between colonialism, transnationalism, and the birth of Puerto Rican cinema. I also address how Puerto Rican film historians have constructed the narrative of Puerto Rican national cinema around the idea of filmmaking patriots, ignoring the importance of exhibition and transnational circuits of distribution for the development of a local cinema. I also consider how colonial relationships, particularly discourses in and about film, have marked the way Puerto Ricans construct national identity, and how the complex bonds with the colonizers (Spain and the United States) create inconsistencies in the ways scholars define Puerto Rican cinema and its beginnings, and national culture more broadly.

2

Cinema Comes to Puerto Rico

Historical Uncertainties and Ambiguous Identities (1897–1909)

Cinema arrived in Puerto Rico quite soon after its initial parallel development in France, Germany, and the United States beginning in the mid-1890s. However, scholars have to date both underresearched and arguably overtheorized about the earliest phases of Puerto Rican cinema history, including early exhibition on the island. The few records of cinema's early manifestations in Puerto Rico have over the years gained the status of fact largely through frequent citation by subsequent authors, often without careful verification or cross-checking, even as new resources have surfaced in recent decades. At the same time, that received history has served some film and other historians as a basis for elaborating arguments about the national identity and cultural functions of cinema on the island, in some cases without their ascertaining that the available evidence really supports such interpretations. This chapter presents newly verified or discovered evidence to offer a better-detailed account of cinema's earliest developments in Puerto Rico than previously available. Such a fresh history can, I argue, provide a foundation for understanding the phenomenon of Puerto Rican cinema historically within local and transnational as well as important national contexts.

The construction of early Puerto Rican cinematic history to date has followed to a considerable extent an article written by Juan Ortiz Jiménez published in 1952 in the magazine *Puerto Rico ilustrado*, titled "40 años de cinematografía puertorriqueña." Although Ortiz's article deserves recognition as possibly the first historical account of Puerto Rican cinema, thoroughgoing researchers working a half-century later can identify many elisions and errors in the work. Many of those gaps arise from the limits of its primary sources, specifically from recollections of some surviving participants in early cinema that Ortiz Jiménez enterprisingly gathered through interviews but probably did not verify with research into other historical records. For example, in the article Ortiz Jiménez notes that the first film exhibition in Puerto Rico occurred in 1901. Ortiz bases that 1901 date on an interview he conducted in 1952 with the pioneering filmmaker Rafael Colorado, by then an octogenarian. Colorado recalled in the interview that a French man had introduced film exhibition in Puerto Rico.[1] While a French man did come to Puerto Rico to project films in 1901, he was certainly not the first person to do so. Newspaper announcements of cinema programs reveal that several years earlier at least three other people had already staged moving picture exhibitions on the island. In this article, Ortiz also asserts that Juan Emilio Viguié made the first Puerto Rican film in 1912, and that Rafael Colorado soon followed him with a production of his own. Both "firsts," which have become standard "facts" in historical accounts of cinema in Puerto Rico, are unfortunately unverified assertions apparently based on Colorado's and Viguié's recollections many years after the events.[2]

Ortiz Jiménez's work, nonetheless, is truly groundbreaking historiography and has served as a basis for scholars to develop more detailed historical narratives. Thus, for example, Joaquin "Kino" García extended the date for the origins of cinema history in Puerto Rico to 1898, albeit based only on speculation that the U.S. military first undertook filming (but not exhibiting) during the Spanish-American-Cuban-Filipino War.[3] Given the existence of battle "footage" containing views of American troops in both Cuba and the Philippines archived in the Library of Congress, and presumably shot by Americans in those territories, it seemed reasonable for film historians like García and José Artemio Torres to expect that the cameramen accompanying the U.S. military also shot scenes in the Puerto

Rican archipelago.[4] However, unfortunately no filmic evidence exists (in the Library of Congress or elsewhere) that any such footage was made in Puerto Rico; regrettably, if such was made, it has not survived.

Although such previous accounts of the introduction of cinema to Puerto Rico prove valuable points of departure, my own research has yielded a rather different historical construction of Puerto Rico's film history. In relation to archival research, Giuliana Bruno argues that absences in historiography and even in the archives do not necessarily impede the historical reconstruction of cultural practices.[5] A close analysis of such archival silences can reveal much about how societies have valued and consumed specific cultural products and can actually aid us in identifying unusual but productive sources of information. Thus, Bruno argues that this method "suggests overcoming the *horror vacui*, exposing the blank, the limit, and the edge of discursive formations and creating a system of interconnections with textual remanence."[6]

In the case of Puerto Rican cinema, I will demonstrate, we can retrace absences only by restructuring how we approach the Puerto Rican national cultural narrative. To generate a supportive web of knowledge that will help to productively grasp the absences in the historiography, I have turned to alternative transnational resources that have extended my archival search outside the geographic confines of Puerto Rico. Framing Puerto Rican history as intricately connected to the histories of other nations has enabled me to create alternative stories that complicate, but also expand, our knowledge of the process of nation building in the island. Thus, to understand the transnational dealings that in the earliest years helped construct the Puerto Rican nation and its film culture, I have consulted Latin American, European, and North American sources ranging from editorial columns to ships' manifests. I have also pursued leads in government records and court proceedings, as well as literature and photography. Without claiming to have filled in all the gaps, I hope that this approach can help develop new questions and address the old ones from a different perspective.

Film Exhibition in Turn-of-the-Century Puerto Rico

Movies came to many of the principal cities in Latin America rather promptly after public film exhibition began to spread as a novel entertainment practice in Europe by early 1896. Ana López notes that by the end of September 1896 exhibitions had already occurred in the cities of Buenos Aires, Rio de Janeiro, Montevideo, Mexico City, Santiago de Chile, and Guatemala City.[7] The first recorded film exhibition in the Caribbean, which took place in Havana in January 1897, thus seems comparatively delayed.[8] Given the violent turmoil Cuba had experienced since 1895 because of its Independence War, however, it is actually quite remarkable that the delay was not longer.

As I argued in chapter 1, Cuba and Puerto Rico, as the last Spanish colonies in the Atlantic, shared some aspects of their economy and culture. The historically well-established connections between the islands render surprising the belief for many years among Puerto Rican scholars that film exhibition in Puerto Rico did not take place until 1901.[9] As I note in the text that follows, exhibitions in Puerto Rico actually occurred at an earlier date in line with the commercial and traveling patterns in the Caribbean, specifically in May 1897 (thus four months, rather than four years, after cinema's debut in Cuba), proving that the circulation of early cinema certainly did not operate in Puerto Rico, or anywhere else, as a discrete national phenomenon.

As noted, the 1901 date previously held as foundational derives from Ortiz Jiménez's historical account of film's development in the island. However, neither Ortiz nor the interviewee Rafael Colorado names the supposedly groundbreaking exhibitor. Based on historical records, along with film researcher Rose Marie Bernier, I deduce that the unnamed French man whom Colorado referred to was a Mr. Eduardo or Edouard Hervet, who did arrive in Puerto Rico with his traveling film show in May 1901.[10] Despite Colorado's claim, however, Hervet was not the first film exhibitor in Puerto Rico. Nonetheless, his coming to the island in 1901 does affirm San Juan's commercial significance as a stop on the circuit of early traveling film exhibitors. Furthermore, the figure of Hervet (or the unnamed French man) has long held rhetorical value, given that some scholars highlight his nationality to demonstrate the limits on U.S. influence in Puerto Rican film history.[11]

Historical records suggest that between 1898 and 1905 Eduardo Hervet made several film exhibition tours through parts of Latin America and stopped in Puerto Rico in 1901 on at least one expedition. I have found records of Mr. Hervet aboard the ship *La Bretagne* arriving in New York City in April 1894. Although this year predates the development of the Lumière cinematographic apparatus, which was by all evidence the equipment he brought in 1901, the record does establish a precedent for Hervet's business travels to the Americas. The ship's manifest shows him to be a merchant intending a "protracted sojourn" in the United States, during which time he could conceivably have come across the Kinetoscope machine that Edison had put into public use by May 1893.[12]

The records also show Hervet in Mexico City as early as February 1896, and, thanks to Luis Recillas Enecoiz's work in the Mexican archives of public entertainment licenses, we can also locate him in July 1898 in Toluca, about 65 kilometers to the west of Mexico City. In Toluca, Hervet clearly staged a cinematograph show, possibly his earliest exhibition in the Americas.[13] San Juan newspaper accounts show that in 1901 Hervet advertised his show as "the best cinematograph traveling the Antilles," which means that he must have stopped on other Caribbean islands before coming to Puerto Rico. The claim to offer "the *best* cinematograph" also clearly suggests the presence of other traveling shows in the area.[14]

Newspaper archives reveal that before 1901 Hervet had already made a cinema projection tour in the Caribbean, at least to Cuba, for the Havana newspaper *Diario de la Marina* mentions him in January 1900: "In the last two nights Mr. Hervet has received the public's acclaim because of the precision, clarity and stability of the views presented."[15] The archives also show that he continued making such commercial circuits after his 1901 visit to Puerto Rico, as the Brazilian newspaper *Estado de São Paulo* mentions Hervet offering a tour program called "Viagem ao travez do impossivel" (trip through the impossible) in April 1905.[16] In the interval between 1901 and 1905, I have found him traveling from Havana to New York in 1903, en route back to Paris.[17] The record of Mr. Hervet's repeated business trips from France to the Americas, his Puerto Rican advertisement's reference to competing presentations, and the well-established commercial importance of the other cities he visited cumulatively give me strong reason to believe that other traveling film exhibitors may also have stopped in San Juan on their way to or from other cities in the Caribbean or in Central and South America.

Despite Eduardo Hervet's importance for film history in Puerto Rico, I cannot credit him with offering the first film exhibition. Rose Marie Bernier has recently conclusively demonstrated that the 1901 date given and widely repeated for that event over the past six decades is mistaken.[18] Historical records show that the earliest *known* film exhibition in Puerto Rico happened four years prior, in May 1897, offered by a man named Luis Pío.[19]

The reports about Pío's show make apparent that this cinematic exhibition was the first of its kind in the island. For example, the author of a newspaper article about Pío's exhibition exclaims, "What a difference between the cinematograph and the *silforamas* [possibly the praxinoscope] that until now we had seen here!" The phrasing suggests that before Pío's cinematographic showing, only devices that created the illusion of movement through the use of mirrors (rather than actual film being projected) had come to San Juan.[20] In another report published in San Juan in May 1897, the writer asserts that the cinematograph will be "an interesting and new show for our public" and then explains how the device works. That article thereby further indicates the novelty of Pío's exhibition in San Juan.[21]

Based on an interview Bernier conducted with a claimed descendant of the film exhibitor named in the 1897 articles, Luis Pío Sánchez Longo, the full name of the exhibitor mentioned in the articles was Luis Pío Sánchez Rivera.[22] Following Bernier's lead, I have learned further from Dr. Sánchez Longo that the family's oral history narrates that his grandfather (who apparently sometimes used Pío as a business name) held the debut show in the San Juan municipal theater, presently called the Teatro Tapia, located in Fortaleza Street in Old San Juan. An 1897 article in the newspaper *La correspondencia* supports Dr. Sánchez's assertion that the first exhibition was staged in the San Juan Municipal Theater.[23] In our conversation Dr. Sánchez also declared that Pío had brought the cinematic apparatus from Europe.[24] However, another article in *La Correspondencia* contradicts that assertion by stating that the film *Dolorita en la danza del vintre* (*The Dolorita Passion Dance*, 1897) was part of Luis Pío's show.[25] Because the Edison Manufacturing Company produced this particular film, it is almost certain that Pío used a Vitascope, a cinematic apparatus produced in the United States.[26] The assumption of a European origin for the projector probably stemmed from the long-standing accounts of the French origins of cinema in Puerto Rico.

Whatever the specific origins of the projector, available evidence does strongly suggest that Luis Pío, the exhibitor, was in fact Luis Pío Sánchez, who, as his grandson asserts, had a career as a man of the theater around the turn of the century.[27] Even if the family histories that Luis Pío Sánchez Longo recollects are not precise, the informant is incontestably the grandson of Luis Pío Sánchez Rivera (1848–1927), who was in fact a maternal first cousin of the resident commissioner to Washington, D.C., Luis Muñoz Rivera.[28] Exploring colonial records (including U.S. census data) as well as

U.S. ship manifests yields a detailed picture of the entrepreneur. The existence of such records showcases how transnational relations have influenced the production of Puerto Rican national culture.

Through the U.S. Puerto Rico census of 1910 and 1920 I verified some of the background and activities of Luis Pío Sánchez Rivera. The census of 1910 documents his living as a prosperous citizen of the town of Comerío, forty kilometers inland from San Juan.[29] The census record further shows him to be the son of a Venezuelan father and Puerto Rican mother and himself the head of a large household with extended family living nearby. A combination of census records documents that Sánchez Rivera and his wife had at least ten children, the seventh among them Julio Sánchez y Ortiz, the father of Dr. Sánchez Longo. The 1910 record gives Sánchez Rivera's profession as a merchant dealing in foodstuffs. That profession, as well as the elite position of his extended family in Puerto Rican society, would certainly have made it possible for him to travel extensively. Through his role as a merchant, Sánchez Rivera would have likely come into contact with foreign goods and services, a point further supporting family claims that he was the "Luis Pío" listed in the 1897 newspaper articles.

The 1901 *First Annual Register of Porto Rico* lists Luis Pío Sánchez as a councilman of Comerío; that role coupled with his family relation to Muñoz Rivera signal that Sánchez held a prominent position in his town.[30] In fact the 1903 *Third Annual Report of the Governor of Porto Rico* praises Sánchez for his work on the education council of Comerío. The U.S. government–appointed post suggests that Sánchez knew English and that perhaps he had made political connections with Americans in the past, possibly from past travels to the United States.[31] Certainly Sánchez appears to have had sufficient wealth and contacts to travel widely and could thereby have interacted in the mid-1890s with early cinema exhibitors, materials, and equipment. In sum, whether or not we can further verify that Luis Pío Sánchez Rivera was indeed the exhibitor Luis Pío, and whatever that enterprising figure's nationality, certainly film came to Puerto Rico at least four years earlier than previously held.

Further underscoring the significance of the year 1897 (and further displacing Hervet as the initial exhibitor in Puerto Rico), Puerto Rican newspaper archives evidence a film exhibition offered that same year in Ponce by an unnamed Englishman.[32] In the late nineteenth century, the southern coastal city of Ponce was arguably the cultural center of Puerto Rico and the principal town of the "criollo" elite, rather than San Juan, the seat of the military and colonial bureaucracy. Thus, Ponce was an important and distinct market in Puerto Rico.[33] As was the case for Pío in San Juan, however, the visiting English exhibitor, according to newspaper ads, used "Edison's projector," which at that point referred to the Vitascope.[34] But while Mr. Pío's show seemed to have been successful (running from May until August), the public did not receive the Englishman's exhibition well. An article following the Vitascope's exhibition complains that "there is too little stability of focus and the light is weak. If the businessman remedied these defects and lowered the prices, he would get a bigger audience."[35] These critiques of Edison's projector fall in line with Charles Musser's findings that one of the difficulties of marketing the Vitascope was its poor photographic quality caused by problems with the Blair Company's film stock that Edison used.[36] I found no further mention of the Englishman's show in Ponce or anywhere else on the island following this report from the dissatisfied journalist. It appears that audiences shared the journalist's negative views, and the show stopped in Ponce, not reaching San Juan and probably not touring elsewhere on the island.

After this failed show, the newspaper *Boletín mercantil* records another exhibition, occurring in March 1898, with Salvador Negra named as the exhibitor in charge.[37] This man was very likely a Salvador Negra listed in an 1897 ship's record as an American citizen residing in the Dutch colony of Curaçao.[38] Although a March 6, 1898, article in *Boletín mercantil* predicts that the San Juan public will appreciate Mr. Negra's show, a follow-up article three days later comments that the show "does not appear to be pleasing the public."[39] Looking at the negative reception of Negra's show together with the reception of Pío's, the Englishman's, and Hervet's, the accounts of the four different instances of public film exhibition through 1901 give the impression that the Puerto Rican audience's response to film exhibition was quite "hit or miss" in the earliest years, with Pío's clearly being regarded as the most successful. To some extent Pío's success in attracting reportedly large audiences throughout the summer of 1897 in San Juan may have arisen from the novelty of his apparatus and show, in effect because he appears to have been the first. Conversely, the outcome of the first exhibition in Ponce and others through 1901 suggests that the comparative novelty of the film projector could not alone captivate audiences across the island, certainly not in any sustained way.[40]

Given the cumulative evidence, one can fairly conclude that Puerto Rico was a well-established stop on the trade route of commercial representatives of a range of nationalities: American, English, French, and of course Spanish (as Luis Pío Sánchez Rivera of Puerto Rico would have been under Spanish rule in 1897). In sum: by the time Hervet offered the cinematographic show that historians long considered "the first" on the island, Puerto Ricans in at least the two major cities had already had occasion to acquaint themselves with the cinematographic invention. Also worth noting, the cinematographic apparatus made its way to Puerto Rico before the Spanish-American-Cuban-Filipino War, contradicting earlier attribution of the introduction of filming technology to Puerto Rico by American soldiers presumably covering the conflict.[41] Additionally, given that some early projectors had the capability to operate as movie cameras and the evidence available from many other traveling projectionists that they often shot footage in each locale, we might well suppose—even without any intact film to prove the point—that one or more of the exhibitors who came to the island between 1897 and 1901 may have filmed some material locally.[42]

Rumors of War Footage

Even though the newspapers' records allow the maintenance of, and even strengthen, the long-standing Puerto Rican national historiographic disavowal of credit for cinema's local introduction to any American exhibitor, entrepreneurs from the United States appear to have conducted the first documented filming in the island. There is no extant footage proving that Puerto Rico was the subject of any U.S. military filming in 1898–1902 (in contrast to such footage that does survive from Cuba and the Philippines), but newspaper reports do indicate that Puerto Rico figured as a subject of magic lantern shows and also of footage made by private companies from the United States that sought to capitalize on the curiosity generated about the Spanish-American-Cuban-Filipino War. For example, in December 1898, the *Trenton State Gazette* (in New Jersey) announced a free exhibition of "fifty war pictures . . . taken from scenes of the battlefield in Cuba, Porto Rico and Manila."[43] The Clark Brothers of Trenton, New Jersey, owners of the Clark Brothers' Lamp, Brass and Copper Company, sponsored the exhibition, which news reports categorized as the first free exhibition of war films in town.[44] Further, the article proclaims that the films varied in length, "the shortest moving picture shown will be fifty-five feet long, and the longest 115 feet."[45] The mentioned length of the reels reveals that these films were short scenes lasting no more than two minutes. Since the article does not offer any description or the titles of the individual films, I cannot ascertain if the films were re-creations or actual footage.

One clear reference to filming near, if not in, Puerto Rico during the war of 1898 does appear in a feature article in the *Atlanta Constitution* entitled "Photography That Is Perilous." The following long passage from said newspaper recounts in detail the experience of Arthur Marvin, a cinematographer with the American Biograph Company who shadowed General William T. Sampson, the general in charge of supervising the Cuban blockade and the May 12, 1898, bombardment of the city of San Juan, Puerto Rico:[46]

> We [Arthur Marvin and fellow Biograph cinematographer F. S. Armitage] had followed Sampson's fleet eastward from Key West to Porto Rico. It was at the time of the bombardment of San Juan. As the bombardment was the first opportunity to do any work, we were anxious, naturally, to get some good views. When the firing began we steamed up toward the battleship and got where we could take in the whole range of operations pretty well. We kept urging the captain of the yacht to get in nearer the shore, and he gradually did so.
>
> Pretty soon the Spanish batteries began a reply to the American fire. Some of their shells came within three or four hundred yards of us, I presume, and we began to congratulate ourselves on the fact that there might be a good exhibition before long. Presently the Spanish shots began to come faster and to splash up the water a little nearer to us. We were interested in watching the argument between the ships and the batteries, and didn't notice what was happening to ourselves until our yacht had got under pretty good headway and was making rapid time away from the shore.
>
> We shouted to the captain to hold up and veer around, but he didn't hear us. We tried to argue with the crew, but they were equally deaf. By the time we got these scared fellows to listen to us we were twenty-five miles out at sea. When we got back the performance was over, and the American fleet had sailed away.
>
> Although we missed the main show we figured in a principal role for a side performance that followed. There were two small Spanish gunboats, and we

> weren't certain as to whether a moving picture apparatus would be considered contraband of war or not. So this time we made no effort to discourage the energies of the crew. In fact we turned to and poured oil over the coal that was spread out on the deck, and then passed it down below until we had flames coming out of the top of the smokestack and were leaving Porto Rico in our wake at the rate of fifteen knots per hour.[47]

Although giving the impression that in this instance Marvin did not get the desired shots, his narrated experience attests to attempts to shoot actualities of the war along the shores of Puerto Rico. However, the American government did not make these films; they were made by private companies, such as the American Biograph Company. That private citizens made such filming and not the U.S. military challenges early Puerto Rican historiographic suppositions that imagined these "war films" as part of the invasion itself, and not as quasi-journalistic enterprises. However, the existence of this newspaper article also suggestively bears out what film scholars in Puerto Rico, without concrete evidence, have assumed: the filming by Americans of Spanish-American-Cuban-Filipino War footage about Puerto Rico.

Another film company, operated by a Jewish American named Siegmund Lubin, took advantage of U.S. excitement about the war. Lubin, having emigrated from Poland, became an optician in Philadelphia, from which he turned to producing films from 1897 to 1917. At the onset of the Spanish-American-Cuban-Filipino War, Lubin started to make moving pictures about the conflict, eventually producing forty films on the 1898 subject.[48] Among those was a three-hundred-foot-long film (ca. five minutes at silent speed) called *The Capture of Porto Rico*, which Lubin advertised in January 1899 in the *New York Clipper*.[49] Though film scholars well know that Lubin staged his war films rather than shooting actual footage in the purported locations, his decision to make a film about Puerto Rico demonstrates the demand for this kind of production in the United States.[50] If indeed this film was a re-creation (rather than, perhaps, a re-edited and retitled length of actuality footage shot by another company), it might count as one of the earliest imaginative representations of Puerto Rico in a motion picture. Its existence and that of similar films deserve mention in our accounts of the history of cinema in Puerto Rico, especially because the events of 1898 have so profoundly shaped the process of nation building in Puerto Rico. After all, these cinematic representations formed part of the

U.S. political discourse regarding the country's relationship to the former Spanish colonies; as such they are an integral part of the rhetorical construction of Puerto Rico and its inhabitants.

A second mention of a possible Lubin production depicting Puerto Rico appears in the *Omaha World Herald* in April 1900. In this instance the newspaper does not explicitly name Lubin but rather the cineograph, the cinematic apparatus that he invented.[51] The advertisement announces the exhibition of "the latest moving pictures of the Spanish-American War—scenes of Cuba, Porto Rico and the Philippines."[52] The language used in the advertisement presumes that they could convincingly promote in the American Midwest scenes from the 1898 war as up-to-date and popular almost two years after the end of the conflict. In 1899–1900, any really "latest" war scenes would have necessarily been re-creations, but probably the moving pictures were not actually new. Rather, the films advertised were very likely the same that appeared in Trenton, New Jersey, and New York, with the description being justified only by their being newly arrived in Omaha.

The evident sustained interest in the subject beyond the year 1898 underscores the importance of the colonial wars of the late nineteenth century and their representations in American political discourse and national ideology. The pervasiveness in film, literature, and journalism of the war theme highlights the importance of this conflict for the nation-building process, not in this instance of Puerto Rico but, rather, distinctively of the United States. As Kyle Evered explains, tensions between the North and the South resulting from the American Civil War found a resolution in the conflicts of 1898. Soldiers from all regions of the United States managed to gather for the common goal of establishing U.S. supremacy in the Americas.[53] Still, despite the therapeutic effect that the war might have had inside the United States, it also created a new quasi-enemy that needed submission in the new colonial territories, the position that the South had played recently. However, just like in the U.S. South, the resulting wounds of the "defeated" side promoted a further sociocultural identity divide between the metropolis and the colonies.

Lacking the government or the industry and the means or willingness, the Puerto Rican people did not have the opportunity to represent themselves in film for many years after the Spanish-American-Cuban-Filipino War ended. That is, although cinema had arrived in Puerto Rico before the war, with the exhibition of U.S.- and French-made products, by all evidence no production made in Puerto Rico by a Puerto Rican nor any with

Puerto Rican actors appeared until more than a decade later. Undoubtedly the lack of Puerto Rican film productions does not mean the complete absence of any other identity-forming discourse throughout the first decade of the twentieth century. Nonetheless, we should recognize that in its silent period through the late 1920s, cinema did serve as a more effective cultural ambassador and site of discursive transnational negotiations than many other forms of cultural production.

Representing U.S. Colonial Puerto Rico

As of now, I have identified a Selig Polyscope Company production of 1898, an "actuality" entitled *Washing the Streets of Porto Rico*, as the earliest film that purportedly contained footage of Puerto Rico.[54] The American Film Institute (AFI) catalog briefly describes the subject of this apparently lost one-shot film: "A very unique scene showing the method of washing the streets in Porto Rico and of special interest now that this country forms part of Uncle Sam's domain. This is a particularly brilliant film, perfect in every detail and being something out of the ordinary has proved very successful."[55]

From this description I can make some conjectures regarding the making and promotion of this footage: first, that it was advertised (but not necessarily made) after August 1898, for the summary lists "Porto Rico" as a new U.S. possession; and, second, that the filmmakers considered the scene as arguably "out of the ordinary." That last statement implies that Puerto Rico was not a common subject filmed at the time, or that Americans would presumably find Puerto Rican cultural practices amusing, or both. If in fact audiences "well-received" the short film as the description from the company claims, such an outcome could have triggered further filming in or about the island. The great number of books published during that period about the Spanish-American-Cuban-Filipino War and the islands' incorporation into the U.S. federation indeed suggests great interest in the "new possessions" from the American public.[56] However, I have not found any mention of this particular actuality in any of the available archived newspapers of the time. During 1898–1900, however, newspapers across the United States mentioned purported "war films" containing images of "Porto Rico," as I have already discussed.[57] *Washing the Streets*—which appears to have consisted of a single shot—is then the first known footage shot in Puerto Rico (not on its coast), and even though we do not know who shot it or when or precisely where, it marks a foundational moment in Puerto Rican cinema history: filming in the geographical territory of Puerto Rico. Further, the anonymity of its cinematographer opens up the possibility that any of the exhibitors previously mentioned (Luis Pío, the anonymous Englishman, or Salvador Negra) could have shot this film.

Although the film's description in the AFI's catalog mentions that *Washing the Streets* shows "a unique method" of accomplishing this sanitary task, I have found U.S. military references that suggest that the new military government's health code called for this practice, and thus it was likely imposed by the United States. Indeed, the 1901 *Report of the Military Governor of Porto Rico from October 18, 1898, to April 30, 1900* declares, "The streets in the cities or towns of Porto Rico must be kept clean. Dirty streets are not only unhealthful, but are very unsightly, and give any city a bad reputation in the eyes of strangers."[58] The report goes on to say that anyone caught dirtying the streets will receive the punishment of a fine of "not less than $5 nor more than $200, United States currency, or imprisonment for not less than five nor more than ninety days, or by both," suggesting that the new government considered the act a substantially serious offence.[59] Therefore, it seems likely that this film captured the enforcement by military policy after the U.S. occupation of Puerto Rico in the summer of 1898. It also seems very likely, then, that *Washing the Streets* forms part of a discourse of hygiene and health linked to the justification of U.S. colonization of the island.[60]

Despite its political implications, Puerto Rican historiography has surprisingly overlooked this film. I find it revealing that footage of a battle of the 1898 war, even though nowhere archived that I can find and even though presumably shot by Americans and not Puerto Ricans or Spaniards, somehow came historiographically to stand as foundational imagery for Puerto Rican national culture, whereas that of an urban sanitary routine did not, even though both reveal important aspects of the process of colonization. It seems that the collective infatuation with 1898 has discursively transformed a shocking but not exactly gruesome political transition into a traumatic moment. That is, although 1898 does not really represent a trauma of extreme physical violence (as it might represent in the Philippines), it does stand as the mark of a supposed lost identity. In the Puerto Rican case, intellectual elites have rallied around this particular historical event, pointing to it as a cathartic moment of identity formation. Dominick LaCapra explains that "a memory site is generally also a site of trauma, and the extent to which it remains invested with trauma marks the extent to which memory has not been effective in coming to terms with it, notably through modes of mourning."[61] The nation's memory or narrative includes many accounts of hard power but does not include this particular film account, a recorded ethnographic moment (however minor it may be) of the performance of equally traumatic soft power.

In addition, *Washing the Streets* as a documentary, and arguably an ethnographic one, purports to represent historical-cultural practices as they "factually" occurred (memory caught on film). Given the popular assumption of truth-telling associated with documentaries, José B. Capino argues that such films "must be treated not only as historical facsimiles or social documents but also as literary expressions and historiographic imaginings—in other words, as objects both to interpret and to think with."[62] I would add that embracing or rejecting ethnographic images from the national "canon" reveals a great deal not only about a given film and those who made it but also about how we, the depicted, might like to imagine ourselves. The popular narratives of war link it explicitly with violence—the physical subjugation of a people—giving a tangible reason for that sense of incompleteness, but they also typically ignore the more subtle, but still effective, means of enforcing colonization.

In relation to rhetoric, *Washing the Streets*, for all its inconsequential subject, highlights the ways in which colonization helps to construct both the colonized nation and the one that colonizes. In promoting and making exotic aspects of everyday life in the colony, the resident colonizers also open themselves up for an equal amount of gawking from the colonized at their own seemingly mundane practices. Instead of mutual recognition of coexisting cultural differences, the treatment of the mundane as a spectacle reveals a polarization of two different cultures that thenceforth stand opposed (as is the case between the United States and Puerto Rico). For instance, one can find in other cultural productions examples of this process of reciprocal exoticization. U.S. writer Stephen Crane's account of a U.S. soldier's burial in the city of Ponce illustrates the point:

> There was a carriage containing two American women and upon the pavement stood a little group of officers, with their battered old hats in their hands. The natives began to accumulate in a crowd and from them arose a high-pitched babble of gossip concerning this funeral.

> They stretched their necks, pointed, dodged those who would interfere with their views. Amid the chatter the Americans displayed no signs of hearing it. They remained calm, stoical, superior, wearing the curious, grim dignity of people who are burying their dead.[63]

Crane's voice, equally judgmental and amazed, communicates both amusement and offence at the Puerto Rican crowd's reaction. A colonizer himself, Crane interprets the crowd's infatuation with the burial as a mark of inferiority and low-class behavior rather than as curious observations evoked by the occurrence from the crowd's perspective of an equally "exotic" event.

Aside from showing no knowledge of Puerto Rican burial traditions that called for neighbors to join in walking processions and from making essentialist claims about the differences between Americans and Puerto Ricans, Crane's account demonstrates how otherness supplants marks of class in colonial situations. Thus, acts of recording the other (on paper or film) seem to occlude any will to understand and preserve cultural traditions, but instead only further reify and mark difference between the recorder and other divergent perspectives or practices. As Edward Said argues, "the difficulty with theories of essentialism and exclusiveness, or with barriers and sides, is that they give rise to polarizations that absolve and forgive ignorance and demagogy more than they enable knowledge."[64] Thus adding this film to the national narrative can help generate knowledge to depolarize the less "glamorous" aspects of colonial practices.

Additionally, the production of *Washing the Streets* and other novelty films about the Spanish-American-Cuban-Filipino War, like those created by Edison, Biograph, and Lubin, may well indicate the U.S. public's craving for news about their expanding empire.[65] Alison Griffiths argues that early cinema audiences in the United States were attracted to ethnographic films depicting non-Western people because of the curiosity generated by difference. She further contends that such attraction represented both the way cinema made traveling accessible for all Americans and the way it legitimized imperialism by suggesting that Americans had a right to consume and appropriate other national spaces.[66] Because, as Kyle Evered argues "there was a perceived mission for Americans both to decide the fate of others and to prosper, simultaneously," the addition of Puerto Rico as a new member of the U.S. federation helped to build the image of the United States as strong and compassionate.[67] The discourses and acts of benevolence, violence, and hypocrisy surrounding late nineteenth-century U.S. colonialism helped to develop and cement polarized views regarding the relationship between the United States and Puerto Rico, both on the mainland and on the island. Even though we do not know who shot *Washing the Streets,* because of the link these ethnographic images have with early twentieth-century colonial discourses that defined and categorized Puerto Ricans, I argue that they belong to the national cinema regardless of the nationality of those who produced them. Despite the hesitations cinema historians might have about appropriating films that objectify or commodify a national/ethnic group, excluding such works from the national historical narrative serves only to make invisible important parts of the colonial relation. Indeed, turn-of-the-century U.S. film and travel literature reveal a popular fascination with other cultures that likely helped to define how colonial officials discussed and presented the "new possessions" to the American public and even the world.[68]

Although *Washing the Streets,* given its mundane topic, appears to have been a true actuality, U.S. producers actually staged many of these supposed candid ethnographic moments that taught Americans about the world. As Alison Griffiths argues when talking about Biograph's *Asia in America,* the fictional nature of some of these recordings allows the films to reveal more about how the United States imagined the world than about what the world was really like.[69] One such assuredly staged vignette, the American Mutoscope and Biograph Company's *How the Porto Rican Girls Entertained Uncle Sam's Soldiers* (1899), took as its "ethnographic" subject Puerto Rican women. The AFI catalog's description of the film reads: "An officer of the U. S. Navy is chatting with a Porto Rican girl. While two others are doing the characteristic dance of the country, a third joins in and finishes the dance much to the officer's amusement and delight. From the New York Theater."[70] Although the film's advertising poster claims that the movie is "photographed from real life," the summary of the film alone intimates that the film was not an "actuality," but a "fictional" scene.[71] Further, the remarks "from the New York Theater" most likely refers to a theater that had this name—and was located on Mercer Street between Bleecker and Amity Streets in Lower Manhattan—implying that the scene represented in this film was a vaudeville piece.[72]

A surviving photo still of the movie shows that despite the ridiculousness of the two actresses' outfits, which included strange crown-like hats, their costumes also eroticized them through the presentation of plunging

FIG. 2.1 Promotion for *How the Porto Rican Girls Entertain Uncle Sam's Soldiers* (1899)

necklines and bare arms, as they pose with their hands on their hips in coquettish fashion. In addition, the man playing the part of the American soldier holds one of the women at the hip and arm as she flashes a suggestive smile at him. The setting clumsily depicts a tropical garden with what looks like potted palm trees and bromeliads. Both the description of the film and this photo-still make evident that this short film focused on the sexuality of Puerto Rican women, especially in interaction with U.S. men. That these actresses were possibly vaudeville dancers and that they so coquettishly approach men implies a view of Puerto Rican women as sexually available. Although this surviving photo-still does not really involve true ethnographic material (since no one in the films appears to be truly Puerto Rican), as perhaps *Washing the Streets* did, it serves as a clue pertaining to the attitude of U.S. cultural producers regarding the inhabitants of the new colonial possessions, particularly the women.

In fact, the U.S. public showed extensive interest in Puerto Rican women's sexuality. Currently available newspaper archives contain at least twelve syndicated articles printed widely in U.S. papers between 1898 and 1900 that dealt exclusively with Puerto Rican women, under such headlines as "Willing Slave to the Men are our Puerto Rican Sisters" and "Courtship in Porto Rico."[73] A full-page article by Frank G. Carpenter, titled "Pretty Porto Girls" and widely syndicated in July 1899, centers on the beauty and behavior of Puerto Rican women as he experienced on a visit to the island.[74] In the article Carpenter proclaims,

> As I look at these pretty Porto Rican girls I thought of the sensation they would create among our young men when they visit the fashionable watering places of the United States. They will be formidable rivals of the American summer girls. Heretofore many of them have taken their outings in Europe, but now they are talking of coming to the United States. They are taking lessons in English, and already several of them have found husbands among our army officers. I understand they like Yankee beaux better than Porto Ricans, and that they will prefer American husbands because American wives have more freedom and better times.[75]

Carpenter's praise for the looks of Puerto Rican women barely masks the article's colonial concerns about the possible integration of the subjected nations into larger U.S. society. Although "Porto Rican girls" are pretty, their desire for American men signals for the writer the inadequacies of Puerto Rican men and Puerto Rican society more generally. That is, the explanation Carpenter offers for Puerto Rican women purportedly preferring American husbands clearly sets U.S. customs as superior to those of the island, particularly in relation to the status and permissible social behaviors of women. The article further suggests the universal attractiveness of U.S. cultural values and that anyone can recognize their superiority. In addition, this article addresses mainly the beauty of high-class women, describing working-class women only in passing when discussing the cheapness of domestic labor in the island, and referring to such women simply as "clean and nice looking."[76] In the end only rather civilized high-class women, due perhaps to their having higher standards and education, can clearly perceive and appreciate the value of U.S. men and their way of life. Articles like this one, along with photographic collections and political discourses, indicated the possibility of social uplift and integration (at least of some sectors) of Puerto Rican society into the United States.[77]

Both *Washing the Streets* and *Porto Rican Girls* reveal the importance of rhetoric in the colonial process. Although the bombardment of San Juan was a very violent event, the U.S. colonization of Puerto Rico happened rather "tamely," with only twenty-two casualties across both camps.[78] Nonetheless, the Puerto Rican population did experience the invasion of 1898 as a distressing event; likewise, contemporary Puerto Ricans still understand it in this way. Still, rather than focusing on physical violence, I suggest instead that the colonization of Puerto Rico, in its initial decade, happened mostly at the level of rhetoric. Discourses regarding hygiene and sexuality, as Warwick Anderson has extensively documented in relation to the Philippines, were an integral part of the creation of the colonial subject's inferior "nature."[79] Despite the colonialist nature of the films about Puerto Rico produced and distributed, at least in the United States in relation to the Spanish-American-Cuban-Filipino War, those works should form part of Puerto Rico's cinematic history because they still offer the first filmic representations of Puerto Rico and its people.

The initial cinematic shootings in Puerto Rico were sporadic as well as likely of nonnative origin (with no certainty about *Washing the Streets*). Yet these representations came about very soon after the emergence of cinema internationally. With the coming of the Spanish-American-Cuban-Filipino War, Puerto Rico became a profitable film subject for U.S. filmmakers. Although the U.S. productions about Puerto Rico had a colonialist nature and register, they also contributed to and promoted discourses that circulated in Puerto Rico and the United States regarding the nations' new relationship to each other. Even if not of Puerto Rican origin, these films capture a particular, and crucial, cultural moment in the island: the U.S. invasion and subsequent U.S. sociocultural policy regarding its new territory.

After the 1898 war, Puerto Rico continued to receive traveling exhibitors such as Salvador Negra and Eduardo Hervet. However, at the beginning of the twentieth century what had once been sporadic events became a stable form of entertainment. By 1906, a Mr. Vargas regularly operated a film apparatus in San Juan, and in 1908, as Bernier has amply documented, a moving picture house called the Tres Banderas Theater appeared in the Ponce de León Avenue in Old San Juan.[80] By 1909 movie houses had opened in San Juan, Ponce, and Mayaguez, among other municipalities, suggesting the successful spread and likely popularity of film exhibition throughout the island.[81] Still, the first cinematic representation of Puerto Rico and Puerto Ricans by someone arguably local did not happen until 1912. In the following chapter I will discuss the early film career of pioneer filmmaker Rafael Colorado D'Assoy and the importance of understanding Puerto Rican cinema made on the island as a transnational phenomenon.

3

Stateless Nationhood, Transnationalism, and the Difficulties of Assigning Nationality

Rafael Colorado in Puerto Rican Historiography (1912–1916)

In 2011, the organizers of a lecture series sponsored by Producciones Don Pedro and the Ana G. Méndez University System proclaimed the start of celebrations of the centennial of Puerto Rican cinema. The dating of Puerto Rican cinema's beginnings to 1911–1912 seems arbitrary and certainly delayed in light of ample evidence of cinematic activity in Puerto Rico as early as 1897. However, the centennial organizers' choice of that date—and their explanation for it—reveals much about how Puerto Ricans have imagined national cinema: "In 1911 in San Juan the veteran Spanish photographer Rafael Colorado D'Assoy started to film actualities. In 1912 in Ponce the young Juan Viguié Cajas started his career as a cinematographer by filming everyday scenes. The commemoration of the one hundred years of Puerto Rican cinema will center on the importance that these two figures had for the growth and development of the seventh art in our country."[1] Further press releases and articles about the scheduled activities explained setting 1912 as the beginning of cinema in Puerto Rico because it was the year that Rafael Colorado made the narrative film *Un drama en Puerto Rico*.[2] Thus it seems that the organizers selected this date not because cinema in Puerto Rico clearly began in 1912, but rather because both Rafael Colorado and Juan Viguié ostensibly first engaged that year in film production. In choosing to emphasize those two filmmakers, the event organizers joined film scholars such as Ortiz Jiménez and José Artemio Torres in crediting Colorado and Viguié with establishing a native film industry. Thereby the event further asserted the validity of previous discourses that stated that the two men's contributions in producing cinema in Puerto Rico served as the foundational moment.

While recognizing the commendable attempts to open spaces for the communication of knowledge about Puerto Rican cinema history, I would note that the choice of 1911–1912 as a starting point for Puerto Rican cinema highlights an approach to national cinema centered on "auteurs," which ignores the role of exhibitors and audiences in the cultural industry's imagining.[3] Further, the more specific choice of 1912, based on the filming of the first narrative movie in Puerto Rico, showcases how, in discussions about cinema, fiction has traditionally been valued over documentaries and actualities despite the latter's crucial role in the formation and evolution of the film industry.

Still, the most interesting aspect of the event organizers' choice to designate the first known Puerto Rican fictional film as the origins of a national cinema is that its maker, Rafael Colorado D'Assoy, was born in Spain and long publicly self-identified as a Spaniard rather than a "criollo" Puerto Rican.[4] Even acknowledging the importance of appropriating "foreigners'" contributions in writing a given nation's cinema history, it surprised me how easily and completely Colorado has come to anchor the canon of Puerto Rican cinema while the names and contributions of other nonnative producers and productions, particularly those associated with the U.S. industry, are fully excluded. How is it that without strictly "being Puerto Rican," Colorado has come to stand among the pantheon of national heroes? Posing the question does not deny Colorado's importance for

Puerto Rican cinema; rather, quite the opposite, my query postulates the complexity and problematic nature of defining the national, whereby, in fact, the realities of transnationalism permeate all aspects of the construction of the nation. That Colorado remained deeply identified with Spain until his death in 1959 does not mean that he was not also Puerto Rican. As I will show in this chapter, transnationalism has from the beginning pervaded the construction of Puerto Rican cinema—and Puerto Rican national culture more generally—to a greater extent than most scholars of Puerto Rican cultural productions have to date acknowledged.

Despite Colorado's undeniable importance for Puerto Rican cinema (a subject to which I return), historical discourses making and maintaining him as a national figure have tended to dismiss his problematic transnational position. Surprisingly, on the other hand, scholars have traditionally defined Puerto Rican national cinema in ways that exclude transnational interactions. That is, as I had discussed in the introduction to this book, Puerto Rican researchers have tended to limit what Puerto Rican cinema can encompass by defining it in very conservative terms that assign nationality based on ethnogeographical belonging: you have to be born in, live in, and produce in Puerto Rico for your product to be considered Puerto Rican.[5] However, these nationalist terms stand at odds with the transnational reality of the development of cinema in the island (and elsewhere). Given the great involvement of transnational actors and products in the development of cinema in Puerto Rico, we must consider as part of Puerto Rico's national cinema history instances of film exhibition and even production conducted by nonnatives, like Colorado himself. Also, as discussed in the previous chapter, even some productions depicting Puerto Rico and Puerto Ricans by filmmakers who were neither born nor permanently resided on the island, warrant inclusion in the nation's cinema history because of their great influence in the realm of political thought. To fill in some persistent gaps in the historiography and generate a nuanced and thorough account of how cinema arrived and developed in Puerto Rico, we must allocate space within the national narrative for transcultural exchanges and strive to understand the international relations that have shaped the circulation of cinematic products and producers in Puerto Rico.

As noted, the belief that both Juan Viguié Cajas and Rafael Colorado produced their first films in 1912 has led to most accounts taking that year as the birth of Puerto Rican cinema. However, I have found no evidence that Viguié made a film in 1912. Even a 1936 Puerto Rican *Who's Who* publication offers no mention of him making a film in 1912, while offering other cinema industry details like his having worked as a cinema operator (1909–1914) and with Universal Films in New Jersey (1914–1917).[6] In fact, it seems that only Ortiz Jiménez's undocumented claim of the existence of such a film stands as evidence for its existence.[7] Since I have not been able to find any historical or archival reference to Viguié making a film in 1912, I assume for now that he did not make such a film, or at least he did not make or exhibit it that year. Thus, I focus the current chapter about the developments in Puerto Rican film production in the early 1910s on Rafael Colorado's documented work, waiting to discuss in subsequent chapters the later contributions of Juan Viguié Cajas as an important figure in Puerto Rican cinema history.

In contrast to the situation with Viguié, one can find extensive documentation regarding Colorado and his film enterprises in 1912. Analysis of Puerto Rican historiography reveals, however, that it is not the abundance of historical materials about Colorado's engagement with cinema, but rather, paradoxically, his involvement in the Spanish-American-Cuban-Filipino War that early film historians most emphasize and prize. I would suggest that such fascination with Colorado could have its roots in the arguably collective Puerto Rican scholarly fixation with the conflict of 1898 and the resultant cultural shifts, which frequently—and understandably—arise in scholarly discussions about identity and cultural productions.

Though I focus here on the persona of the filmmaker almost unanimously considered the "father" of Puerto Rican cinema, Rafael Colorado D'Assoy, I aim ultimately to broaden our understanding of Puerto Rican cinema as a *transnational* phenomenon. In actuality, we can celebrate Colorado's life and work as a nationalist achievement only by detaching him from the international context in which he lived and produced. Although Colorado undeniably contributed to the process of nation building, such inattention to his transnational connections indicates problems in assigning citizenship, or general belonging, in a stateless nation. An overview of Colorado's life and early work enables analysis of the problematic uncertainty of assigning nationality to cultural productions and producers, particularly when nation and state do not correspond.

Rafael Colorado, Film Exhibition, and the Transnational Circulation of Cultural Subjects

The symbolic function of Rafael Colorado's life and military involvement as an expression of Puerto Rican nationalist sentiments emerges as all the more mythologized given the extent to which he remained a firm supporter of everything Spanish throughout his long life (1868–1959). In an article he wrote the year he died, Colorado asserted that he came to Puerto Rico in 1888 as a then twenty-year-old member of the Spanish military onboard the ship *Buenos Aires*.[8] By that time, he had already received a degree in art from the University of Montesion in Palma de Mallorca, the town of which his father was the military governor.[9] From these details we can glean that Colorado came from a privileged background and thus would likely have maintained a privileged position in Puerto Rico under Spanish rule.

Colorado claimed that he had initially planned to seek his youthful adventure in Cuba, but at the request of his mother, who was afraid of an epidemic of yellow fever there, he agreed to come instead to the neighboring island of Puerto Rico.[10] Although fears of contracting yellow fever seem legitimate, given his family's deep involvement in the Spanish military and government, the decision not to go to Cuba more likely related to the independence turmoil that had brewed there since 1868 than to any potential illnesses. After all, compared to Cuba, Puerto Rico had remained relatively peaceful and stable since its failed revolutionary attempt in September 1868.

In his late life autobiographical article, Colorado notes that he was originally part of the twenty-eighth battalion of the "Cazadores de Cadiz," but due to his skills as a photographer and draftsman, the colonel of the General Staff, Juan Arnal, soon appointed him to the topographic section of the General Staff. After ten years of living in Puerto Rico, Colorado had retreated into civilian life as a photographer, even though he remained a member of the Spanish military. Thus despite his past military career, during which he had attained the rank of lieutenant, Colorado saw action in the war of 1898 as part of the volunteer infantry rather than as an active-duty soldier.[11] Colorado's appeal for film historians may have substantially arisen from Ángel Rivero Méndez's heroic account of the photographer's role in the 1898 Puerto Rican campaign in his *Crónica de la guerra hispano-americana en Puerto Rico* (1922). Rivero's chronicle portrays Colorado not only as a devoted subject of the Spanish crown but also as a loyal friend and superior soldier. For example, in the preface to the chronicle, Rivero describes Colorado in extremely positive terms, notwithstanding the fact that the Spanish military unsuccessfully defended the island from the U.S. invasion: "An artist of worth who was a former distinguished soldier, Rafael Colorado abandoned everything to come to my rescue. . . . Without the help of Colorado, this *Chronicle of the Spanish-American War* would be a harsh book, opaque; he transformed it to become lucid, transparent, almost alive. I owe thanks to this gentle artist, an amateur sportsman, who still bears the scars of the 1898 military campaign."[12] In addition, Rivero also generated Colorado's mythic standing as an unusual and extraordinary soldier by praising his distinctive action in capturing the only American flag seized in the whole campaign (in the town of Fajardo, which the Americans had laid claim to but left undefended).[13] Through the present, that distinction recurs in every account of Colorado, perhaps because, as I argued in chapter 1, Puerto Rican political discourse has set the defense of Spain and Spanishness as tantamount to emphatic Puerto Rican nationalism, despite the irony of valorizing a prior colonizer.

Thus, among accounts of Colorado's importance for Puerto Rican film history, one often finds an iconic picture of him dressed as a mounted cavalry officer. The emphasis on that single photograph—one of many of Colorado that exist—deserves closer analysis. One might argue that the image of Colorado in his officer's uniform distinguishes and characterizes him in a particular militaristic and chivalrous light.[14] Even more dramatically, an account like Roberto Ramos Perea's *Cinelibre* (2008) describes Colorado not only as a soldier but explicitly as a fierce nationalist defending Puerto Rico from the U.S. threat: "[L]ike a good Spaniard, hater of the Yankee (he was a soldier during the invasion), [Colorado] proved that he could fight against the gringo in this forum [film] and here [in Puerto Rico]. If we had preserved his cinema, beyond his photographs, we would know that there was an atmosphere, a movement, a light that is ours. And above all a desire . . . nobody should underestimate the power of the desire to make Puerto Rican cinema."[15] Despite Ramos's claim, Colorado's having fought in the Spanish-American-Cuban-Filipino War does not prove that at the time of the war he had a particular aversion to the United States because of an anticolonialist position. That is, we cannot extrapolate from his fighting in the 1898 war that he was a Puerto Rican nationalist. We can safely conclude only that he was a Spanish soldier from a family line linked to the

FIG. 3.1 Rafael Colorado as a soldier

Spanish military, who was bound to realize a duty to Spain and the defense of its interests by fighting in a Spanish war, regardless of where it was carried out. In Colorado's case, Spain's immediate interest was the preservation of its hegemony over the colony of Puerto Rico.

Certainly, Colorado made many substantive (if less often celebrated) contributions to Puerto Rican history other than his involvement in the war, specifically to the development of photography and cinema on the island. Notably Colorado helped to establish a professional association of photographers in Puerto Rico in 1924. More than a decade previous to that important contribution to Puerto Rican visual arts, however, he had broken new ground in the young Puerto Rican film industry. He first worked in cinema as a local distributor for Pathé productions, by 1912 advertising himself as the "exclusive agent of the Pathé frères house" in the island.[16] The records also show that Colorado had a photographic studio in San Juan where he most likely shot and processed films, initially photographs and later moving pictures. In the summer of 1912 he started advertising his photographic studio as well as a Pathé distribution company under the business name Cine Puerto Rico.[17]

Initially, in 1912, the advertisements for Colorado's enterprise, while still promoting all aspects of his business, particularly highlighted his position as a Pathé distributor. Further, I gathered from a Puerto Rican Supreme Court case that Colorado helped establish the Cine Monte Carlo, which showed exclusively Pathé films.[18] This theater, established in May 1912, was located in the Puerta de Tierra sector of San Juan. Although an investor, Colorado did not himself manage the Cine Monte Carlo; rather, two men, named Ramón Bosch and Luis Ferreras, did so.[19] Still, Colorado's Pathé distribution business most likely exclusively supplied this cinema. By 1913 Colorado had extended his business connections to the Dominican Republic, for he claims in advertisements to be the sole distributor of the "Simpler" brand of film equipment in both Puerto Rico and Santo Domingo.[20]

As a distributor, Colorado engaged in the transnational exchange of cultural goods. His relationship to Pathé links him to the French cinema industry, but the records of many trips Colorado took by ship to New York City suggest that he probably acquired his materials from other Pathé distributors in the United States rather than directly from France.[21] His link to the Dominican Republic, although more expected than any to France given the geographical and cultural proximity of the two islands, further emphasizes the cycle of international exchange related to the cinema and other cultural industries in Puerto Rico.

Rafael Colorado as Cinematic Producer: Negotiating the Local and the Global

The achievement that has raised Colorado to historical eminence and ensured that he appears in every account of early Puerto Rican cinema is his having made the first clearly narrative film in Puerto Rico, *Un drama en Puerto Rico* (A drama in Puerto Rico, 1912). This film's production coincides with and helps explain a shift evident in Colorado's advertising of his business. In November 1912, he began to run a supplementary advertisement in every issue of *Gráfico*, a weekly arts journal that Colorado himself edited, that explicitly promoted the film production side of his company. The advertisement asserts that Rafael Colorado's photographic studio was the "first and only business in Puerto Rico dedicated to the manufacture of cinematographic pictures."[22] Such claims to "pioneering," although not otherwise documented, may well have been warranted given the relatively recent arrival of the cinema industry in Puerto Rico.

Even though archived newspapers contain few detailed descriptions of Colorado's first narrative film, *Un drama*, such sources yield important information about its production and reception. According to the newspaper *La democracia*, the film's story involves a cockfight. The article offers no more details about the plot but does give information about the film's production, noting that the movie was filmed in San Juan and shows "well-known places."[23] The article also mentions that Colorado made other films "despite the high expenses that these productions pose and the poor gains that they yield."[24] A contemporary article in the local magazine *Puerto Rico ilustrado* reveals that before releasing the film for public exhibition, Colorado arranged a private showing for journalists. The anonymous writer of this piece comments that the film "is a work of art which reveals that Mr. Colorado possesses a real vocation for the cinematographic scene."[25] Other reviews of the film, like that in *La democracia*, are also positive. According to the newspaper *La correspondencia*, the premiere film screening sold out, with more than two hundred people left out of the show.[26] One might well question the accuracy of this report, however, due to its function as a movie theater announcement and promotion. Still, the film played for at least a week in at least two theaters, receiving thereby a considerable amount of exposure in the capital city.[27]

Newspapers further document that *Un drama* played in theaters along with two other Colorado productions, *Rosita Realí* (1912), which presented footage of a fashionable dancer and her trademark dance, and *Batallón Puertorriqueño* (Puerto Rican Battalion, 1912), which most likely presented footage of the Porto Rico Provisional Regiment of Infantry, the only native military squadron allowed by the U.S. government before 1917.[28] The exhibition of these two films as well as *Un drama* indicates that Colorado shot actualities alongside fictional dramas; the diversity of production may have aimed to meet varied audience interests and ensure sufficient profit to finance further film projects.

Colorado continued in 1913 with active film production in Puerto Rico, making by August of that year a second narrative film titled *Maffia moderna* (Modern Mafia). An article about the film in *Gráfico* indicates that the film was a comedy shot in, or portraying, the area of Puerta de Tierra in Old San Juan.[29] The same article announces that the Cine Puerto Rico Company had acquired new filmmaking equipment and now aimed to distribute its films throughout the Caribbean: "The artist Mr. Colorado has previously experimented in filmmaking, but today the Cine Puerto Rico Company, which he founded, has a workshop equipped with all the latest equipment to manufacture films and be able to meet the demands of the Puerto Rican market and that of the neighboring Antilles and America."[30] The article employs a clearly nativist rhetoric in claiming that because the advertised film (*Maffia moderna*) was made in Puerto Rico and dealt with "Puerto Rican themes," it would have more success in the island's market than would "foreign" films.[31] As one can deduct from the scarcity of Puerto Rican productions and the great variety of American and European productions that circulated in the island, local audiences did not appear to "crave" films with "Puerto Rican themes" more than films without said themes made elsewhere. For example, in April 1913, the theater Tres Banderas advertised in *Gráfico* an Edison production titled *A Tudor Princess* (1913) and a Pathé production of *Les Misérables* (1913).[32] A month later Tres Banderas advertised a film with the title *Desdemona* (possibly a 1912 Danish production), and a Chicago Essanay production titled *Take Me Out to the Ball Game* (1910).[33] Despite the small sample size, the foregoing

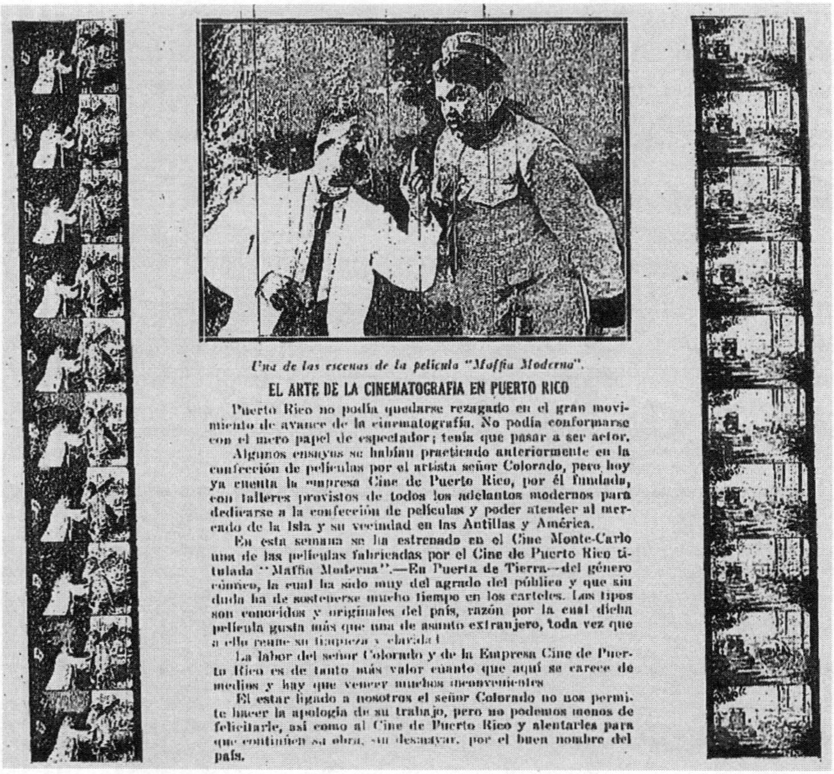

Una de las escenas de la película "Maffia Moderna".

EL ARTE DE LA CINEMATOGRAFIA EN PUERTO RICO

Puerto Rico no podía quedarse rezagado en el gran movimiento de avance de la cinematografía. No podía conformarse con el mero papel de espectador; tenía que pasar a ser actor.

Algunos ensayos se habían practicado anteriormente en la confección de películas por el artista señor Colorado, pero hoy ya cuenta la empresa Cine de Puerto Rico, por él fundada, con talleres provistos de todos los adelantos modernos para dedicarse a la confección de películas y poder atender al mercado de la Isla y su vecindad en las Antillas y América.

En esta semana se ha estrenado en el Cine Monte-Carlo una de las películas fabricadas por el Cine de Puerto Rico titulada "Maffia Moderna".—En Puerta de Tierra—del género cómico, la cual ha sido muy del agrado del público y que sin duda ha de sostenerse mucho tiempo en los carteles. Los tipos son conocidos y originales del país, razón por la cual dicha película gusta más que una de asunto extranjero, toda vez que a ello reúne su limpieza y claridad.

La labor del señor Colorado y de la Empresa Cine de Puerto Rico es de tanto más valor cuanto que aquí se carece de medios y hay que vencer muchos inconvenientes.

El estar ligado a nosotros el señor Colorado no nos permite hacer la apología de su trabajo, pero no podemos menos de felicitarle, así como al Cine de Puerto Rico y alentarles para que continúen su obra, sin desmayar, por el buen nombre del país.

FIG. 3.2 Promotion for *Maffia moderna* (1913)

film list shows that Puerto Ricans consumed films originating from various international sources, and dealing with different cosmopolitan (Hugo, Shakespeare) and regional (British history, baseball) topics. Distributors do not appear to have chosen films based on their particular similarity or applicability to the "Puerto Rican reality" but rather following global trends. Additionally, Colorado's advertisement does not explain what the "Puerto Rican themes" mentioned in the announcement might be. Does the ad possibly refer to films being set in Puerto Rico, or to their iconography and encoded ethnicity? Whatever the implications, the phrase clearly validates the local in contrast to abundant international products circulating in the Puerto Rican market. Further, since Colorado distributed the French Pathé line, his position about the superiority of local products seems to put his two businesses (distribution and production) at odds with each other. Also worth noting, this article contains the first occurrence that I have found of this ongoing nativist argument as used to promote Puerto Rican film production and its consumption in the presence of a globalized market.

Nonetheless, the employment of nativist rhetoric and iconography to promote the local film industry was not particular to the Puerto Rico case. For example, as Bill Rout argues, "Australian films of the 1910s and 1920s . . . capitalized on their Australianness, attempting to attract local audiences with recognizable local landscapes, character types, [and] Australian literature and theatre."[34] Similarly, in Ireland, local filmmakers during the 1910s chose to produce films based on local works and historical events, with, according to Kevin Rockett, the historically themed movies playing a particularly important role in "advancing national consciousness."[35] Thus, filmmakers from around the world recognized the potential of an appeal to the local to make their films stand out amid the many global productions circulating in their local markets.

After *Maffia moderna*, Colorado made an actuality in 1914, as an article published in the November 1916 edition of *Cine-Mundial* comments on a two-year-old film by Colorado titled *Una procesión en el mar*.[36] According to the magazine, the film captured an actual religious procession that took place in the Cataño side of the San Juan bay. The article also comments that the film had "relative success" but does not mention any further details about it or its exhibition.[37] Interestingly, the same *Cine-Mundial* article reveals that another man, Francisco Maymón, the owner of the Yaguez Theater located in the western town of Mayaguez, also made a film in 1914. The magazine gives the title of Maymón's film as *Escenas de Puerto Rico* (Scenes of Puerto Rico), and comments that the most attractive views in the film came from the Guajataca forest in Isabela (another western town), suggesting that the film focused on views of nature. Finally, *Cine-Mundial* observes that the film enjoyed great success in the filmmaker's town, Mayaguez, but that he had not made a film since. The appearance of another filmmaker during the period (even if he made only one film) suggests that at least an elite public had taken notice of Colorado's early work, and that enough interest in the film business existed throughout the island to lead to a filmmaking experiment outside of San Juan.

In 1915 Colorado introduced an important change to his filmmaking business by shooting outside of Puerto Rico on a neighboring island. According to José Luis Sáez, at some point between June 18 and 27, 1915,

Colorado shot an actuality titled *Excursión de José de Diego en Santo Domingo* (José de Diego's visit to Santo Domingo, 1915) in the Dominican Republic.[38] Sáez further relates that Colorado had come to Santo Domingo in the company of José de Diego, who was at that time the president of the Puerto Rican House of Representatives, explicitly to film the event. Colorado's position as a personal companion and official "documenter" of the event suggests that he perhaps had a privileged position inside political circles and conceivably had become a well-known filmmaker in Puerto Rico. In addition, his shooting, and even later exhibiting, the film in the Dominican Republic further emphasizes Colorado's position as a transnational business and cultural figure. Even as Colorado appears to have evolved into a recognized filmmaker, at least in San Juan, he also maintained his business as a photographer and film distributor in and outside Puerto Rico. After an apparently less "productive" period in 1914–1915, Colorado was again very industrious in 1916, producing at least five films that year.

In July 1916 both *La correspondencia* and *La democracia* made reference to a film made by Colorado titled *El milagro de la Virgen* (The Virgin's miracle).[39] *La correspondencia* notes that an actor named Alberto Durero played the film's protagonist and offers a critique which suggests that the film's setting, while beautiful, overshadowed the action and Mr. Durero's performance.[40] Aside from offering this evaluation, the author of the piece does not discuss the film's plot, nor does this article, nor the one that appeared in *La democracia*, describe the film's imagery. The title of the film, however, implies that the plot may have involved some personal crisis averted by a miracle, perhaps called forth by religious devotion.

A couple weeks after *El milagro*'s premiere, another Colorado production, *Fiestas del 4 de julio en San Juan* (Festivities of the Fourth of July in San Juan, 1916), opened and played on the same program.[41] The descriptive title and subject matter, a surprising discovery in light of Colorado's presumed anticolonial stance, suggest that this film was a short actuality. Whether or not the festivities shown were themselves explicitly colonialist in nature, the film probably showed the local distinguished elite meeting socially on the occasion of the U.S. celebration. Still, politically, 1916 was a particularly fraught year: in May, Luis Muñoz Rivera delivered one of his most famous speeches in favor of Puerto Rican independence.[42] Furthermore, on August 29, 1916, the U.S. Congress passed the Jones Law, which allowed the Philippines to create an autonomous local government and initiated legislative discussion of what would become the Jones Act of 1917 (which granted Puerto Ricans American citizenship). The absence not only of surviving prints but also of detailed newspaper descriptions makes it impossible to know the film's precise content or even its approach to the title subject. Despite the temptation to read ideological motives into the film, there are no indications that this film had any political message attached to it.

Whatever the implications of the film about the Fourth of July activities in San Juan, Colorado did make another film, also likely an actuality, with a clear political subject: *Llegada de don Luis Muñoz Rivera* (The arrival of Mr. Luis Muñoz Rivera, 1916). Local newspapers carried extensive coverage of this film, probably because of Luis Muñoz Rivera's status as perhaps the most important political figure in Puerto Rico at the time, holding the position of the first resident commissioner to the United States. An article in *La democracia* preserves a clear description of the film and lists the film's intertitles as follows:

> The watchman pointing at the "Carolina." The steamship going through the canal. Entering the port. Having a glimpse of Muñoz Rivera, we can see thousands of hands applaud. Muñoz Rivera greets from the deck. The public at the dock moving like a giant wave. The rally marching. Muñoz Rivera passing between flags. Cars parade through Fortaleza Street. Text of Mr. Tous Soto's telegram. Muñoz Rivera in the Ateneo's balcony delivering his speech. Paragraphs of the speech. Muñoz Rivera surrounded by misters Barceló, Huyke, Díaz Navarro and other members of the party. The rally dissolving in Baldorioty square. Cars passing through the Colón square accompanying the Resident Commissioner to Washington. In the parterre of Mr. Eduardo Giorgetti's manorial house. Muñoz Rivera meeting with the island's delegates and important members of the party. Parade.[43]

The officials named in the intertitles were all members of the Partido Unión, which at the time of the film's exhibition opposed the extension of U.S. citizenship to Puerto Rico.[44] The emphasis on that party and its officials, while giving an air of popular support to the local government, does not necessarily suggest a particular political stance, for the Partido Unión in fact espoused a range of political relations with the United States, from independence to annexation.[45] Certainly, given the popularity of the party, and the ample newspaper coverage of the political proceedings in the United States relating to Puerto Rico, in making a film about the Partido

Unión and Luis Muñoz Rivera, Colorado made a wise commercial investment. Interestingly, some months later, Colorado joined other Partido Unión members (particularly Luis Lloréns Torres and Nemesio Canales) in forming another film company, the Tropical Film Company, the subject of the next chapter.

The newspaper *La democracia* reports that *Llegada de don Luis Muñoz Rivera* was shot, developed, and exhibited for the first time within less than forty hours following the event depicted.[46] That the topic proved popular with San Juan audiences emerges from the record of the film's running at least a full week, from September 23 through September 30, 1916. The article in *La democracia* indicates that Colorado planned to exhibit the film in both New York City and Washington, D.C., to showcase "what the power of ideas [can] represent and express."[47] I have found no evidence that the film ran in the United States, but the announced plan to export it, particularly to the U.S. capital city, together with the aforementioned "power of ideas" statement, and the contemporaneous U.S. political discussions about the citizenship status of Puerto Ricans, suggests that Colorado may have believed the film could somehow have political appeal. However, it is historically unlikely that U.S. audiences (perhaps not even American politicians in private screenings) would have had any interest in this film. Since the late nineteenth century, though, Puerto Ricans had been regularly sojourning or settling in the United States, particularly in New York City;[48] Colorado may have envisioned such expatriates as the targeted audience, presuming that an infrastructure was available for exhibiting films from Puerto Rico in New York City. In fact, Colorado had a son living in the United States, and he might have thought of him as an agent for the New York market since Rafael Junior had attended Cornell University and possibly made business connections in that state.[49] In addition, throughout his life, Colorado traveled widely between the United States (particularly to New York) and Puerto Rico, and likely made important business contacts there. Although I have not found evidence that Colorado's productions attained international distribution, as his business practices in both distribution and production show, Colorado himself nonetheless clearly was a transnational individual.

Concluding a highly productive year, in September 1916 Colorado released another completed film entitled *Por la hembra y por el gallo* (For the woman and the rooster). Although the film has apparently not survived, a detailed description of its plot appears in the September 20, 1916, issue of the San Juan newspaper *La correspondencia*. According to the newspaper article, the film tells the story of a wealthy man named Méndez who buys a coffee plantation, and, upon arriving to claim the land, falls in love with an orphaned plantation worker, Lucía. However, Lucía already loves one of the hardworking farmhands, Cleto. (Movie stills uncovered by Juan Ortiz Jiménez reveal that the actors playing all of these characters are white).[50] An antagonistic relationship develops between Cleto and Mr. Méndez, with the boss challenging the worker to stage a cockfight. Cleto's rooster is smaller than Méndez's, but despite Méndez's cheating, Cleto still manages to win. Furious, Méndez taunts and pushes Cleto and then pulls a gun on him after the worker, in self-defense, apparently strikes the boss with his rooster—an act that may have generated a comedic moment. Although others prevent a shooting, Cleto gets banned from the premises but cannot resist returning to visit Lucía. A fight ensues when Méndez catches him, but just as Cleto is on the verge of winning the struggle, Méndez's horse charges and knocks Cleto to the ground. Seeing Lucía nearby, Méndez ties Cleto to a tree and then threatens to take advantage of her. In frightened self-defense, Lucía kills Méndez with his own gun, frees Cleto, and flees the scene in panic. Local officials find the wounded Cleto near Méndez's body and accuse him of murder, a charge Cleto accepts to protect his beloved. But Lucía appears at the trial to take the blame herself. Here the description of the film stops, but we can discern from a previous reference in the article's narrative that a witness of the fight who had hidden in the tree would then have appeared by surprise to exonerate both Lucía and Cleto.[51]

Colorado was not the scriptwriter of this film; his brother-in-law and business partner Antonio Capella wrote the screenplay. Still, the choice of antagonist seems somewhat at odds with Colorado's (and Capella's similar) social position. Coming from an elite Spanish family, Colorado belonged to the same social group as the villain Méndez. Furthermore, coffee plantations at the time, unlike, for example, sugar plantations, were typically owned by "criollos," making it one of the few local industries not controlled by absentee U.S. capital. Against the historiographic background asserting Colorado as an anticolonialist, one might well wonder at the feature film taking as its villain the Puerto Rican owner of a coffee farm, rather than an American sugar plantation owner.

Even more remarkable than the national characterization of the villain is the subtle Marxist tone that infuses the plot. The film characterizes the local bourgeoisie, exemplified in Mr. Méndez, as greedy, callous, and abusive, while the workers, like Lucía and Cleto, are industrious, kind, and strong. Curiously, the year *Por la hembra* came out, 1916, is also the birth year of the Puerto Rican Socialist Party, an event that points to a heightened interest among political circles about labor conditions and workers' rights. I do not mean to suggest that Colorado was clearly a socialist, but rather that then prevalent socialist discourses may have influenced the film's privileging of the socially disadvantaged characters, perhaps with respect to potential audience appeal. Yet we can better understand the film's choice of protagonist in the context of the genre of melodrama.

The description of the film narrative reveals numerous characteristics of a melodrama. Geoffrey Nowell-Smith summarizes typical melodrama of the period as "accentuat[ing . . .] moral and dramatic values around characteristic motif-heroes spurred to action by revelations of unspeakable villainy, leading to last-minute rescues of innocent heroines, *deus ex machina* endings, and the like."[52] Historians of American cinema have well demonstrated how, by the 1910s, the film industry in the United States had effectively adapted the highly popular theatrical genre of melodrama.[53] The immense popularity of films like D. W. Griffith's *The Birth of a Nation* (1915) in the United States, or the rise of Italian divas like Lyda Borelli in the 1910s, evidences the great appeal of melodrama to global audiences.[54] Because of the wide circulation of American and European films in the Puerto Rican market as well as his position as a film distributor, Colorado (as well as scriptwriter Capella) must have been exposed to film melodramas prior to himself making *Por la hembra*.[55] Certainly the plot summary points to the screenwriter Capella's and likely director and distributor Colorado's familiarity with the internationally popular genre and that they sought to incorporate it into the nascent cinema industry of Puerto Rico.

Another noteworthy aspect of *Por la hembra* is the film's focus on the local countryside and its imagery. Both Colorado's 1912 film *Un drama* and *Por la hembra* make use of the cockfighting motif and rural life as their setting. By 1910, Colorado lived in the urban space of the San Francisco neighborhood of San Juan and worked in industrially driven professions like publishing and photography; clearly, his films did not depict his own social space.[56] Instead, at least in the 1916 film, he utilized the figure of the white rural agricultural worker, known as the *jíbaro*, which along with rural life has long represented a common trope in Puerto Rican literature. The *jíbaro* circulated widely, for at least a century, from the time Manuel Alonso (1822–1889) published his well-known book *El gíbaro* in 1845 through (and beyond) the 1947 publication of Abelardo Díaz Alfaro's celebrated short story collection *Terrazo*. In its early incarnations, for example, in writings by Alonso or Manuel Zeno Gandía (1855–1930), writers do not portray the *jíbaro* in a positive light: s/he is uneducated, promiscuous, careless with money, and manifests other such character weaknesses. Conversely, by the early twentieth century, poets like Virgilio Dávila (1869–1943) and Luis Lloréns Torres (1876–1944) had made the image of the *jíbaro* a positive symbol of Puerto Rican nationalism: hardworking, proud, and patriotic. Those writers also clearly valorized the *jíbaro* as white.[57]

The romanticization of the white rural worker of the mountain region forms part of the trend of the idealized hispanization of Puerto Rico as a nationalist claim against U.S. colonization. Thus, as Francisco Scarano argues, although initially the *jíbaro* served as a mask from which to criticize the Spanish colonial government by adhering to a local ethnic identity politics, by the first half of the twentieth century the *jíbaro* had acquired paradoxically positive Spanishness.[58] Because of the nationalist meaning that contemporary literary criticism has traced in the figure of the *jíbaro* and the mountainous coffee regions of Puerto Rico, scholars like Ramón Barco and Ramos Perea have found in Colorado's work traces of Puerto Rican nationalism. However, use of the figure of the *jíbaro* is not necessarily tantamount to expressing a political position. Whatever his later views might have been, at the time of the film's production, Colorado had not made any political statements about the status of Puerto Rico in relation to the United States. Thus, one cannot safely assume that the presence of the rural theme meant that Colorado was a Puerto Rican nationalist.

Instead of serving as a clear mark of cultural nationalism, the mixing of Puerto Rican iconography with international elements in the film, like its typing as melodrama, signals an instance of convergence between the local and the global inherent in Puerto Rican culture. Thus we can credit Colorado with introducing the *jíbaro*, a well-known literary figure, into the new cultural and globalized media of cinema. Clearly his film *Por la hembra* elaborated established Puerto Rican cultural traditions in close integration with world trends that he appropriated into the Puerto Rican scene. Thereby, again, Colorado obviously engaged in a transnational exchange of cultural products.

Considering thus the development of melodrama in other locales, one cannot claim that the *jíbaro* figure proves that *Por la hembra* was a product solely of Puerto Rican cultural discourses. Instead, the film represents a cultural negotiation between the international and the national. Still, the transnational influences on *Por la hembra* do not invalidate any role the film played in the process of the Puerto Rican nation building. On the contrary, transnational exchanges are integral parts of the Puerto Rican nation, as is most clearly symbolized in the paradoxical political status and official name of the island: Associated Free State.

Colorado's historiographic status and indeed, I would argue, his documented influence on Puerto Rican cinema extends beyond his negotiating local and global trends in the structure, style, and plots of the films he made. Many have credited and widely praised Colorado as the first person to incorporate a film company in Puerto Rico, thereby laying the groundwork for an industry approach to filmmaking. According to official government business records uncovered by Juan Ortiz Jiménez, Colorado and his brother-in-law Antonio Capella incorporated the company under the name Cine Puerto Rico on March 18, 1916, to produce *Por la hembra.*[59] Notably, the legally incorporated company took the same name that Colorado had used for his film distribution business since at least 1912, under which rubric he had produced his previous films. Thus, while de jure he founded Cine Puerto Rico in 1916, the business had de facto existed since at least 1912. Even if solely family members made up the company, the move to incorporate the business (which he seems not to have deemed necessary previously) appears to be a legal economic protection for himself and his partner and brother-in-law, whether the film failed or proved extremely successful. In fact, by 1920 Colorado had separated from (and later divorced) Capella's sister, breaking the family tie between the two.[60] Also, Colorado might have sought legal recognition for his film business because he had not supplied the entire capital for the production of *Por la hembra*.

Despite his extensive production of films inside the geographic territory of Puerto Rico and his undeniable importance in the development of the film business in the island, Colorado was clearly a transnational figure rather than a presumably unadulterated Puerto Rican cultural producer. Therefore, we can see that the conservative definition that many scholars have assigned to Puerto Rican cinema (films made by a Puerto Rican, depicting and produced in the island) is at odds with the transnational reality of the development of the film industry in Puerto Rico. In his identity as a private lifelong subject of the Spanish kingdom as well as in his work as cinema distributor and producer, Colorado exemplified the transnational connections that have helped to construct Puerto Rican culture, as well as the difficulty of defining what is and who is a national. Yet the complexity of assigning nationality in Puerto Rico extends well beyond individual cases and in fact highlights the problems embedded in defining the nation outside the legal confines of the state structure.

Citizenship in a Stateless Nation: Constructing the Puerto Rican Subject

The coexistence of colonialism and a deep-rooted cultural nationalism entails the simultaneous experience of cross-cultural/territorial development and a homeland-centered nationalist political rhetoric, even though the two political realities are seemingly at odds with each other. Because of these contradictions in the political development of the island, the construction of the Puerto Rican cultural subject masks transnational exchanges within conservative nationalist rhetoric. Puerto Rico's position as a stateless nation means that Puerto Ricans cannot measure belonging in terms of citizenship; rather, we exclusively focus on constructing the nation around unifying myths of shared values and experiences. Homi Bhabha has cogently argued that "the political unity of the nation consists in a continual displacement of its irredeemably plural modern space . . . into a signifying space that is archaic and mythical."[61] Bhabha's point elucidates why cross-cultural/transnational relations might be rhetorically ignored or deemphasized in the service of a unifying and incontestably nationalist discourse.

The popular nationalist rhetoric, with its emphasis on geographical markers of belonging, makes it easy for film scholars to formulate narratives of uncontested Puerto Ricanness when the subject discussed resides within the geographical limits of the islands of Puerto Rico. In other words, although a strong ethnic component helps to determine who does and does not belong (which can sometimes become xenophobic when dealing with marginalized groups such as Dominicans), most Puerto Ricans in the island do not define nationality based on blood lines like many ethnic nationalisms do. Instead, its people conceive Puerto Ricanness as a cultural discourse that nearly everyone living in the island—despite their actual birth place—can deploy within the geographical confines of Puerto Rico. Interestingly, ethnic/national definitions of Puerto Ricanness inside the United States do not follow the same pattern. While a Spaniard can come and reside in Puerto Rico, effectively becoming Puerto Rican after a decade of living in the island, the same does not hold true for a Spaniard residing in a traditionally Puerto Rican neighborhood in, for example, the Bronx.

However, despite the accessibility of Puerto Ricanness today, at the turn of the century and into the 1910s, declaring oneself a Puerto Rican national was a much more controversial position. As noted in chapter 1, U.S. officials, in fact, imprisoned many nationalist leaders as a result of their political positions. Therefore, although one can retroactively assert that Rafael Colorado actively contributed to the national cultural project, one must also acknowledge that he very unlikely considered himself a Puerto Rican nationalist. As Carlos Pabón has noted, not until the mid-twentieth century, with the ascendance to power of the Popular Democratic Party (PPD for its Spanish acronym), did "the national" become an official position of the local state.[62] Historians have easily traced the institutionalization of Puerto Rican culture and the political consensus over nationalist symbols to the PPD's Operation Serenity and its promotion of cultural nationalism, which developed forty years after Colorado produced his first films.[63]

Adding to Puerto Rico's complicated political position, the lack of a state-supported cinema industry further obscures the categorization of productions as Puerto Rican. Nonetheless, this lack of state support also means the absence of a clear-cut space of national definition as well as an extremely hard economic reality that deters production in the island. Given the circulation of so many discourses about what constitutes the national cinema, I would argue that any film involving a trace of Puerto Ricanness—geographic, linguistic, thematic, or ideological—could count as a Puerto Rican film.

When it comes to assigning nationality to cultural producers such as Colorado, many Puerto Ricans tend to look at how their acts affect the construction of cultural history under nationalist models. More than delineating a formula for determining who belongs and does not belong, as is the case with legal citizenship, the designation of "nationality" may relate to perceived cultural "productivity." Because he produced and lived inside the island for an extended period of time, despite his legal nationality (which in 1917 became de facto American), Colorado and also his productions are categorically assigned (even awarded) Puerto Rican nationality. Further, Colorado's use and command of the Spanish language (constructed historically as a strong marker of Puerto Ricanness) accelerates his acceptance among film scholars as Puerto Rican. By contrast, most scholars deny U.S. films produced or depicting the island a space in the national imaginary because of the inability to adapt these films into the current nationalist rhetoric that claims uniqueness and difference from the United States.

Yet Colorado's recurrent contacts and travel between Puerto Rico and the United States and to the Caribbean (with documented trips to the Dominican Republic and Cuba), even if only for professional reasons, raise questions over traditional discourses that restrict Puerto Rican culture to a certain territorial space. To be precise, the cultural flow of American and European products through noncolonial agents suggests a somewhat agreed-upon cultural exchange that predates the great Puerto Rican migratory waves of the mid-twentieth century. Although Puerto Rican film historians tend to overlook the importance of exhibition inside the historical narrative of the development of cinema in the island, filmmaking did not spontaneously appear in Puerto Rico. Instead, the exposure to nonnative products that circulated in the island for years motivated individuals to engage in the production of films. Further, Colorado—as someone who worked in selling cinema equipment and films before becoming a filmmaker—had frequent and constant contact with non–Puerto Rican productions and products (especially American ones), and thus his works manifest transnational interactions. Moreover, I contend that the case of Rafael Colorado symptomatically reveals trends and events in cinema on the island that require us to develop a consciously transnational approach to Puerto Rican historiography.

The following chapter discusses how the political climate surrounding the passage by the U.S. government of the Jones Act of 1917, which eventually led to American citizenship for Puerto Ricans, affected how Puerto Rican filmmakers and critics as well as audiences more generally envisioned local productions. There I demonstrate that the tense political climate of 1916–17 transformed filmmaking into an explicitly active agent—if primarily in the realm of discourse—of the nation-building project.

4

In the Company of the Elites

The Discourses and Practices of the Tropical Film Company (1916–1917)

During the late 1910s, cinema's presence in Puerto Rico grew steadily as numerous movie houses opened, not only in San Juan but also in other important cities in the island. Newspapers of the period document the names of many early film theaters: the Tres Banderas, the Ideal, the Luna, the Norma, the Montecarlo, all in San Juan, as well as the Delicias (Ponce), the Habana (Ponce), the Beliograph (Cataño), and the Variedades (Bayamón), among many others.[1] With the growth of movie theaters came increased interest in the social capabilities of film. More specifically, educated circles began to see filmmaking as an intellectual activity or an educational tool for the budding nation. Although Rafael Colorado had already explored the artistic and economic potential of making films in Puerto Rico, not until 1916, when he joined two Puerto Rican intellectuals, Nemesio Canales and Luis Lloréns Torres, did filmmakers delve into the politicocultural potential of cinema. The Tropical Film Company, as they named the new film production company, represented a novel intellectual outlook about the role that filmmaking could effect in the nation-building process in Puerto Rico.

The short-lived Tropical Film Company (1916–1917), the first indisputably "native" film company, emphasized national-cultural concepts in its production work. Yet the company's activities also reveal multiple and sometimes contradictory impulses and goals, which in fact characterize subsequent Puerto Rican filmmaking and its association with the nation-building process more generally.[2] Lloréns and Canales, two intellectuals known for their involvement in the national independence movement, initiated the company (along with Colorado), with the aim of reaching both local and international audiences, particularly in the United States. Archival documentation reveals that the company completed four productions, of which no copies remain. However, counter to received Puerto Rican film historiography, I find the short-lived Tropical Film Company's contributions historically significant, not primarily because of the filmmakers' explicitly stated political/cultural commitment (which some historians have acclaimed), nor for its exceptional aesthetic achievements (which we cannot verify), but rather because of the company's negotiation of conflicting educational, cultural, and economically focused discourses within the limitations of the financial and infrastructural resources that then existed, and still persist, for locally based cinematic production, distribution, and exhibition in Puerto Rico. Moreover, the company's vision of the role of film primarily as a cultural ambassador has surprisingly remained the standard conceptualization for the island's filmmakers to this day.

Unlike Colorado's Cine Puerto Rico, established and headed only by Colorado (later joined by Antonio Capella), the Tropical Film Company involved many individuals who evidently fulfilled specific business roles. In a 1917 article published in the local literary magazine *Juan Bobo*, the company announced its board of directors as follows: on the business side, Ernesto López Díaz as president; Enrique Vidal, treasurer; and Ricardo Casal, secretary; as well as two additional board members, Antonio Pérez Pierret and Manuel Camuñas. Further, on the artistic side stood Rafael Colorado, technical director; Luis Lloréns Torres, scriptwriter; and Nemesio Canales, artistic director.[3] It appears that Lopéz Díaz provided at least some of the capital, given that he was a wealthy plantation owner (which also makes it unlikely that he was directly involved with productions, since plantations functioned year round in Puerto Rico).[4] To date, I have not found descriptions of the extent to which the other board members were involved.

Most scholars place the founding of the Tropical Film production company in 1917; however, I have discovered evidence that the company had already produced (or at least appropriated) a documentary by late November 1916.[5] Regardless of the precise date of its founding, the company clearly operated in years contemporaneous with the passing of the Jones Act in the U.S. Congress (signed into law by Woodrow Wilson on March 2, 1917), which granted American citizenship to Puerto Ricans, a locally elected congress, and, to men, the right to vote (although not for federal positions). I highlight this historical event because it laid the groundwork for the relationship that Puerto Rico and the United States have today. The Jones Act tied Puerto Ricans to the United States (without any form of consultation) by making them citizens, but at the same time it granted a certain degree of autonomy by allowing the space for a Puerto Rican Congress to be established, one that would be composed of and elected by Puerto Rican men. It was in this climate of political ambiguity that this production company incorporated and produced its films. According to company promotion, its purpose was "to create the most patriotic labor that can be conceived by making entirely Puerto Rican films in which our customs, our traditions, our landscape, and all the eclectic details that constitute our disputed national entity, palpitate."[6] The item makes clear that the company considered Puerto Rico's political status and its cultural traditions extremely significant, to such an extent that they dared to deem their project the most patriotic undertaking ever in Puerto Rico (placing it even above the Grito de Lares!).[7] This statement functions as the first express association between filmmaking in Puerto Rico and a nation-building project. Although by 1913 Colorado had made explicit his view that Puerto Rican "themes" would attract Puerto Rican audiences, his statements did not disclose any conviction about the patriotic value of his work, as the declarations of the Tropical Film Company clearly did.[8]

Significantly, two of the artistic directors of the Tropical Film Company, Lloréns and Canales, had previously begun to produce and edit *Juan Bobo*, an intellectual literary magazine. Namely, Lloréns and Canales, both then already well-known and respected writers and journalists, had in 1915 already succeeded in publishing that magazine and, as I discuss in this chapter, then, in 1916, used it as a platform from which to launch a new

FIG. 4.1 Nemesio Canales

artistic project, the Tropical Film Company. Although the magazine had already featured articles about film industries in other countries (such as the United States and Spain), along with a list of film showings in local theaters, after the inauguration of the Tropical Film Company, it ran numerous articles and advertisements geared to promoting this specific company. The relationship between Tropical Film and the literary magazine *Juan Bobo* echoed the relationship that Colorado had established between his own magazine, *Gráfico,* and his film company, Cine Puerto Rico. In both cases the magazine preceded and was more successful than the film company it promoted. Historically, the popularity and status of locally produced literature greatly exceeds that of locally produced cinema, even to this day. A careful analysis of the goals and experiences of the Tropical Film Company makes clear why cinema has not shared the success of other cultural forms in the identity-building process of the popular Puerto Rican imaginary.

FIG. 4.2 Luis Lloréns Torres

Inconsistencies in the Received Histories of the Tropical Film Company

Although resources are limited, with no films surviving and little contemporary material available, several scholars (García, Ortiz Jiménez, Ramos Perea) have conducted important initial historical research on the Tropical Film Company. However, these scholars all seem to follow an entangled line of argument, at once praising the attempts of the company as patriotic and enterprising, while generally dismissing those efforts as having little consequence. For example, Kino García in his book on Puerto Rican film asserts that "through the years, the efforts were always isolated, without continuity or any major consequences in the international filmic arena."[9] Yet, in another essay published in *Sargasso*, he argues that "from those first films which no longer exist, we learned there is a need to understand the importance of a sense of history and the study of history, in order to rescue our cultural heritage piece by piece."[10] In sum, García appears to argue that early film production in Puerto Rico matters only to Puerto Ricans, without it having broader impact elsewhere. Yet he calls for the creation of a national cinema, arguing that such a development has not yet occurred due to Puerto Rico's colonial situation: "Puerto Rico is an invaded country in every sense of the word and this fact affects the development of a national cinema."[11] Ultimately García implies that the history of Puerto Rico's (limited) film production can aid our understanding of the island's colonial relationship with the United States and the local cultural effects of that dynamic. Thus, he treats early cinematic endeavors largely as skirmishes on a sociopolitical battleground.

Film historian Juan Ortíz Jiménez similarly vacillates in the views he expresses about the significance of early productions. Ortíz contends that "what cinema has been produced in Puerto Rico has unfortunately not had major consequences. Every attempt has become something like a bad recollection that no one wants to confront, especially when someone among us shows interest in the economic and artistic potential of this fascinating mode of expression."[12] However, when discussing the Tropical Film Company, he in effect condemns the venture with faint praise as "a great effort."[13] Like García, Ortíz presumes a distinction, even a disjunction, between historical and industrial importance. To be exact, the two film historians separate cultural from economic value. They also share a vision of the film-production undertakings as nation-building projects. Both authors further posit the indispensability of cinema for the assertion of Puerto Rican cultural independence. Moreover, both researchers assert that filmmakers themselves have sought, historically as well as more recently, to highlight that distinction between the political-cultural and the industrial-aesthetic values of film production.

More radically than García and Ortíz, Roberto Ramos Perea sees even greater (post)colonial significance in film history in Puerto Rico. In his view, to its detriment, film in the island looks too much like American film: "For the last one hundred years we have been the idiot followers of a *gringo* cinema that has told us how to make our cinema, and of national filmmakers, themselves faithful lovers of Yankee cinema, who have wanted to claim with their works that only *that* cinema is "well done," and is the kind of cinema that should distinguish us, and the one before which we should lower our heads in shame for being a miserable colony that only knows to make films about its bandits and its low esteem for its women."[14] Although his comments express a clearly polemic view not necessarily shared by most scholars, Ramos's phrasing reveals the scholarly predilection toward addressing Puerto Rican films in relation only to the island's political status. These comments also raise the question of whether critics disdain those who might emulate the cultural productions of the United States because of the country's particular political situation and power, or because they perceive in such imitations a lack of creativity.

Although Ramos criticizes most contemporary Puerto Rican films and filmmakers, he makes an exception and reserves a place of honor for early films. In his opinion these productions reflect the best Puerto Rico has to offer because they had a "nationalistic" character.[15] Furthermore, he proposes that the early filmmakers were adventurous and fearless because they "made these movies with the purpose of showing that it could be done."[16] But he does not acknowledge, or had not discovered in the available record, that Tropical Film intended as part of the company's business strategy to have its films viewed by American audiences. Yes, the company showed an interest in creating a national culture dedicated to film, but as I demonstrate in the next section, the company also paradoxically looked to the American film industry as a business model. Thus, available evidence does not really support Ramos's claim that these early films were more nationally conscious than more recent undertakings. Ramos probably relies on the well-known reputation of the artistic directors of the Tropical Film Company, Lloréns and Canales, as pro-independence leaders as a basis for these assertions, rather than on company publicity and other documentary evidence of the company's goals and operation. Although the company had national and cultural aims, it also saw itself as a business, and for that matter a business that depended on the U.S. market. As I will discuss later, Tropical Film openly declared through its promotion in *Juan Bobo* its desire to export its material to the north, and it also argued for the powerful public relations service it considered its films could provide abroad through representing the "real" Puerto Rico.[17]

The Educational/Cultural Project of the Tropical Film Company

Despite my points of disagreement with scholars like García, Ortiz, and Ramos, I concur that, as they all suggest, it comes as no surprise that a company with Canales, Lloréns, and Colorado on its board (apparently as leading members) would attempt to create a project directed at establishing autonomy for the island. This conclusion follows due to Canales's and Lloréns's well-known pro-independence and Pan-American leanings, as well as to contributions Colorado made through his previous involvement in independent filmmaking. As literature and history scholar Arcadio Díaz notes, "[Lloréns], as well as Nemesio Canales, polemically parted ways from the more conservative members of the patriotic elite, to postulate a less abstract nationalism, and on occasion, to directly attack the notion of 'homeland' of the 'lyrical tribunes.'"[18] As Díaz notes, both Canales and Lloréns understood nationalism as an actual political project, not just a declaration of cultural identity. Therefore, when the publicity for the Tropical Film Company, which Canales and Lloréns disseminated through *Juan Bobo*, refers to a "patriotic" or nationalistic endeavor, they reference, most likely, an actual emancipatory project.

Despite this outwardly clear expression of patriotic, nationalistic sentiments, the Tropical Film Company was full of contradictions, starting with its name. The New York City directory of 1917 reveals that in mid-1916 (when the information was compiled for the 1917 publication), a Tropical Film Company existed in the United States. The directory discloses that William F. Cox and Carl Deforest Pryer then owned the company. The New York Tropical Film Company made what appear to be two pro-U.S. intervention films: *Following the Flag in Mexico* (1916) and *United States Marines under Fire in Haiti* (1916).[19] Of the two company members, William Cox seems to have provided the capital for the films, for the New York City directory lists him as an investor (and his 1917 required registration for possible drafting into the U.S. military gives his occupation bluntly as "capitalist").[20] However, he may also have been involved in the making of the company's films, as ship records show that he traveled to Haiti (the shooting location of one of the films) twice in 1915.[21] Still, his position in the company must have been that of a producer, since Cox, originally from Massachusetts, appears to have settled in New York City working as a stockbroker (not an artist).[22] By contrast, the 1910 census describes Pryer as a photographer, and newspaper reports credit him as the films' director, documenting his involvement in the artistic aspects of the film.[23] In addition, during the 1910s, Pryer, who was originally from Kansas, had traveled to Mexico, Central America, the "West Indies" and Cuba, where he worked in what he called "Industrial and Historical Photography." Newspaper records also show that he continued to work as a filmmaker into the 1930s.[24]

The two films the U.S.-based Tropical Film Company produced ostensibly presented U.S. military interventions in Mexico and Haiti positively, glorifying American soldiers and calling for cooperation among American nations. The American Film Institute describes the plot of the first film, *Following the Flag in Mexico*, as follows:

> At the northern Mexico border, General Francisco "Pancho" Villa poses. After Villa's raid on Columbus, New Mexico, dead men and horses lie in the streets, and ruins are in smoke. Major General Frederick Funston, of Fort Sam Houston, San Antonio, Texas, poses. American troops pass by the Alamo as they leave for the border. General Venustiano Carranza, Mexico's provisional president, sends a large army to cooperate with U.S. troops, led by General John J. Pershing, who poses at Columbus. Refugees crossing the Rio Grande are searched, vaccinated, and marched across the desert to internment camps at Fort Bliss, Texas. After some battles, Carranza triumphantly enters Mexico City. A federal soldier is captured and shot by a rebel firing squad. After a battle that lasts six days, Juarez is occupied by rebels. Street fighting occurs in Torréon. Villa's commanders are defeated. The American Red Cross treats wounded. Peaceful noncombatants, including an American and an Englishman, who were executed by Villa troops, hang in trees. Finally, a military funeral for American dead at Columbus is conducted.[25]

As the description indicates, this film appears to have presented Mexican soldiers as violently depraved and American ones as empathic saviors. According to the American Film Institute's description of the second film, *Marines under Fire in Haiti*, this film expressed an equally positive attitude toward U.S. military occupation in the hemisphere:

> The Monroe Doctrine is the rationale given for U.S. intervention in Haiti. Scenes at Port-au-Prince include wrecks of ships from 1804, the shore where Christopher Columbus landed, his home, the church Columbus erected during his stay, and the Cathedral Market. Dr. Bobo, the revolutionary chief,

> is shown. Marines fight against Dr. Bobo's "Cacos," or guerrillas, at Cape Haitien and Jacmel. A shell explodes killing several Cacos dashing up a mountain pass. Rear Admiral William Banks Caperton receives U.S. Charge D'Affairs R. B. Davis. At Jacmel harbor, the U.S. Consul and Lieutenant John Quincy Adams, a marine, are shown. Sisters of Mercy treat the injured poor. Marines are shown at review. An awkward Haitian squad drills. In the interior, a marine field hospital operates. The last fighting of the revolutionaries occurs near Cape Haitien, after which the peace pact is signed. Haitian industries, including bananas, coconuts, coffee and sugarcane, are presented. President Philippe Sudre Dartiguenave states that he intends to make Haiti a prosperous, enlightened and progressive nation. A call for U.S. preparedness to protect rather than to conquer is issued.[26]

Although apparently more sympathetic toward the Haitians than the previous production seemed to have been toward Mexicans, this film also glorified U.S. troops and their involvement in the American hemisphere. Additionally, the U.S. Army's evidenced use of the American Tropical Film Company's films in recruitment efforts and official events indicate that these films represented, or at minimum accorded with, the military's official stance on its involvement in Latin America and the Caribbean.[27]

The New York City directory reveals that by 1917 the American Tropical Film Company had disbanded; Cox disappears from the directory, and Pryer remains in the same Brooklyn location but is associated with a different enterprise, The Exploration and Research Film Company. Though the evidence is by no means definitive, it seems likely that Cox and Pryer had sold the Tropical Film Company and divided the assets by the end of 1916. Furthermore, the organization *Cinemovida* cites a report from Antonio Colorado, grandson of Rafael Colorado, noting that sometime before 1916 Colorado's studio had burned, forcing him to buy new equipment.[28] A New York–bound ship's manifest indicates that in December 1916 Colorado had traveled to New York, possibly to replace his lost equipment.[29] Although I can place Cox, Pryer, and Colorado in New York City at the same time, I do not have evidence of contact between them. Thanks to preserved passport applications and ship's manifests, I can also place both Pryer and Colorado on the island of Hispaniola between late 1915 and early 1916, but again have no evidence of direct contact.[30] Nonetheless, two filmmakers working in the mid-teens on the same Caribbean territory seem likely to have had opportunity to meet. Very plausibly, Colorado may have bought the American company's equipment and also its name, which could explain why a Puerto Rican–owned firm bore an unlikely English name. Further supporting this theory, in early 1917 an article in *Juan Bobo* about the creation of the film company declares that it had bought Rafael Colorado's studio and equipment, which "had been reinforced with the recent acquisition in New York of the latest apparatuses for filming, developing, and copying film."[31] If, in fact, as seems probable, the Puerto Rican filmmakers bought the New York company's name along with the equipment, the Puerto Rican Tropical Film Company would also have acquired other possible assets (even previous productions and other materials and business contacts) of a company that had made films directly contradicting the Puerto Ricans' anti-imperialist claims.

Further displaying contradiction in the Puerto Rican company's narrative, Tropical Film's stated target audience was not Puerto Rican, not even Latin American; instead announcements asserted that "the filmed dramas would be presented in the Yankee and European markets."[32] I find this ambition fascinating because, as Lloréns scholar Arcadio Díaz has argued, Lloréns was driven by "the opposing and vindicating words of a culture, the attack, at a literary level, of one of the aspects of imperialism, or, to say it in another way, the defense of the symbols that to them constituted the 'national culture.'"[33] And what bigger national symbol than people, film audiences?

However, though the Puerto Rican company bore a name in English, the titles of the movies that it produced did not. In addition, despite its desires to export, the company's main interest was clearly to produce films in and about Puerto Rico. In a 1917 issue of *Juan Bobo*, a contributor called "Lys Amencio" described the purpose of the Tropical Film Company as "the production of motion pictures primarily with subject matters and scenes of the country, both current and historic and with a tropical spirit."[34] That is, the company wanted to highlight Puerto Rico's culture and geography in an attempt to prove the island's social riches, both artistically *and* economically: "[the company] want[s], with enthusiasm, to make art and reveal to the masses the beauty of our country and what we can do here with this industry, which today is one of the most powerful industries in the world."[35] The filmmakers recognized film's political power and wanted to use it to assert the value and capacity of Puerto Rico and its inhabitants, in an international context.

Nonetheless, although the Tropical Film Company saw cinema's potential to express the island's right to sovereignty and autonomy, at least the artistic directors also understood cinema as an educational project for Puerto Ricans. Film scholar Luis Trelles's research has shown that in Puerto Rico, "the elites considered the new entertainment medium overly vulgar, and they reserved their own participation, following old traditions and customs, for the 'big shows,' meaning important theatrical and musical events."[36] Therefore, the Tropical Film Company faced a big task, not only of producing well-made, marketable films but also of attracting an audience from among the cultural and political elites, then a resistant public. Even *Juan Bobo,* Lloréns and Canales's magazine, expressed a negative perception of popular cinema: "Up to this date, mediocre authors have invaded this field, and thus the great bulk of films are coarse creations that resemble the cheap romances that are written for vulgar people. But the day that the great creators of beauty put their effort into not making film a select art of aesthetic emotions, exploiting for this the adequate subject matters for cinematography, on that day, which is not far off, film art will occupy a prominent rank alongside the most prominent aristocratic speculations."[37] The foregoing statement reveals that cultural elites, among them also Lloréns and Canales, generally saw film as a low form of entertainment, similar perhaps to current perceptions of television soap operas. Therefore, for the Tropical Film Company to make successful films, the company first had to change the opinion of investors capable of financially sustaining the enterprise. It appears that even though movie theaters proliferated, the film industry in Puerto Rico, as elsewhere, initially appealed to the middle and lower classes and not the elite capitalists who could fund filmmakers' ambitious projects.[38]

Nonetheless, despite the difficult task at hand, the magazine *Juan Bobo* seemed to have played an important role, particularly in cultivating public relations to attract the unenthusiastic upper class to the company's film projects. Since Canales and Lloréns were well known, and also recognized as belonging to the Union Party (the one with the most intellectuals affiliated), I can safely say that, at the very least, the intellectual elites of the country were aware of the duo's projects as expressed in their writings.[39] Nemesio Canales scholar Servando Montaña has concluded, "*Juan Bobo* was in its time the most lucid conscience of the Puerto Rican situation and the most valiant spokesman of liberty and justice against the political and social mediocrities of the times."[40] Montaña's analysis provides the context for understanding Canales and Lloréns's critical words and simultaneous defense of the visual medium and an educational campaign regarding the potential benefits of cinema for the nation.

Notably, *Juan Bobo*'s campaign promoting cinema did not begin with the incorporation of the Tropical Film Company, for the editors had joined the debates somewhat earlier. For example, in 1916, the secretary of Puerto Rico, Martín Travieso, had proposed the creation of a film censorship board. The writers of *Juan Bobo*, evidently outraged by the suggestion, published an ironic statement authored by "César Borgia" which rhetorically demanded, "What would you gain by moralizing the movie theaters, if you leave our eyes and ears exposed to the infernal contamination of the books, the newspapers, the theater, the oratory and other artistic mediums?"[41] This critical statement documents not only that Canales and Lloréns sought to defend artistic liberties but also that they rhetorically set film as equivalent to then more socially acceptable forms of popular entertainment. Their statement defined cinema as an artistic medium (as opposed to just a commercial product) as a strategy to defend films from censorship. However, they also took this opportunity to criticize the misuse of cinema and to suggest possible avenues for improvement, "and you, Mr. Travieso, still want us to take lightly the excess of morality in cinema, and you pretend to further inject films with more morality, even more pedestrian morality of the flock, of that idiotic morality of beatitude that causes nausea to every modern spirit gifted with any form of perception."[42] Although the editorials in *Juan Bobo* implied that the economic and political elites disliked film because it was full of sappy melodrama, the writers—almost certainly Canales and Lloréns—nevertheless saw potential in the medium and set out to make it a useful tool not only for artistic expression but also for political projects.

In order to make the higher classes (the primary readers of *Juan Bobo*) understand and respect film as an art form, the editors proposed means of bettering the medium, for, in their words, making it "less vulgar." Further, because, for the most part, intellectuals—themselves members of the economic elite—headed this company, they unavoidably tied film production's success to its consumption by this social group. Also, considering the capital-intensive nature of filmmaking, clearly only people with ample economic means could risk entering this business enterprise. Even to this day, the number of Puerto Ricans making films remains low. However, I do not agree with Francisco González's assertion that Puerto Rico has a constant and long-standing tradition in which "the industrial vision of cinema precedes its artistic mission," because the statement of intent of the Tropical Film Company manifests the participants' aspiration to associate their productions primarily with a cultural project and only secondarily focus on economic concerns.[43] More than a moneymaking enterprise, they saw their venture as a political and artistic mission. Nonetheless, company leaders needed to consider the marketing of their productions and may have considered the exportation of their works as central to their objectives, economically as well as politically.

The Tropical Film Company's Commercial Aims

In its less than one year of operation in Puerto Rico, the Tropical Film Company worked on the production of four films, all of which are lost: *Los funerales de Muñoz Rivera* (Muñoz Rivera's funeral, 1916), *Paloma del Monte* (1917), *El tesoro de Cofresí* (Cofresí's treasure, 1917) and *La viudita se quiere casar* (The widow wants to marry, 1917). Apart from one announcement in the New York–based magazine *Cine-Mundial* and two in the local newspapers *La democracia* and *La correspondencia*, all information I have gleaned about the Tropical Film Company's productions and goals comes from a series of articles published in *Juan Bobo* between December 1916 and March 1917. Although, as I will show in this section, there is insufficient evidence available to ascertain whether these films actually played in theaters (or were even finished), the advertisements and articles primarily published in *Juan Bobo* do document that the Company's expressed intention (if not their actual result) was not only to release the productions in Puerto Rico but also to export them to the United States and other markets.

From the Tropical Film Company's beginning, the filmmakers set the goal of showing the films they produced to both American and European audiences.[44] However, the company considered the productions' export as more than a way to increase profit. For them, the sales of the films in foreign markets offered a means to carry out two political objectives: first, to display the island's rich resources and culture to attract tourism, and second, to show that Puerto Ricans were a capable and self-sufficient people who could do things on their own. The *Juan Bobo* contributor writing as

"Lys Amencio" cites the views of Ricardo Casals, administrative director of the Tropical Film Company, on the economic concerns associated with the new film endeavors:

> If the North American public likes our productions, as has already been proven by the success we have obtained with other films, the result will be flattering. But essentially, the company will accomplish more important patriotic work than all the advertising and journalistic campaigns, which are excessively costly and limited. As you already know, a film on tour can be exhibited throughout the Union's territory and speaks with the public through the eyes, to those watching who know how to read and those who do not, of which there are not a few in North America; and this is what interests us, that people see that Puerto Rico is not the "pig's ear," as Champ Clark would generously say.[45]

Here Ricardo Casals describes the main goal of the company as the political defense and "authentic" representation of Puerto Rico, alongside profitability.

According to the company's publicity, the films would generate financial returns not only through the distribution of the films themselves but also through the tourism to Puerto Rico that the films would inspire. The company believed that "showing films [in the United States] would provoke a desire to know the country in those who can travel and would attract a great deal of American tourism to [the] island."[46] Therefore the enterprise sought to portray Puerto Rico as something culturally and geographically different from the United States, in an attempt to repudiate then dominant (North American) political arguments about the necessity and productivity of U.S. political intervention. Specifically, the company undertook to separate the acknowledged need for some U.S. economic investment from the strongly disputed need for political intervention. After all, during this time Nemesio Canales wrote in the local newspaper *La democracia* the following lines rhetorically addressing U.S. President Wilson: "Puerto Rico wants to be independent, like the rest of the American countries. And if it is true that your magnanimous Republic does not need to gain any profit from us, what prevents you from doing us justice, giving us the independence that we want?"[47]

In light of the filmmakers' clear commitment to Puerto Rican independence, the company's appeal to an American audience need not automatically signal an interest in closer involvement with or by the United States. In fact, despite the company's announced intentions, I have to date not found any evidence that the films the Tropical Film Company produced ever circulated outside Puerto Rico. I could not find any mention of the company or its films in the *New York Times*, *Variety*, or *Motion Picture World* of 1917. The only mention of Tropical Film in a U.S.-based trade magazine appears in the Spanish language *Cine-Mundial*. Although *Cine-Mundial*'s article announces the founding of the company and the future production of *El tesoro de Cofresí*, it does not mention the screening or even the actual production of any film.[48] However, since I do not know the English titles that possible distributors might have given the productions, there still remains a slim possibility that one or more played in the United States.

Even though I doubt that the Puerto Rican Tropical Film Company achieved the stated goals of exporting its productions, I propose to read that projected appeal as a strategic move toward a separation of "Puerto Ricanness" from "Americanness." Thus, as Kino García contends, "the common element of these productions seems to be the search for a theme and a self-image which could identify us as people."[49] At core, these films were indeed an attempt at a filmic creation of the nation. As Rafael Colorado had claimed before in relation to his film *Maffia moderna* (1913), the members of this company appear to believe in the existence of a Puerto Rican "essence," and in the difference and separation of this fundamental nature from that of the United States.[50]

Despite recurrent interest in cinema's potential for nation building, the status of the new medium remained socially controversial through the 1910s. In her study of film in Puerto Rico, Silvia Alvarez has found that "in the early days of film in Puerto Rico, debate centered on the cultural power of the new medium, the possibility of transmitting values, or subverting them, of contributing to domestication or to revolution."[51] Even if Puerto Ricans did not debate cinema as hotly as other national audiences did in the 1910s, the fact that some leaders thought the new medium influential enough to warrant censuring suggests why the Tropical Film Company considered cinema a potentially effective educational and political instrument. Certainly, as *Juan Bobo* reported the Tropical Film Company's thinking on the subject, films could reach a very broad audience, also abroad, in part because viewers need not be literate. The point was highly relevant also when considering circulation of the company's works within Puerto Rico, for, as Alvarez further argues, "for a population that until the middle of the century was for the most part illiterate, film provided a special kind of literacy and knowledge of the world."[52] Even though the promotion of the four films in an elite/educated magazine like *Juan Bobo* suggests that the company's targeted audience belonged to the higher classes, it also seems clear that the Tropical Film Company wanted to produce material that could interest and take the island's general population in the direction of asserting their (sociocultural) differences from the colonial power.

Certainly the Tropical Film Company's productions did emphasize "Puerto Rican" themes that could have immediate local appeal and relevance, in keeping with the company's stated goal of educating audiences. For example, the company's debut release to theaters was not a fiction film but rather a documentary about the funeral of autonomist leader Luis Muñoz Rivera, *Los funerales de Muñoz Rivera* (1916).[53] As I have discussed in the previous chapters, the Puerto Rican public knew Muñoz Rivera as one of the leaders of the Union Party and one of the most famous politicians in Puerto Rican history; the public widely celebrated him for his struggles to secure for Puerto Rico greater political autonomy, under both the Spanish and the American regimes.[54] In fact, as I discussed in chapter 3, Rafael Colorado, working then for Cine Puerto Rico, had released earlier in that same year (1916) a rather successful documentary centered on Muñoz Rivera. The choice of subject for Tropical Film's first production invites two possible explanations: either the producers thought the popularity of the leader would make a documentary about him a profitable enterprise, or they sought to portray the leader as a Puerto Rican hero who deserved to have his funeral immortalized. Evidence I have found strongly suggests the latter rationale, in addition to the historical fact that Canales and Lloréns both knew and sympathized with Muñoz Rivera and belonged to the same political party as he.[55] At the time of his death on November 15, 1916, Muñoz Rivera was in the United States, where he lobbied for Puerto Ricans to gain the right to have their own local government.[56] Thus it seems quite plausible that the Tropical Film Company promoted this documentary film to pay homage to this very influential and beloved leader and to make sure that the masses got a chance to ritually mourn the deceased.

Although no copy of the film has survived, the newspaper *La democracia* indicates that it was five thousand feet long (running approximately sixty to eighty minutes at silent speed), and premiered on December 7, 1916, at the Cine Luna in San Juan.[57] The Tropical Film Company was clearly somehow associated with *Los funerales*, but the film's production circumstances are complex. The initial advertisements and reviews refer to Colorado as cinematographer and do not mention the Tropical Film Company as the producers. The newspaper *La correspondencia* declares in acclaiming *Los funerales*, "Now as never before we can call for the most enthusiastic applause for Mr. Colorado, who has once more demonstrated his complete mastery of the difficult art of cinematography."[58] However, the article makes no reference to any other artistic figures involved in the project, leading me to believe that Colorado worked independently in producing this film. In any case, the reported content of the film resembles Colorado's previous film *La llegada de Muñoz Rivera* (The arrival of Muñoz Rivera), exhibited only two months earlier.[59] Nonetheless, the December 16, 1916, issue of *Juan Bobo* announced the film's release in an article and elsewhere in the same issue advertising it as a Tropical Film Company production.[60] The strong evidence of connection around the film's promotion leads me to conclude that the making of *Los funerales* prompted Colorado to unite with other intellectuals interested in filmmaking, particularly Lloréns and Canales, into what became the Tropical Film Company. Yet *Juan Bobo* did not announce the organization of the Tropical until February 24, 1917, which suggests that the legal constitution of the company happened after the making of *Los funerales*.

The film, in any case, appears to have received positive reviews, at least from the critic in *La correspondencia*. That newspaper declared of *Los funerales*: "As a cinematographic work, it is the best that has been produced in Puerto Rico, not only because of the choice and diversity of the scenes, but also because the photography is clear and perfectly detailed."[61] Further, the newspaper affirmed that the film would have great historical value because "all the currently socially important people in Puerto Rico, regardless of political party or hierarchy, can be clearly seen in this film, and in many scenes, and thus in whatever moment anyone wants to see them, even after death, we can contemplate them again."[62] In addition to showing important Puerto Rican figures, the film reportedly depicted a great variety of geographic places, following the funeral procession from Eduardo Giorgetti's house in Santurce (San Juan, on the northeast coast) to Barranquitas (in the central mountains), Muñoz Rivera's burial ground, having passed along the way through the towns of Río Piedras (in the northeast region), Caguas (east central), Coamo (south central), and Ponce (south coast), among others.[63]

However important and widespread this film proved in Puerto Rico (for which, unfortunately, too little evidence is available), it did not represent a work that could carry out the Tropical Film Company's agenda abroad. At least two of the film serials that the company next undertook seemed shaped to achieve that combined educational, political, and at least partially economic, goal. The company produced as its first fiction film a romantic drama titled *Paloma del Monte* (1917).[64] An article in *Juan Bobo* discloses that Italian actors Aquiles Zorda and Clara Zorda (a father–daughter duo then touring in Puerto Rico) played two of the film's lead roles, described as two mountain *jíbaros*, with Gabriel Tejel playing the other lead character (most likely the love interest for Clara Zorda's Paloma).[65] Judging from previous local productions, the film probably made use of a recognizable melodramatic plot adapted for the Puerto Rican market through the use of local iconography. Still, because no copy of the film remains, I cannot offer more details about its narrative.

Magazine articles do reveal other information about *Paloma*, for example, that the film was released early in 1917, for an advertisement dated February 10, 1917, in *Juan Bobo* mentions the timely finish of the last episode of the serial later that month. That article also mentions that the film consisted of five episodes fully filmed in Puerto Rico. Since in the articles the writers use the terms "episode" and "reel" interchangeably, it seems likely that each episode consisted of one reel (approximately twelve to sixteen minutes). Furthermore, part of the filming took place at the University of Puerto Rico in Río Piedras, apparently because the filmmakers thought that it would portray Puerto Rico as an educated place: "[In this film] we can see the extremely sympathetic scene of Puerto Rico's university life, through which we will promulgate abroad something which will give great pleasure and will rehabilitate the country from the prejudice that exists against it of being inhabited by an uneducated and inferior people."[66] The filmmakers' comment suggests that they wanted *Paloma* to give the impression that Puerto Rico had a rich cultural and intellectual life. In addition, in referring to *Paloma* as another sign of the Tropical Film Company's "merit in its artistic and patriotic labor," the *Juan Bobo* reviewer (again, likely Canales or Lloréns) clearly viewed the film as integral to the process of nation building.[67] By extension, one might reasonably conclude that the filmmakers regarded the film as a demonstration that Puerto Rico did not need the United States to manage its affairs since it had capable and knowledgeable citizens that could do it themselves.

Clearly, the producers saw the film as realizing the "good" artistic taste necessary to an educational project. Although like other intellectuals of their class, Lloréns and Canales had expressed disdain toward the imported vulgar melodramas, they, unlike others, wanted to change the situation and evidently believed that they succeeded in their first fictional movie in moving away from the dominant coarse trend. For that purpose, another article in *Juan Bobo* emphasizes the artistic achievement of Gabriel Tejel, a Puerto Rican actor playing one of the lead roles in *Paloma del Monte*.[68] Paradoxically, the article characterizes Tejel as even more accomplished for enduring the unfortunate circumstance of having performed only in Puerto Rico! "Despite the inauspicious environment in which he has developed, he has realized the artistic parameters of a refined temperament and an exceptional dramatic comprehension [. . .] it is truly a pity that the young Gabriel Tejel wastes and squanders his talent in this our traditional atmosphere of village banality in which a shrill commercial tone reigns."[69] Noticeably in this statement, the Tropical Film Company wanted to separate itself from previous films presented in the country. Advertisements in *Juan Bobo* reveal that American, French, and Italian films dominated cinema exhibition in 1916–17 in San Juan. The many U.S.-made films shown included *The Yellow Menace* (1916, Serial Film Corp.), *The Mysterious Rose* (1914, Universal Film), and *The Supreme Impulse* (1915, Independent Moving Pictures). A significant number of European productions played as well, such as *Rocambole* (1913, Pathé, France), *Le pickpocket mystifié* (Nick Winter: 1911, Pathé, France), *La bestia umana* (1916, Cinema-Drama, Italy), and *Ultima rappresentazione di gala del Circo Wolfson* (1916, Amando Vay, Italy). From this small sample one can appreciate the variety in provenance and genre of the films shown in the island. Hence, in describing its films as offering a new, genuinely artistic approach to film, the Tropical Film associates distinguished themselves and the company from the competition in a way that could not only give their endeavors cultural legitimacy but also attract the educated sectors, in whose eyes film "was a degenerate form of theater, not much above a mere travelling show."[70]

Along with integrating aspects of Puerto Rican culture that local audiences might value, *Paloma del Monte* apparently presented the land as an attractive tourist destination. Descriptions of the film in *Juan Bobo* boasted that the film was "embellished by the abundant landscapes of the island."[71] Besides the urban landscape of the University of Puerto Rico, the film also presented coffee plantations in the countryside of Cayey and Juana Diaz, showing the varied beautiful scenery as well as the economic potential of the island.[72] The film therefore promoted Puerto Rico as both a cosmopolitan city with a university, and a beautiful agricultural wilderness that could appeal to every type of tourist. This appeal to tourism realized the tradition of early travelogues, which, as Paula Amad has suggested, the U.S. public understood "as an edifying tool for crosscultural understanding," even if in fact they created a "transvaluation of the other into a potential consumer."[73] In highlighting the beauty as well as the civility of Puerto Rico, the Tropical Film Company offered, whether by explicit design or not, a counterdiscourse to cultural exhibits popular in the United States at the time, which portrayed Latinos literally as sideshow freaks. As historian Fredrick Pike describes the practice, "by the end of the century, Cubans, Filipinos, Puerto Ricans, and Mexicans had been added to the specimens exhibited on the midway. One could view them along with bearded ladies, sword swallowers, and grotesquely fat men and ladies."[74] In the Tropical Film Company's productions, the apparent desire to defend Puerto Rico from misrepresentation got mixed, in somewhat contradictory ways, with the "cult" of travel and capitalist practices.

Besides in the setting of *Paloma* and other films, the Tropical company productions incorporated other supposedly authentic Puerto Rican elements. An article in *Juan Bobo* recounts an incident to demonstrate that the "genuineness" of the human portrayal also played a part in the decisions of the company to cast particular actors. According to the magazine, "when one of the most striking scenes of Mr. Luis Lloréns Torres' drama was being shot, the need arose to solicit one of the jíbaros to enact a role with all the local realism."[75] Although the use of nonactors could have related to budget constraints, the article's report of the incident asserts the film's authenticity in a way that resonates with Tropical Film's previously expressed concerns about American depictions of Puerto Rico. Yet the article itself treats the "authentic" *jíbaro* more as a joke than as a dignified human. The article recounts how the local man did not understand how to distinguish acting from "real life": in a mock fight, the man hit Zorda, who played the leading character, so hard that the punch propelled the actor down the hill.[76] In addition, the journalist took pains to report the *jíbaro*'s language as "naturally" as possible, ridden with grammatical and syntactical errors.[77] Even if the film itself did not play abroad, such condescension toward the rural population in the pages of the journal edited (and largely written) by the leading Tropical company members again contradicts their stated aims of dignifying the Puerto Rican people in the eyes of foreigners.

The Tropical Film Company's next film also focused on a local setting and character. In this instance, however, the filmmakers appear to have based the film on a famous (and mythologized) Puerto Rican historical figure, the "Robin Hood-esque" pirate Roberto Cofresí.[78] The company advertised the ten-episode serial (running a total of approximately 120–160 minutes) *El tesoro de Cofresí* (Cofresi's treasure, 1917) simultaneously with *Paloma*. Nonetheless, the advertisements refer to *El tesoro* as being in production, while describing *Paloma* as ready for exhibition.[79] To date I have not found proof that *El tesoro* played in any theater; it may have foundered at the production stage and never been released. The promotion material for the film is nonetheless significant in relation to my assessment of the company's complex and often contradictory workings. Although the film took a mythologized figure with political connotations as its subject matter (for Cofresí allegedly championed separatist and anti-U.S. positions), the publicity emphasizes the film's setting rather than its local historical theme.

The description of the film in *Juan Bobo* draws attention to the photographic quality of the landscape scenes Rafael Colorado had shot, but it does not mention anything about the film's plot.[80] The critic "Amencio" claims in discussing the production of *El tesoro* that the company had filmed a 360-degree view of the island from the top of El Yunque Mountain.[81] Although I find it highly unlikely that even a panorama shot could have captured the whole island from this location, such a shot could have shown most (if not all) of the northeast coast as well as the central mountain range. Thus the filmmakers might have captured an extreme long shot view of rainforests, beaches, valleys, and urban areas of Puerto Rico. Indeed, the film likely included closer shots of one of the island's many beaches, given its apparent focus on the life of a famous pirate. Such scenes may have featured the beaches of Arecibo, where according to Juan Ortíz the company shot part of *El tesoro*. However, the beaches of Río Grande or Luquillo could also have served as locations given their proximity to El Yunque, the site of filming mentioned in the *Juan Bobo* article.[82] The production must have featured (or aimed to, if it remained incomplete) vistas of nature and beautiful landscapes that the company evidently thought could promote foreign tourism.[83] The point must remain speculative, but if the filmmakers did indeed complete and exhibit *El tesoro* in Puerto Rico, given the large number of theaters by 1920 (at least in the biggest cities), such a film could have provided the many viewers who did not travel frequently outside of their towns with their first view of the country's rich geographical diversity.

The End of the Beginning: The Tropical Film Company's Demise and Legacy

The final known production of the Tropical Film Company, entitled *La viudita se quiere casar* (The widow wants to marry, 1917), appears to have deviated in pronounced ways from the company's previous films. In *Juan Bobo*, "Amencio" describes the film as a short (two-reel) comedy and suggests that its plot involved a happy, rich widow, who, to judge from the title, searched for a new husband.[84] The writer this time makes no mention of the film serving as an instrument of tourism or cultural edification and promotion. It seems likely that the company sought in making the film to achieve commercial success through pleasing the local public. A Puerto Rican actress with the stage name of Bety Varezal (real name unknown) played the lead female role of the film, instead of Clara Zorda, who had starred in both *Paloma* and *El tesoro*.[85] *Juan Bobo* also notes that filming took place in the metropolitan area of Santurce, and that the filmmakers planned to release the film around the second week of March 1917 to exhibit in a program with *Paloma*.[86] I have not been able to learn whether the company actually managed to exhibit the film. Still, I have found other artistic details, for another article in *Juan Bobo* declares that Aquiles Zorda wrote the film's script: "[*La viudita*] is studded with bewildering comedic scenes through which its author, Mr. Zorda, has invested all the pieces of his southern genius."[87] The writers in *Juan Bobo* declared, as they had done about the other Tropical productions, that *La viudita* formed part of the patriotic work carried out by the Tropical Film Company; the journal also unsurprisingly predicted the comedy's success.[88]

Whether or not the film proved commercially successful (or was even completed and released), the company had disappeared by the summer of 1917. Many scholars have attributed the company's demise to the United States having entered the First World War that March.[89] According to this theory, "the scarcity of virgin film stock due to the United States entering World War I spelled doom for Tropical Film's projects."[90] Because research has not yielded any official records of the company's bankruptcy, I can at best theorize reasons for the San Juan–based Tropical Film Company's disbanding after less than a year. Certainly, the most likely explanation is that the company simply ran out of capital, for the four films reportedly made probably could not offset the high cost of production (a point some newspapers refer to in discussing films made in the 1910s in Puerto Rico), given that the company had to rely for its returns on the local film market, which U.S. and European distributors controlled. In addition, the outbreak of the First World War in Europe had caused the decline of productions in important industries in England, France, and Italy and had helped U.S. producers to expand their business globally.[91] Thus entering the already saturated U.S. market, and profiting, would have been difficult. As noted, it is improbable that the company managed to export its productions to North America (nor have I found evidence that any went to Latin America, where the narratives might have anticipated cultural resonance). But even if one or another of the titles did get released in the United States and exhibited in one or more cities (in New York City, for example), there is no evidence (and perhaps should have been no anticipation) that American audiences had any interest in the productions.

Regardless of actual outcomes, scholarly debates about film in Puerto Rico have from early on centered on the medium's impact on local culture, education, and the development of a national consciousness. It is noteworthy that also from early on many Puerto Rican intellectuals, especially those directly involved in film production and promotion, have linked cinema to a nation-building project, thereby positioning film as a key step toward defining "Puerto Ricanness." Perhaps filmmakers and critics have posited this connection so widely and apparently easily due to film's standing as popular culture: in contrast to locally composed or distributed literature, for example, cinema has from the 1910s at the latest attracted an enthusiastic following among the illiterate as well as (more gradually) among the literate living in Puerto Rico.

However, although the Tropical Film Company claimed interest in Puerto Rico's image around the world, it also functioned as a business, making compromises between sociopolitical ideals and economic sustainability. Therefore, instead of trying to look back at the Tropical Film Company as an idyllic beginning, unfortunately cut short, we should recognize the many contradictions and problems in the way its members imagined and construed it. This does not mean that the Tropical Film Company did not mark an important moment in Puerto Rican film history. On the contrary, we have to recognize the Tropical Film Company's foundational work, particularly in its conception of national cinema as a complex balancing act of promoting and displaying culture, education, politics, and business.

The Tropical Film Company associates did not further engage in filmmaking following the company's closing. Luis Lloréns Torres continued to have an active career in the local political and literary circles until his death in 1944.[92] Nemesio Canales left Puerto Rico and lived in the United States, Venezuela, Panama, and Argentina, where he worked as a writer and journalist. He came back to Puerto Rico in 1921 where he continued his work as a writer and political figure until his early death (at the age of 44) in 1923.[93] Rafael Colorado continued working as a photographer until his death in 1959, having in 1924 helped to found the Puerto Rican Association of Photographers, over which he initially presided.[94] Despite the Tropical Film Company members leaving filmmaking, they continued to engage in the production of culture and nation building through other mediums.

In the years immediately following the closing of the Tropical Film Company, filmmaking in Puerto Rico developed in a markedly different direction. The years 1919 to 1925 saw the coming of U.S.-based production companies to film "on location" in the island, but also in some instances to set up co-productions involving local investors, cast, and crew members. The visiting companies, unsurprisingly, did not share the Tropical Film Company's commitment, however short-lived, to exploring film's cultural-educational value or potential toward building a national identity for Puerto Ricans. The next chapter approaches this cultural turn and focuses mainly on U.S. productions made in or about Puerto Rico during the period from 1917 (*Heart and Soul*) to 1925 (*Aloma of the South Seas*).

5

Perilous Paradise

American Assignment and Appropriation of "Puerto Ricanness" (1917–1925)

After the Tropical Film Company disbanded in 1917, Puerto Rican filmmaking went through a period of very low productivity. In the 1920s local companies produced only one feature film, *Amor tropical* (*Tropical Love*, 1921), and even this film came about as a result of the involvement of an outsider. Nonetheless, cinema attendance continued to be high during the 1920s. María E. Ordóñez, writing for the magazine *Cinema*, notes that by 1923 San Juan theaters were making "approximately three thousand dollars a day, or around one million dollars a year."[1] That theaters made great profits indicates that the Puerto Rican public regularly attended movie houses. These figures also show that local distributors and exhibitors actively worked to generate and maintain public interest in their products.

At the same time, during 1917–1925, the industry saw a rise in the production of American films with Puerto Rico as their fictional setting, several of which were actually shot in Puerto Rico. In this chapter I will discuss how during the 1920s filmmakers in Puerto Rico changed their approach to film production from an exclusively local cultural undertaking to an enterprise that sought to attract U.S. investment. By soliciting and actively pursuing the involvement of U.S. filmmakers, local producers aimed to gain valuable technical and business knowledge, infrastructure, and other resources from the more developed, and commercially more successful, film industry in the United States. For, by the end of the First World War, the United States had successfully captured the global film market, so much so that in Latin America and parts of Asia American productions occupied up to 90 percent of screen time.[2]

Three U.S.-based producers—Playgoers Pictures, Edward A. MacManus, and Famous Players-Lasky—came to Puerto Rico during the 1920s to shoot a total of four films. These four films included one widely advertised and discussed "hit," *Aloma of the South Seas* (1925), featuring the American actress-dancer Gilda Gray.[3] In addition, another U.S. filmmaker, Sam Roth, filmed a travelogue-style documentary on the island in 1923. Although the producers of these films did not have as their primary aim to contribute to the advancement of the island's film industry, nor even to create an adequate representation of Puerto Rico, in practice, media institutions on the island appropriated these U.S.-financed productions as local. As Andrew Higson has famously argued, film's ability to cross borders and be read in relation to multiple contexts provides the opportunity for adopting the foreign as local.[4] Local audiences seeing Puerto Rican settings, and even in some cases Puerto Rican actors, on the screen, interpreted these U.S. films as if they were actively participating in the construction of the nation, and thus as if they were Puerto Rican cultural productions. Therefore, following Higson, in this context "the foreign commodity [was not] treated as exotic by the local audience, but [was] interpreted according to an 'indigenous' frame of reference; that is, it [was] metaphorically translated into a local idiom."[5] Discursively, in the local arena, these films became fully Puerto Rican, also in their consistent inscription by local media.

The U.S. film industry's interest in Puerto Rico, which brought U.S. filmmakers to the island, found its initial form of expression in the realm of fiction. Before doing any actual shooting in Puerto Rico, U.S. filmmakers used the island as an exotic fictional setting. Even though these films do not form an active part of the catalog of Puerto Rican productions (since they were made by Americans in the United States and with U.S. capital), Puerto Ricans nonetheless responded to the discourses regarding race and imperialism that these films brought forward. In other words, these U.S. cultural products became an integral facet of the national political discussion about the "nature" of Puerto Rican identity and the United States' need to intervene in the Caribbean. Addressing African American representation in early U.S. films, Jacqueline Stewart has argued that, "African Americans recognized that stereotypical media images worked hand in hand with other 'images' of Black people in the white imagination (i.e., in legal discourse, political debates, public policy, social customs) to determine the treatment of Blacks in the real world."[6] Similarly, Puerto Rican audiences understood that U.S. cultural products worked as one of many discursive strategies relating to the United States' colonial project.

Despite the many representational problems that these U.S. productions exhibited, their circulation in Puerto Rico in fact profoundly influenced (inadvertently or not) the development of the island's cinema infrastructure. I demonstrate in this chapter that the American public's evident curiosity about the new colony (which the production and circulation of these U.S. films strongly suggests, and U.S. newspaper discourses of the time further document) helped to bring U.S. capital to support the Puerto Rican film industry. More specifically, the U.S. interest in Puerto Rico as a filming location propelled the development of the first "Hollywood style" film studio in the island. Thus, even though in comparison to the works made in the 1910s the number of films made by local producers declined during the 1920s, the island's cinema industry continued to develop, as through the building of the studio mentioned here.

Although the exact reasons for the decline in local film production in Puerto Rico during these years remain elusive, I will demonstrate connections between the active involvement of the U.S. film industry in the island and an easing of the local understanding of the pressing need to "accurately" represent Puerto Rico on film. In turn, the use of Puerto Rico as a fictional and actual setting for U.S. film productions may relate to changes in U.S. foreign policy. The political transformation that Puerto Rico had gone through in 1917 with the passing of the Jones Act cast the island as a metaphoric U.S.–Latin American hybrid, in effect inviting U.S. producers to benefit from the social consequences of an institutional change in American foreign policy.

From Big Stick to Good Neighbor: Puerto Rico as Test Site for American Foreign Policy

Before World War II, Puerto Rico experienced two predominant historical moments in which the island figured as a popular topic in political discourse in the United States. Understandably, in 1898, and during the initial decade of U.S. colonization, Puerto Rico, Cuba, and the Philippines emerged as prevalent topics for travel and history books as well as press coverage and film actualities, as discussed in chapter 2. The decade following 1917 and the passing of the Jones Act (which granted Puerto Ricans American citizenship) seems to have had a similar impact in generating increased interest in the island within the United States. Historically, this decade also corresponds with the end of World War I and the subsequent supposed "isolationist" period of U.S. foreign policy during the interwar years. However, historians have revealed that during the 1920s and 1930s, the U.S. government very actively pursued its national interests in Latin America.[7]

As historians Thomas Skidmore and Peter Smith have affirmed, by the end of World War I the U.S. had laid the groundwork for an active presence in the American hemisphere.[8] According to Skidmore and Smith, by the 1920s, "The United States now exercised virtual hegemony in the Caribbean basin, as could be seen in the military occupations of Nicaragua (1912–25 and 1926–33), Haiti (1915–34), the Dominican Republic (1916–24), and Cuba (1917–22). Even when the United States did not occupy these countries, it deeply influenced their development, wielding veto power over their domestic policy."[9] The importance of Latin America for the U.S. economy was such that "by the close of the neocolonial period in 1929, 40 percent of all U.S. international investments were in Latin America."[10] These economic and political connections served as a major incentive for U.S. sociocultural activity in the region.

Because Puerto Rico, as an internationally recognized U.S. possession, did not appear violently occupied or manipulated, the island could readily serve North American interests as an example of the positive outcomes of maintaining an active relationship with the United States. In 1934 Theodore Roosevelt III (son of Teddy Roosevelt), who had previously served as Puerto Rico's governor (1929–32), proclaimed, "It must be admitted that Puerto Rico is not and most certainly never will be an economic asset to the United

States. She is far more likely to continue to be in need of federal aid. On the other hand . . . from the broad aspect of international relationships she can be of great value both to our country and to this hemisphere. She can and should serve as a connecting link between the two great cultural divisions."[11] Evidently, Roosevelt imagined Puerto Rico as a charming (but otherwise useless) daughter that could attract Latin American suitors into the U.S. family. This attitude toward foreign relations reflects a distancing from the past aggressive "big stick diplomacy" and a move toward a new "gentler" direction. Historian Dennis Merrill even asserts that "the predominant conversation during the decade [1920s] did not in fact center on whether the country should engage the world but rather on how to do so: whether to honor America's long standing tradition of unilateralism and expansionism at others' expense or to transition to a softer, more multilateral mode of interaction."[12] As we know, the United States during the 1930s eventually chose the latter, "softer" expression of power, as epitomized by Franklin Roosevelt's 1933 Good Neighbor Proclamation.

Although the new soft power diplomatic approach may have aimed to create an encouraging cultural bridge between North and South America, it also continued to clumsily exoticize Latin Americans in support of interpretations of the hemisphere as consisting of binary opposites. In Philip Swanson's words, the spirit of this new "friendly" diplomatic stance resembled "an exotic yet sinister cocktail of admiration, attraction and desire mixed with patronizing snobbery and underlying sexual, moral, ethnic and political anxiety."[13] During the first third of the twentieth century, prior to the official establishment of the Good Neighbor approach, Puerto Rico figured as an exotic, yet real, site on which to dispel sexual, racial, and other social anxieties. Films depicting fictionalized Puerto Rico reveal how U.S. popular culture perceived and rhetorically constructed Puerto Rico, allowing us to understand the discourses that Puerto Rican producers (like the aforementioned Tropical Film Company) potentially sought to combat with their work. Two films made in the United States in the late 1910s, *Heart and Soul* (1917) and *The Liar* (1918), took Puerto Rico as a fictional setting for stories that reveal deep concerns with the implications of the U.S. colonization of Puerto Rico, particularly with regard to issues of miscegenation and potential political defiance.

Fictional Puerto Rico and Colonial Angst

Heart and Soul, directed by J. Gordon Edward for Fox Film Corporation and starring Theda Bara, was an adaptation of the 1887 novel *Jess*, an early work of English colonialist author Sir Henry Rider Haggard.[14] Although contemporary film audiences knew Bara as a "vamp" figure, she appears to have departed from that particular characterization for this production.[15] Instead of a tale of wicked sexual seduction, Haggard's novel tells the story of an English colonist in the Transvaal region of South Africa and his two nieces, Jess and Bessie, and an English soldier, John Neil, who comes to live with the colonist family during the First Anglo-Boer War.[16] Captain Neil is engaged to the beautiful Bessie, but in love with Jess, a smart and sensitive but plain-looking woman, who sacrifices herself for her sister's happiness. Frank Muller, a ruthless and violent Boer who wants to marry the reluctant Bessie, serves as the novel's villain. Muller's infatuation with Bessie is so extreme that he willingly starts a war to marry her! Through its melodramatic plot, the novel offers a clear critique of the British response to the war as well as of the "uncultivated" Dutch settlers.[17] The film version, on the other hand, has nothing to do with the Anglo-Boer War. Instead, Puerto Rico serves as the fictional setting of *Heart and Soul*, for which Saint Augustine, Florida, stood in. The film takes as its villain a corrupt American planter, Drummond, who incites the natives to rebel.[18]

Although the American Film Institute's catalog and the 1917 review of the film in *Variety* describe Puerto Rico as the setting of *Heart and Soul*, reviews in the *Atlanta Constitution* and the *Washington Post* describe the film as taking place in Hawaii.[19] Since the film is no longer extant, it remains unclear if the filmmakers left the setting ambiguous (just some tropical island under U.S. control), if the intertitles were changed at some point to indicate different locations, or if the reviewers simply could not appreciate the difference between Puerto Rico and Hawaii. After all, the two territories had many similarities: both archipelagos show a distinctive Iberian influence, were annexed to the American Union in 1898, and by 1917 were both colonial territories of the United States controlled by U.S. sugar agricultural interests. Whatever the setting of the film narrative, the adaptation's use of an actual U.S. colonial location, whether Puerto Rico or Hawaii, rather than a completely fictional one, suggests that the filmmakers saw a similarity between British interests in South Africa and U.S. interests in the Caribbean and possibly the Pacific, as evidently also did some film reviewers.

Since the review in *Variety* states that the film "runs barely an hour," it seems likely that the movie was a highly condensed, at best loose adaptation of the 350-page novel.[20] Given Bara's film reputation as a seductress, even in the absence of a surviving copy, one might speculate that the film focused on the love triangle among Jess (Theda Bara), Neil (Harry Hilliard), and Bessie (Claire Whitney). However, based on the archival information I have gathered, it seems likely that the filmmakers deployed Bara's "exotic" reputation in conjunction with the film's setting rather than primarily to characterize Jess. Reviews of *Heart and Soul* describe the film as being "full of *primitive* Southern scenery, replete with uprising and plantation fights."[21] According to Gaylyn Studlar, much of Bara's appeal derived from her "oriental" associations, for the East "like the vamp . . . was also regarded in the Western imagination as 'Other,' decadent and immoral, aligned with primitive, even perverse, sexuality, and with extremes of power."[22] Despite Puerto Rico's many geographic, historical, and cultural distinctions from "the Orient," U.S. as well as other Western writers and politicians of the period frequently stereotyped tropical Puerto Rico, and Latin America in general, in a very similar fashion to the "Orient," particularly as sexually attractive but brutally uncivilized, a point to which I shall return later.

Rather than focusing primarily on women's sexuality, as Bara's casting might imply, the film appears to engage the colonial/racial concerns foregrounded in Haggard's novel, after notably displacing those issues geographically. Newspaper reports describe the film as having "mob scenes, [and] burning of houses," as well as "uprising and plantation fights," implying that, as in the novel, the rivals are both colonial farmers, and that the villain incites a war between the natives and the colonists.[23] Based on what I have gathered about the film's plot, which involves corrupt planters, simple-minded but violent natives, and military heroes, the narrative seems symptomatic of U.S. anxieties about its new colonized lands and their local populations. That the "natives" are so "primitive" and can be so easily driven to insurgence suggests the need for more active U.S. intervention in its colonies. This message appears to follow the line of Theodore Roosevelt's "Big Stick Diplomacy" already enforced in Latin America since the turn of the nineteenth century.

However, as the British in South Africa encountered with the Boer, supplanting another "white" colonizer required justification, achieved through the construction of a hierarchy of "whiteness" affirmed by superior colonial prowess and benevolence. Because the Spanish had colonized (and procreated in) Puerto Rico prior to the U.S. possession of the island, many white Puerto Ricans lived among the black and biracial populations; thus the distinction between "native" and colonizer based on phenotype could not be so easily demarcated. In racial terms, Puerto Rico proved a very different setting than other U.S. colonized territories, including the Philippines, despite that territory's former occupation by the Spanish. Puerto Rican anthropologist Jorge Duany explains how the United States managed the situation: "Census reports showing that the Island's population was predominantly white bolster legislation conferring U.S. citizenship to Puerto Ricans, but not Filipinos. In Puerto Rico a more centralized colonial regime emerged than in the Philippines, where local elites were used to keep the peace and raise revenue."[24] However, despite the U.S. government's willingness to allow the island some administrative autonomy and to recognize Puerto Ricans as Americans (a "favor" not awarded to most other colonial populations), as César Ayala and Rafael Bernabe argue, the island's inhabitants were still "seen as dark and 'only a few steps removed from a primitive state of nature' and/or as products of a decrepit Spanish-Catholic obscurantism [and further] Puerto Ricans were [still] considered by many to be incapable of self-government."[25]

In sum, much of American cultural discourse addressed Puerto Ricans as flawed in character despite their comparative "whiteness," especially because of their exposure to the uncivilized and disease-ridden tropical setting.[26] Juan F. Perea makes the point that "throughout the years of debate regarding Puerto Ricans' capacity for self-government, concerns focused on the effects of climate and racial mixture." He further notes that, for example, "Representative Slayton attributed the incapacity for self-government to 'the character of the people and the climate. The tropics seem to heat the blood while enervating the people who inhabit them.'"[27] According to medical discourses of the time, the tropics were infested with maladies that made people lazy and unfit for refinement. Newspaper articles sometimes made such claims in pseudoscientific, positivist terms: "[American] scientific treatment ha[s] made a whole people 50 percent better physically and has caused a 400 percent increase in Porto Rican commerce."[28] Headlines declared that the "Lazy Bug Gets Porto Ricans" even years after U.S. armed forces had undertaken "Fighting the Porto Rican Microbe of Laziness."[29] Under the pretext of bringing medical and economic benefits, the U.S. government asserted the necessity of its intervention and continued presence on the island. For example, an article in the *New York Tribune* praised General Leonard Wood (who served as military governor of both Cuba and the Philippines) for "help[ing] clean Cuba, the Philippines and Porto Rico of deadly diseases and ma[king] them fit for Americans."[30]

By narrating the locals' supposed inability to deal with their unproductive sickness, popular discourses in the United States constructed Puerto Rico and its inhabitants as deeply in need of saving. Given the inadequacy of the island's administration and infrastructure, these writers argued, the United States needed to bind the island more thoroughly to the American ways. In the end, just as the British had incorporated the Boers into their empire, the U.S. government had given Puerto Ricans U.S. citizenship. Arguably, popular perceptions of U.S. involvement in Puerto Rico at the time of the production of *Heart and Soul* did evince many similarities with those of the English–Boer relationship in South Africa.

Moving away from literary sources, Fox studios produced a second feature film during the late 1910s that took Puerto Rico as a fictional setting called *The Liar*. The film, directed by Edmund Lawrence, starred Virginia Pearson, another actress who often played a "vamp" type but in *The Liar* appeared in a sympathetic role.[31] The film, shot in the Blackstone Studio in Brooklyn, was about sixty minutes long.[32] According to the review in *Variety*, *The Liar* tells the story of Sybil Houston (Pearson), who lives in the United States but goes on a trip to visit her father on his plantation in Puerto Rico. There she meets Franklin (Edward Roseman), her father's secretary, who falls in love with her and asks for her hand in marriage. Sybil refuses Franklin and instead marries her boyfriend back in the United States, John Carter (Victor Sutherland). The scorned lover then fabricates a plan to convince Sybil that her mother was black so as to shame her into leaving John and marrying him instead. The film ends with Sybil faking suicide and Franklin revealing that the whole miscegenation story was a lie, allowing for a happy ending for John and Sybil.[33]

Remarkably, Sybil's belief in the possibility that her mother could be black comes about because her father has provided a pension to a black man he had brutally beaten when that man was a boy.[34] That is to say, Sybil gives Franklin's story some credence because her father "inexplicably" takes care of a black man. In addition, the film suggests that racial tensions are more visible and problematic in the far-off space of the colony; Sybil faces danger only when she leaves the United States and enters Puerto Rico.

After Franklin harasses her on the island, she returns to John's comforting embrace on the continent. The real trouble develops when John and Sybil decide to go to Puerto Rico to live and there encounter Franklin again. Had they stayed in the United States, the film proposes, none of the racial problems would have arisen since Franklin would have been out of the picture and had no occasion to forge the birth certificate he uses to document his claim.

As a markedly problematic racial space, the colony represents an imagined eminent threat to U.S. "civilized whiteness." The anxiety about miscegenation expressed in *The Liar* is indicative of what Ann Laura Stoler calls "the colonial politics of exclusion."[35] According to Stoler, colonization generated racial–sexual codes to ensure the maintenance of power: "legal and social classifications designated who was 'white,' who was 'native,' who could become a citizen rather than a subject, which children were legitimate progeny and which were not."[36] In other words, racial markers served as a way for colonizers to determine who could and who could not gain access to privileges; hence interracial sex was proscribed to maintain established status markers.

In having strained their family ties through living in different spaces, both Sybil and her father expose themselves to suspicions about their blood relationship. Adding to the already dubious associations between the father and daughter, which undercut colonial exclusionary practices, the father engages in an "inappropriately" close relationship with a local black man. However, Sybil's fears regarding her "racial makeup" cannot be said to be exceptional. As Stoler explains, since it was common for white male colonists to have sex with "nonwhite" women, "social and legal standings derived not only from color but also from the silences, acknowledgments, and denials of the social circumstances in which one's parents had sex."[37] Because her mother died, Sybil must rely on her father's credibility to maintain her social standing and claim to whiteness. In the Caribbean, Stuart Hall argues, "Africa was a case of the unspoken, Europe was a case of that which is endlessly speaking- and endlessly speaking *us*. The European presence thus interrupts the innocence of the whole discourse of 'difference' in the Caribbean by introducing the question of power."[38] After the war in 1898, the United States found itself with a new problematic social issue/power dynamic caused by the colonization of different ethnic groups: how to maintain racial and cultural supremacy without forcibly dominating the "other." Patronizing benevolence, the "white man's burden," seemed the proper answer.

Even though these two films aimed to portray American characters as morally upright and benevolent, and hence as sympathetic, Puerto Rican audiences, at least in the United States, did not seem to appreciate their colonial message. In his memoir, labor leader Bernardo Vega describes how Puerto Rican spectators in Brooklyn became enraged after watching one of these productions: "[T]he Puerto Ricans who were there began to protest, and midway through the film we got together in the lobby of the theater. Panchito Carballo, a tabaquero from Caguas . . . spoke for several minutes in very correct English. He made it clear that he was not blaming the owner of the theater but the film company for producing what he called such 'crass stupidity.' He condemned that kind of trashy film which only stirs up hatred and prejudice among people. He explained briefly the cultural situation in Puerto Rico, and when he was through he received a long round of applause."[39] As this anecdote evidences, Puerto Ricans were very concerned with the American narratives about their island and people. While Americans might have perceived films like these as mindless, sentimental fun, Puerto Ricans consumed them as dangerous political statements that needed to be refuted.

Puerto Rico's Commercial Production Model

Although U.S. interests in Puerto Rico increased in conjunction with the granting of American citizenship to the island's inhabitants, that circumstance did not translate into an interest in Puerto Rican cultural productions aside from ethnographic curiosity. After all, in Duany's words, "to the new conquerors, Puerto Ricans were the last representatives in America of a decaying Spanish empire and as such belonged to a degraded culture and race."[40] The low esteem in which the colonizers held Puerto Rican culture translated into a systematic process of Americanization through education during the first decades of the twentieth century.[41] Thus it is understandable that, after the decline of the local Tropical Film Company, aspiring film producers in Puerto Rico would seek to build the island's cinema infrastructure in keeping with that found in the United States and look specifically to the United States for capital investment to achieve such development. For the first time in the short history of the development of film in Puerto Rico, local filmmakers and investors showed interest in constructing a studio that could attract foreign filmmakers and investors to the island's cinema industry.

During the 1920s, besides one locally funded company called Porto Rico Photoplays, three U.S.-based production companies capitalized on the island as a filming location: Playgoers Pictures, Edward A. MacManus, and Famous Players-Lasky. Among them, the three companies produced four films in Puerto Rico between 1921 and 1925. Unlike the setting of the one film made by Porto Rico Photoplays, those films did not actually feature Puerto Rico as their narrative settings. Rather than aiming to represent Puerto Rico itself, these small production companies sought to shoot locations with exotic scenery (for example, the unidentified "tropics") that might attract their North American and other potential audiences who had an ever-broadening choice of films. By 1917, courts had ruled that the Motion Picture Patents Company (also called the Edison Trust) violated antitrust laws, enabling many of the so-called independents to flourish profitably in California near the core of the burgeoning Hollywood film industry.[42] Perhaps inspired by the rise to the top of the former so-called independents, one American man came to Puerto Rico with the evident hope of convincing the locals that with his help they could transform the island into the next Hollywood.

An interesting and odd individual, F. Eugene Farnsworth was the first U.S.-based filmmaker to promote exploring Puerto Rico as an alternative filming locale to California. Farnsworth came to Puerto Rico in September 1919 to advance the idea of opening a movie studio in the island, because, he announced, "the American public did not see [California] as a novelty anymore, and thus many businessmen are anxious for new locations."[43] He sold himself as a man with very extensive, indeed quite incredible experience; according to his own account, he had held a position as the artistic director for Universal Studios as well as for a company called "Mastercraft" and was also a renowned travel film lecturer.[44] Though his claim to being Universal's artistic director appears to be a complete fabrication, Farnsworth had in fact served as president of the short-lived Mastercraft Photo-Play Corporation, which in 1918 produced the film *The One Woman*, based on Thomas Dixon's play of the same name and directed by Reginald Barker. The film, by all evidence the company's only production, likely attempted to capitalize on Dixon's name following the success four years earlier of the adaptation of his play *The Clansman* as *The Birth of a Nation*

FIG. 5.1 F. Eugene Farnsworth

(D. W. Griffith, 1914). As to his final claim, Farnsworth had in fact performed as a travel film lecturer in 1911 but according to the *Boston Globe* did so without success.[45]

However, a fuller account of Farnsworth's life reveals a truly bizarre series of engagements that might help us understand why he came to Puerto Rico and what his intentions were. An obituary published in the *Boston Globe* reveals that after initial stints as a barber and Salvation Army volunteer, Farnsworth turned to "the study of Hypnotism and grave exhibition."[46] He toured New England with his hypnotist show but had to quit in 1901 after one of his partners, Thomas Bolton, died on stage as a consequence of an act gone wrong.[47] After the unfortunate event, Farnsworth, who had previously gone by the name Frank, reinvented himself as F. Eugene, now a travel film lecturer. According to the *Boston Daily Globe*, the travel talks "proved far from remunerating and he turned to the movies, operating a studio in Medford [Massachusetts]."[48] That last claim, like many he made, seems an overstatement, for the Mastercraft Photo-Play Corporation of Medford dissolved after producing *The One Woman*.[49]

As newspapers narrate the story, in the early 1920s Farnsworth became one of the leaders of the Maine chapter of the Ku Klux Klan, being elected as King Kleagle. Reportedly he proved such a good recruiter that during his term "the Klan took in new members at the rate of 1,000 a week," rising from "a handful of men in 1921 to 15,000 to 20,000 in two years."[50] However, Farnsworth's tenure in the KKK was short-lived, for in 1924 the organization expelled him, apparently for "not having a personal character in accord with Klan principles."[51] Accounts suggest that Farnsworth may have stolen membership fees and also tried to open his own chapter of the Klan Ladies without official approval.[52] In a 1924 statement to the *Boston Daily Globe* that apparently forms the basis of his obituary in that newspaper, Farnsworth claimed that he "enjoyed attacks upon [him]self . . . as a leader of the most talked-of organization in the country," suggesting that perhaps, more than anything, Farnsworth relished being in the spotlight.

Curiously, the newspaper coverage of Farnsworth's death left out any account of his involvement in the Puerto Rican film industry. After myself reconstructing that aspect of his activities, I find Farnsworth's involvement in Puerto Rico in keeping with his apparent overarching ambition to become a successful showman. To be precise, his undertakings seem all to have aimed toward gaining public recognition and possible fortune in show business. Farnsworth offered an account in September 1919 to the San Juan newspaper *El mundo* about how he became interested in the island in the early 1900s, when he filmed scenes of the U.S. Panama canal construction. He recounts that while in Panama he met and quickly befriended Colonel George Shanton, who later came to work in Puerto Rico and who, Farnsworth claimed, had personally informed him of the island's great business opportunities.[53] Newspaper coverage of Farnsworth's 1911 lecture tour does document its inclusion of scenes from the Canal's construction, and ship manifests also reveal his travel from Panama to New York City in 1908 and 1910. Thus this aspect of Farnsworth's tales does seem well grounded.[54] In an initial visit to Puerto Rico, Farnsworth acquired a plot of land in Hato Rey (San Juan) of a little less than 30 acres (30 cuerdas) where, according to the report in *El mundo*, he planned to build a film studio and eventually even found a film school.[55]

At least three months before his interview with the Puerto Rican media, Farnsworth had begun promoting his Puerto Rican business venture in the United States. In a clearly press release–based item that appeared on June 1, 1919, through syndication in newspapers as far removed as Washington, D.C., and Bisbee, Arizona, Farnsworth called attention to himself and to Puerto Rico:

> Porto Rico may become to the motion picture industry all that Southern California has been. There's plenty of "atmosphere" of the artistic type, and it only remains to demonstrate that the atmosphere of the climatic type is right.
>
> F. Eugene Farnsworth, of New York, one of the pioneers in the picture business, here investigating, says "Porto Rico's coast line, mountains, vegetation and buildings are more varied and attractive than California. It offers new themes and plots that will prove of fascinating value.[56]

It thus appears clear that Farnsworth sought to attract U.S. capital before approaching local investors, and that his subsequent appeal to Puerto Ricans interested in developing the island's film industry, with special focus on their sense of national pride, was a calculated strategy.

Notwithstanding Farnsworth's supposed thorough study of the island's business potential, a careful reading of Puerto Rican newspaper coverage of his activities suggests that he was most likely trying to run a quick money-making scheme on the island rather than actually undertaking long-term local development. For, as soon as he had proposed the building of the film studio, Farnsworth also encouraged the selling of company stock. The company "offered easy acquisition of stocks for the sympathetic business, for the country at large, [for] . . . the purchase could be done in four easy payments of $25.00, so that the stocks could be easily acquired by the more modest households."[57] Rather than being a capitalist looking for an investment opportunity (which is how Farnsworth had sold himself), he seems to have operated as an idea man looking for willing and gullible investors wherever he could find them. The image of the island he promoted both in the United States and in Puerto Rico, as having "a great climate and enchanting landscapes, with the green of the mountains, and the varied architecture of its building," resonated with a local elite that resented the images that U.S. newspapers had presented of Puerto Rico since acquiring the colony.[58]

Soon after *El mundo* reported Farnsworth's plan to develop the cinema industry in the island, it published an editorial piece written by a local doctor, Jesús María Amadeo, touting Farnsworth's project under the headline "Cinematography in Puerto Rico, Patriotism and the Dollar: An Issue of Dignity." From the title of the piece alone we can perceive that the local elites considered the development of a film industry more than just a business opportunity. In his piece, Amadeo begins by describing what he perceives as a key public relations challenge for Puerto Rico in the United States: "It is known by all that a certain type of tourist has come from the United States with a fatal mission for us: the mission of photographing, copying or painting everything ugly and disgraceful in the country, from the vases made from the higüera tree to the Black Englishmen from [the neighboring British Virgin Island of] Tortola, and then returning north with those items bearing the sad caption of the 'real portorrican.'"[59] Amadeo then argues that "only through the screen we can dispel the fatal concepts that some Americans from the continent have formed of us [Puerto Ricans]."[60] In spite of Amadeo's deeply racist utterances regarding Black Caribbean people and local crafts, his reasoning highlights the combined goals for a national cinema that the Tropical Film Company had espoused just two years earlier: educating North Americans and attracting tourism (presumably for Amadeo of a more cultivated or insightful type of traveler).

Perhaps due to Farnsworth's flattering descriptions of Puerto Rico, the local elites evidently overlooked any discrepancies they might have perceived between the American's proposed lucrative business venture and their own ideals relating to cinema's potential for cultural ambassadorship. After the meetings with local entrepreneurs described in *El mundo*, Farnsworth apparently remained involved in the company as a business representative in the United States, while a local businessman, Enrique González Beltrán, served as acting president of the joint venture, eventually named Porto Rico Photoplays.[61]

Possible discrepancies in the local investors' aims and Farnsworth's dubious motivations aside, a film studio did in fact get built within a year. According to an article published in *El mundo* in early September 1920, the Puerto Rican public received well the venture: "The new buildings lack nothing in comparison to similar ones seen in New York, and we can even say that sometimes they exceed those in degrees of perfection and otherwise. . . . From now on it can be said that the island has one of the most complete cinematographic studios, and certainly, without comparison, the best in the Antilles."[62] Although the proposed infrastructural developments had proceeded quickly, the next phase of attracting companies to film in Puerto Rico was not as effectively realized. The article in *El mundo*, while optimistic about the new business, reveals that the studio did not operate as promised. It refers to the supposed new capitalists attracted to the business venture only as "prominent United States citizens," without mentioning any individual or company names.[63] By that time the company had changed names from the rather unwieldy "Porto Rico Motion Pictures Productions" to the more succinct "Porto Rico Photoplays."[64] It is under that latter name that the company's single film production appeared in 1921, entitled in English *Tropical Love*, directed by Ralph Ince and starring Ruth Clifford.[65]

U.S. Cinema Falls in Love with the Tropics

The director of Photoplays' only feature, Ralph Ince, was the brother of the much better known film producer, screenwriter, and director Thomas H. Ince. That family relation is relevant for tracing Farnsworth's activities in Puerto Rico, for it seems likely that he had met one or both Ince brothers through his association a few years earlier with the Mastercraft Company.[66] Possibly related to Ince's involvement, a U.S.-based company called Playgoers Pictures worked in conjunction with Porto Rico Photoplays in producing *Tropical Love*.[67] The Porto Rico Photoplays' recruitment of U.S. talent, producers, and distributors appears to have been a deliberate effort to bring the industries of Puerto Rico and the United States closer. In an article appearing in the U.S.-based Spanish-language magazine *Cine-Mundial*, a company representative declared, "[T]his is the era of the author-producer, in association with known stars, a fact that the Porto Rico Photoplays has found to be significant and the reason why it has recruited Miss Clifford and Mr. McConnell [the screenwriter]. . . . The intention of the Porto Rico Photoplays is to bring the two Americas to a better understanding of each other."[68] In this way, the appearance in the film of recognizable names for a public familiar with U.S.-made movies served not only as a marketing strategy based on stars but also seemed to respond to regional changes in approaches to foreign policy, using Puerto Rico as a U.S. bridge to Latin America, as discussed earlier.

Surprisingly, advertisements for *Tropical Love* reveal that the company credited with the production shifted according to the region of its distribution. In Puerto Rico, the film appeared as a Porto Rico Photoplays production, while in the United States it publicly circulated exclusively under the Playgoers Pictures name. In India the film showed under the Pathé banner, probably due to distribution arrangements with the French-based company.[69] However, records from the New York State's Motion Picture Commission list the film as solely a Porto Rico Photoplays production, distributed in the United States by Pathé.[70]

Intriguingly, the Puerto Rican press does not mention any outside investment aside from Farnsworth's involvement in the production of *Tropical Love*, called on the island *Amor tropical*. Most crucially for Puerto Rican film historiography, the island's press actively and consistently claimed the film as Puerto Rican. Apparently out of ignorance or in the service of hyperbolic rhetoric, an advertisement for the film in *El mundo* declares *Tropical Love* as "the first Puerto Rican production."[71] However, an article in *La correspondencia* exhibits more historical knowledge in its carefully qualifying the movie as the "first Porto Rico Photoplays production."[72] Despite that divergence, both newspapers announced the film's opening on October 25, 1921, in all theaters in San Juan (listed as The America, The Rialto, The Luna, and The Tres Banderas).[73] In addition, *La correspondencia* notes that after October 28, the film would open in all theaters in Santurce.[74] The film's extensive exhibition in the San Juan metropolitan area suggests local business expectations that it would have guaranteed success in Puerto Rico.

Reviews in both *La correspondencia* and *El mundo* praised *Amor tropical* for the "veracity" of its depiction of Puerto Rico.[75] While *El mundo* asserted that the film offered a positive representation of the island, *La correspondencia* dramatically elaborated its importance in influencing global views of Puerto Rico.[76] The writer of the piece in *La correspondencia*, Obdulia de Lázaro, describes *Tropical Love* as an important turning point for the perception of the island abroad:

> The moving pictures travel all over the world, going from one part of the world to another, and through this medium it is possible for our [Puerto

> Rico's] rural and urban life to be known. And today, more than ever, it is necessary for the world to know our well-loved Puerto Rico.
>
> It would be a great pity for the Porto Rico Photoplays to stop its efforts, because we believe that a good collection of movies filmed in Puerto Rico would help make the U.S. and the rest of the world familiar with this enchanted little Caribbean island.[77]

Although the business structure of cinema production in Puerto Rico had undergone broad change through direct engagement with U.S. investors, the expectations of the intellectual elite appear to have remained the same. Farnsworth had promoted the idea of making money, that is, of building a commercially driven industry, but the island's intelligentsia and possibly even the local investors persevered in their belief in cinema's potential to act as Puerto Rico's "cultural ambassador" to the world.

Newspaper writers were so set on the idea of film as "travel agent" that the reviews of *Tropical Love* neglected to discuss the film's plot, focusing instead on the beauty of the settings. Accordingly, *El mundo* proclaimed that "both the beauty of our landscapes and the typical grace of our jíbaros and peasant huts throb on the canvas with the deep force of intense reality," while *La correspondencia* declared "there are beautiful detailed landscapes in which one can admire the exuberant vegetation of our land; rich expositions of our city and its surrounding neighborhoods, which allow us to admire the best of our buildings."[78] Although Puerto Rican newspapers described the film as an impressive public relations achievement, that basis for local acclaim may have been lost in North America, for U.S. historical sources suggest that the filmmakers cast all of the main characters, played by North Americans Ruth Clifford, Reginald Denny, and Fred Turner, as Americans living in Puerto Rico rather than themselves as Puerto Ricans. Thus audiences could not have appreciated the desired "true Puerto Rican people."[79]

Reviews of the film in U.S. newspapers reveal that the action of the film revolves around the circumstance that Clifford's character, Rosario, does not know that she is the white daughter of a mentally unbalanced American planter living in Puerto Rico. Rosario has lived as a native on the farm owned by her father, whom she does not know, until the film ultimately reveals that she is not Puerto Rican at all.[80] If indeed, as seems likely, the film's intertitles in North American distribution effaced the characters' local connections, the publicity value of the film for the island's interests diminishes. The available evidence does not mention if any Puerto Ricans worked on the production as minor cast members or crew, but the lack of commentary on the subject in Puerto Rican newspapers suggests they did not. Thus, despite the location shooting in Puerto Rico, rather than actually presenting Puerto Rico as a cultured, refined, and friendly society, *Tropical Love* appears to have used Puerto Rico simply as an exotic setting. Nonetheless, emphasis on the motif of the "island paradise" could indeed potentially advance the local entrepreneurs' hopes of promoting profitable tourism to Puerto Rico.

The advertisements for the film in the United States disclose that the promoters there, too, had a tourism angle in mind. U.S. newspaper advertisements for *Tropical Love* highlight the setting's particular appeal, as one in the *Bemidji Daily Pioneer*, which reads, "If you ever stood in front of a steamship office window, with longing gaze glued on pamphlets of 'Winter Cruises,' you'll not miss 'Tropical Love.'"[81] Other newspaper advertisements stop short of casting the film viewing as a substitute for a costly trip to the island, but still wax eloquent in describing the romantic setting. The *Coconino Sun*, for example, carried an ad that reads: "Beneath Porto Rico's tropical sky—moonlight, palm trees, a beach sparkling like a circlet of jewels, native music, silences broken by passionate whispers of love! A powerful story, swift action and beautiful scenery."[82] In neither case, however, did the U.S. advertising campaign for *Tropical Love* really promote active travel to Puerto Rico, which was in any case out of reach for most moviegoers at that time.

Although most North American publicity for the film focused on the scenery in *Tropical Love*, others did recount the story's narrative as a selling point. Promotions like that in The *Pullman Herald* reveal aspects of the lost film's plot:

> The common bond of loneliness drew together Rosario, the Seeker and the Drifter, the three principal characters of "Tropical Love" . . . with Ruth Clifford starred as Rosario, and Reginald Denny as the Drifter and Fred Turner as the Seeker.
>
> Rosario, beautiful child of nature, wondered why her skin was fair and her mother's brown. The Seeker knew not who he was, whither he came from, nor where he was going. It was instinct that, after 20 years, guided him to the scene of the tragedy that had bereft him of his mind. The Drifter, young and educated, had cut away from the bonds of society to find adventure.

> On a sugar plantation in Porto Rico Fate threw these three together, and each became something precious to the other during the adventure and mystery that followed.[83]

The newspaper's description indicates that, like both *Heart and Soul* and *The Liar*, *Tropical Love* cast Puerto Rico as a context or pretext for addressing issues of race and ancestry. The American Film Institute's catalog notes that (as implied in the *Pullman Herald*'s description) the Seeker is Rosario's father who lost his mind (and his wife) following a tropical storm, that a man named Clifford Fayne tries to steal Rosario's land after discovering gold there, and that the Drifter both reveals the white parentage and saves Rosario from Clifford, while himself winning her heart.[84] The plot of *Tropical Love* resembles that of *The Liar*—uncertain, possibly dubious ancestry, conflicts around inheritance, unscrupulous businessmen, and a colonial tropical setting—but the Puerto Rican media heralded *Tropical Love* as an achievement of realistic representation. Apart from the possibly impressive quality of the direction, acting, and script (for which I have no evidence), it seems clear that the praise for the film in Puerto Rico directly relates to its use of the island as a location. Namely, the press coverage expresses excitement and gratification at finally seeing the "real" Puerto Rico touring the world through cinema. In other words, Puerto Rican economic and cultural elites seemed clearly to have considered the film an artistic and critical success without regard to the exoticizing qualities of the story and possibly acting.

In economic terms, *Tropical Love* appears to have brought international attention to the island's newly erected film studio. Just five days after the premiere of the film (October 8, 1921), Pathé, based in Paris, made an offer to rent the Porto Rico Photoplays' film studio for the company's own future productions.[85] The negotiations apparently went smoothly, as in 1922 Pathé made *The Woman Who Fooled Herself*, and in 1923, *Tents of Allah*, both filmed in Puerto Rico and directed by Charles A. Logue. As to the fate of F. Eugene Farnsworth, the Puerto Rican newspaper coverage of him ceases after the release of *Tropical Love*. Although ship records show Farnsworth traveling between San Juan, Santo Domingo, and New York during 1922, suggesting either that his business interests might have shifted to include the Dominican Republic or else that he departed from Puerto Rico through a neighboring port, he appears to have had no further involvement with the film industry in the island. By late 1922, according to his published obituary, he already had achieved his position in the Maine chapter of the KKK.[86] Further, *Variety* announced in a 1950 article that the Porto Rico Photoplays company was "dissolved by court order in 1923."[87] The *Variety* article does not explain why the company disbanded. Puerto Rican film historian Juan Ortiz Jiménez posits that the cause was a struggle between the company's president, Enrique González, and his brother.[88] However, an article in *Cine mundo* reveals that Ruth Clifford, the lead actress in *Tropical Love*, had sued the Porto Rico Photoplays for breach of contract.[89] The article also mentions that Clifford asked for $139,200 in restitution and that the case would be heard in the New York Supreme Court.[90] Although I have no evidence of the final resolution by the New York court, the court-ordered dissolution of the company suggests that Ruth Clifford may have won the suit, forcing the company into bankruptcy. Even though Farnsworth had not developed Puerto Rico into a viable alternative to Hollywood and had not even managed to establish a lasting film production company, the construction of film infrastructure did ultimately aid the eventual growth of the local industry.

The MacManus/Pathé Productions

Although the Porto Rico Photoplays company name does not appear in the credits of any other known film, the studio facilities in Hato Rey may not have lain fallow following the completion of *Tropical Love* in 1922. Though it is conceivable that, presuming the film's successful exhibition in Puerto Rico, the monies foreseen as the studio's return somehow got redirected to the legal case involving Clifford, the studio remained open. Whether or not the company's disbanding by court decree in 1923 came about due to bankruptcy, a local affiliate of Pathé appears to have benefited directly from Porto Rico Photoplays' economic loss by leasing the defunct company's facilities. Thanks to an accord negotiated in the fall of 1921, Pathé acquired the rights to use the Hato Rey studio to make a film on the island.[91]

At this point the historical record shows the engagement of an additional North American film producer/director in Puerto Rico. A man named Edward A. MacManus, produced *The Woman Who Fooled Herself* (1922), which Pathé distributed. MacManus had worked in some relation with Pathé since 1914, when that company struck a deal with his then employer, Hearst's International Film Service, for the production and distribution of newsreels.[92] An experienced man in the film world, MacManus had served as the general manager of the International Film Service (1914) and as secretary of The Motion Picture Board of Trade of America (1916); by 1919 he had established his own production company, The MacManus Corporation.[93] Before coming to Puerto Rico, MacManus had already produced two films, *The Lost Battalion* (1919) and *The Gray Brothers* (1920).[94]

MacManus appears to have made business arrangements with both Pathé and Enrique González of the Porto Rico Photoplays, for by April 1922 both the *New York Tribune* and the *Film Daily* reported that MacManus would shoot four productions in Puerto Rico, to be distributed by Associated Exhibitors (then a division of Pathé).[95] The *Film Daily* declared that "MacManus [had] a fully equipped studio located on 34 acres of property in San Juan, and access to about 2,000 acres of tropical land owned by his associates, a number of wealthy Porto Ricans."[96] Although I have found no definite evidence, the description of the studio and the "associates" closely fits the circumstances of the Porto Rico Photoplays company and its Puerto Rican investors. The *Film Daily* article also reveals that MacManus had come to the island with a full U.S. cast and crew, signifying that his film productions employed little, if any, local talent.[97]

In contrast to the response to *Tropical Love*, *The Woman Who Fooled Herself* (circulated in Puerto Rico as *La mujer que se engañó a si misma*) received very little coverage in Puerto Rican newspapers, perhaps because of the lack of local involvement in the production. Despite the small attention it received, theater advertisements for the film in San Juan newspapers did promote it with nationalist lines like "you will see the most picturesque landscapes of your own country" and "we are exhibiting the purely Puerto Rican film." Nonetheless, the local newspapers did not report on the production process or even publish a descriptive review.[98] In the United States, however, newspapers did discuss MacManus's film, often associating it explicitly with Puerto Rico.

For example, an article in the *Washington Post* describes the setting of *The Woman* as having "a virgin wealth of magnificent outdoor scenery" and declares, counter to historical evidence, that it was "the first picture to be made in Porto Rico and released in this country."[99] Certainly, Pathé, the distributor of the film also in the United States, would have known of the existence of at least *Tropical Love*, making clear the claim's function as hyperbolic rhetoric supporting commercial interests rather than any basis in accurate historiography.

Another review in the *Washington Post* seems to echo the arguments that Farnsworth had made in promoting Puerto Rico as providing resources that California could not: "The tropical scenes are completely convincing, by reason of the picture having been filmed on the island of Porto Rico, which, while not equatorial, is in no sense sub-tropical. The exterior views, which play a large part in the development of the story—having to do with vast coffee, sugar, and tobacco plantations—are marked by a more luxuriant tropical verdure than even southern California can supply."[100] A review that appeared in the *Colorado Springs Gazette* similarly emphasized the novelty of the Puerto Rican location: "[the film] was produced on the beautiful tropical island of Porto Rico, which is virgin soil for photoplay production and therefore offers to the screen some new scenic beauties."[101]

Many reports implied an understanding of the Puerto Rican setting as more symbolic than specifically geographic, and in fact the fictional tropical setting of *The Woman Who Fooled Herself* was not actually Puerto Rico but instead a general South American "equatorial" location. The film's description in the American Film Institute's catalog explains the plot of *The Woman* as follows: "Desperate for a job, New York showgirl Eva Lee accepts an offer from Cameron Camden and Eban Burnham to go to South America to dance and capture the heart of Fernando Pennington so as to get an option on his Grandfather's Casablanca's land. Eva succeeds in snaring Fernando but also falls in love with him. Persuading Camden to surrender the papers, she takes them to the Casablanca residence, only to find it being attacked by Burnham. Fernando repulses the attackers, kills Burnham, and finds happiness with Eva."[102] Apart from the overgeneralized "southern" setting, the use of the name "Casablanca" for the plantation suggests an amalgamation of exotic locations. Although "Casablanca" literally means "white house" in Spanish, the public may well have connected the name with the Moroccan city.

Aside from the film's nonspecific Latin, exotic setting, its marketing also engaged in other orientalizing practices. For instance, an advertisement in the *Baltimore Sun* relied on the image of Latin men as violent and sensual and the newspaper's plot description further promulgated those stereotypes:

> When it comes to getting the woman he loves, the Spanish-American hero of "The Woman Who Fooled Herself," . . . has a startling method.
>
> This hero walks boldly on the stage of the cabaret where the girl he wants is doing the "Dance of the Golden Helmet." Before everyone he snatches her by the wrist.
>
> When a friend tries to interfere with a revolver, the thing he holds in his hand is disclosed as a rawhide lash, with which he snaps the gun from the other's hand. Then he slings the girl over his shoulder and, slashing his whip, he beats his way through the crowd and carries her off.
>
> You can't blame the young man, for the girl had deliberately flirted with him, and then, when he had fallen madly in love with her, she laughed at him.[103]

Such a description and the writer's approving tone unquestionably would disturb current readers for its sexualized violence as well as ethnic stereotyping. Certainly the Puerto Rican critics who had prized the potential of cinema to act as cultural ambassador did not have this type of characterization in mind. Yet, as Gaylyn Studlar discusses, "Hollywood Orientalism of this period was constructed to appeal strongly to women, trading on female fantasies in relation to the indulgence of both consumer goods and sexual desires beyond the established boundaries of proper social norms."[104] Without question, as Rudolph Valentino's remarkable stardom documents, the sexually raw "Latin lover" certainly fits this orientalist mold. Furthermore, as Ana M. López has pointed out, the U.S. film industry continued to treat the tropics as a mysterious, savage land of romance and adventure well into the 1950s.[105]

The next film that Edward MacManus made in Puerto Rico for Pathé, though also an orientalist fantasy, differed significantly from the previous two U.S.-funded productions on the island, particularly in that the narrative takes place in Tangier, Morocco. Entitled *The Tents of Allah*, this film involved the same director as *The Woman Who Fooled Herself*, Charles A. Logue, who probably completed it by October 1922, with its release coming in 1923. Besides on *The Woman*, Logue had worked with MacManus since the company's founding, writing the script for their first film *The Lost Battalion*.[106] Logue worked successfully as a scriptwriter both prior and subsequent to his involvement with MacManus, with a total of seventy-nine titles to his credit.[107] He, however, ended his directorial career with *Tents of Allah*.

As the film's title certainly invited, reviews in U.S. newspapers regularly discussed *Tents of Allah* in relation to the popular 1921 film *The Sheik* (Famous Players-Lasky Corp.), starring Rudolph Valentino. According to the film reviewer writing for the *Chicago Daily Tribune* under the pseudonym Mae Tinée, "The story [of *Tents of Allah*] is something like 'The Sheik' in that a son of the desert turns out to be the son of a white man. And, as in the 'The Sheik,' he becomes enamored of a white girl. As in the story referred to, there is an abduction. Aside from these points in common, the trails diverge and you have Monte Blue as SOME desert lover."[108] In a similar fashion, the reviewer of the *Los Angeles Times* declared that *Tents of Allah* "is one of the stepchildren of 'The Sheik.'"[109] These descriptions strongly suggest that Charles Logue (who also served as the scriptwriter) sought to capitalize on the popularity of Valentino's film when he came up with the concept for *Tents of Allah*.

The film tells the story of an American tourist, Elaine Calvert, who unintentionally insults the sultan of Tangiers and consequently gets kidnapped by a sheik, named Chiddar Ben-Ek, under the sultan's command. Chiddar and Elaine eventually fall in love, and later the film reveals that he is the son of an American commander, allowing for the two to have a relationship.[110] As with the other films discussed in this chapter, the exotic location masks a preoccupation with interracial relationships. Again we see that the beautiful American woman is in constant danger of being sexually tempted by the seductively mysterious Other. The transformation of the racial other into a white American arguably could assuage the anxiety for white audiences about the "attractive brutality" projected onto that other. As with the revelation in *The Sheik* that Valentino's character Ahmed is of European heritage (British and Spanish), the disclosure that Chiddar is American allows for the transference of "exotic" sexual attraction into a proper white suitor, thus preserving racial integrity.

Apparently unconcerned with *The Tents of Allah*'s orientalist tones, which I have argued got extended in films of the period to representations of Puerto Ricans and other Latin populations, local critics received it as a highly commendable achievement. Advertisements in Puerto Rican newspapers even congratulated the film for its success in the U.S. market. For example, advertisements in *La democracia* declared that the film was "praised by the American cinema critics," and *El mundo* raved that it was "classified as extraordinary in the United States."[111] However, I have not found any positive U.S. reviews for the film except the one in the *Chicago Daily*

Tribune comparing it to *The Sheik*, printed months after the film had premiered in Puerto Rico on January 28, 1923. Besides the historical record's contradicting the claims of those advertisers (presumably Pathé), the American Film Institute's catalog lists the film as premiering on March 4, 1923.[112] Records of the Motion Picture Commission of New York show that the New York State film censorship board approved the film for exhibition on January 19, 1923.[113] However, the advertisements in Puerto Rico asserting American approval appeared as early as January 18, 1923, suggesting that Edward MacManus or a MacManus/Pathé representative had invented the enamored U.S. critics' responses to convince Puerto Rican audiences of the film's value based on North American attitudes. Such a sales strategy implies a racist, colonial vision of a hierarchy of artistic tastes and values, positioning U.S. film critics as necessarily superior to native critics (and supposedly recognizably so to Puerto Rican readers).

Still, reviews in Puerto Rican newspapers did exalt the film, using phrases like a "Puerto Rican triumph" and "a work of art, a drama of profound design."[114] A local Puerto Rican film magazine, *Cinema*, ran an extensive positive review of the picture asserting that "the novelistic plot awakens a great interest from its opening scenes, and the film ends with such a strong lyricism that it turns out to be one of those that makes the spectators cry involuntarily."[115] In addition to acclaiming the emotional story, reviews as well as ads in Puerto Rican newspapers highlighted the presence of a local actress as a secondary character in the film. The Puerto Rican actress Amalia Rivera Muñoz played Chala, a character who goes unmentioned in U.S. reviews and so must not have been central to the plot.[116] Yet all advertisements in Puerto Rico featured "Amalia Rivera" in big bold letters along with a line declaring her Puerto Ricanness. Without even mentioning the film's female lead, the reviewer in *Cinema*, Mary Thurman, dedicated a section exclusively to Rivera, in which she declared: "Amalia Rivera Muñoz demonstrates with her performance that she has the aptitude for the world art."[117] It appears that advertisers in Puerto Rico saw Rivera's presence in the film as a way to attract audiences to the theaters and to indicate that the island's industry was indeed moving forward. The strategy the film company employed in Puerto Rico appears to have been a common one, for as Ruth Vasey documents, since the 1920s, American producers recruited international talent for U.S. projects as a strategy to capture the sympathy and allegiance of global audiences. Vasey further argues, as seems to be the case in Puerto Rico that "foreign audiences often responded particularly warmly to their own compatriots when they appeared in the international context of the Hollywood industry."[118]

Contrasted to the local assertions about the wonders of *Tents of Allah* and its innate Puerto Ricanness, the eventual reviewers in the United States paid scant attention to Puerto Rico as the filming location (since the film's story takes place in Tangiers), and when they did note the island location they did so only disparagingly. For example, a reviewer in the *Los Angeles Times* writes that it was evident that *Tents of Allah* was filmed in the tropics, as the horses in the film look so small. The reviewer goes on to declare that, "it is said that the problem of horses is one of the hardest in the making of pictures of a locale other than America, as the type and size vary in each country."[119] The Los Angeles critic's giving attention to such a minor element of the film, in oblique justification of Hollywood or other domestic locations for shooting, may suggest the critic's concern with "offshore" economic threats to the local film industry. Still, newspapers in other areas of the United States offered other criticisms. In lieu of criticizing the local horses, the *Boston Globe* centered on Puerto Rico's oppressive heat and its adverse effect on film stock. The critic's dramatic account of the hardships of processing the film in the island included the following description: "when the trade wind failed for two days and the heat was intense, great oblong cakes of ice had to be placed in the drying room with electric fans behind them so as to blow the cold air directly on the negative. A difference of two degrees in temperature would have ruined the whole film."[120] Although the *Globe*'s comments probably formed part of a marketing strategy to attract audiences to "the film that almost did not survive," such an attitude could also have worked to dissuade investors from producing in such a "volatile" climate.

Nonetheless, U.S. producers kept coming to Puerto Rico. Records of the Motion Picture Commission of New York indicate the production of a travel film with the title *Picturesque Porto Rico* arriving there by December 31, 1923.[121] The records also note the names of a filmmaker, Sam Roth, and a distributor, John J. Iris, associated with this project. Worth mentioning, a film program for the Rialto Theater in San Juan notes that *Picturesque Porto Rico* (*Puerto Rico pinturesco*) played along with *Tents of Allah* at the feature film's local premiere on January 28, 1923.[122] Thus, the scenic film appears to have opened in Puerto Rico months before it arrived in the Unites States (or at least New York). I have found no further details about this scenic film or its makers, but its potential appeal for American audiences must have arisen from its depiction of the tropical/Spanish-influenced setting. The pairing of the two films may also have made obvious to audiences, at least at the Rialto, some of the ways that *Tents of Allah* equated Puerto Rico with the Orient.

After completing *Tents of Allah*, MacManus appears to have left the island and did not complete the final two negotiated films. According to *Variety*, a split between MacManus and Charles Logue had left the studio idle.[123] The article does not detail the events that led to the fallout between MacManus and Logue, and their reasons for leaving the island remain a mystery. However, the *Variety* article does mention that by July 1923 representatives of the studio's manager, González, visited New York in an attempt to lease it to other production companies. It seems likely that during the visit to New York, the Puerto Rican studio managers reached a deal with Famous Players-Lasky/Paramount to film in Puerto Rico *Aloma of the South Seas* (Dir. Maurice Tourneur, 1925).

Famous Players-Lasky/Paramount Comes to the Island

Even in comparison to the fanfare that the other already mentioned productions received in Puerto Rico, the filming of *Aloma of the South Seas,* starring Gilda Gray, in October 1925 constituted the biggest local cinema event of the 1920s. *Aloma* provided Gray her first film-acting opportunity and gave Puerto Rico much-desired coverage in U.S. newspapers. Before starring in this film, Gray had successfully performed as a vaudeville dancer, where audiences recognized her by her signature dance, "the shimmy."[124] In fact, *Aloma*'s allure relied on Gray's dance scenes and display of her body. An article in the *New York Times* reported that "Miss Gray gives an exhibition of dancing in person prior to the screening of 'Aloma of the South Seas,' and in the picture she is again beheld in the same dance."[125] The wording of the *New York Times*' article does not make it clear whether Gray performed the live dance before every New York screening or just during the premiere, but considering that the article appeared ten days after the film's first screening, it seems likely that she performed the live show on more than one occasion. In addition, the film's reviews comment on Gray's costumes and how they reveal her body with quips like "her

FIG. 5.2 Gilda Gray as Aloma

impeccable form is seen to good advantage," and picture captions such as "a costume picture—without much costume."[126]

In keeping with the evident aim of other films shot in Puerto Rico, the makers of *Aloma* attempted to attract U.S. audiences with the promise of exotic locations and characters. The American Film Institute describes the formulaic plot of the film in the following terms:

> Aloma, a beautiful dancer on Paradise Island, is jealously guarded by her lover, Nuitane. When Red Malloy, a dishonest trader, annoys her, Bob Holden, an American seeking to forget an unhappy love affair, defends her and wins her allegiance. Andrew Taylor, learning that his niece, Sylvia, who deserted Bob, is coming to the island with her husband, Van Templeton, sends Bob and Aloma to his plantation, though Nuitane objects. Aloma comes to love Bob but is tricked by Van, a sodden flirt, into "marriage," while Bob realizes that he still loves Sylvia. Bob and Van are lost in a canoe that capsizes during a storm, and the jealous women are drawn together in a common bond of sympathy. Then Bob reappears, announcing that Van has drowned; he is reunited with Sylvia; and Aloma continues her relationship with Nuitane.[127]

As the description makes evident, this film presents another instance of the use of setting not only as a novelty but also as a means by which to evoke the threat of miscegenation. Aloma, like Gray herself, is a sensual and appealing woman, but unlike the actress who plays her, she is not white. Bob's attraction to her (and vicariously, the public's), and her attraction to him, while entertaining, cannot be the film's resolution. Therefore, although Gray drew the patrons into the theaters, her character Aloma could not be the one to end with an American husband. Although the other films discussed in this chapter used men as racial others, *Aloma* makes the menace female. Still, like its predecessors, *Aloma* also ultimately concludes with the coupling of characters based on their ethnicity.

Revealingly, reviewers linked the filming in the "tropics," as they referred to Puerto Rico, with barbarity. That is, U.S. reviewers appear to have imagined the island as an uncivilized, naive, and primitive place. (In fact, many images—both photographs and cartoons—in books, newspapers, and magazines appearing at the beginning of the twentieth century presented Cuba, the Philippines, and Puerto Rico as naked children, often a metaphor for underdevelopment).[128] Although the United States had acquired its colonies twenty-five years prior to the making of this film, opinions regarding the "natives" seemed unchanged. For example, an article appearing in the *Washington Post* describes Puerto Rican participation in the making of *Aloma* in ways that emphasize American superiority. The director reportedly wanted to simulate lightning hitting a coconut tree, for which he asked a local man to climb a palm tree and set up dynamite at the top. After the crew exploded the dynamite, the locals ran off, scared by the explosion, and refused to do a second take, prompting the journalist to conclude that "Porto Rican men [could not] be depended on."[129] The *Post's* narrative describes Puerto Ricans as easily scared by modern technologies (even if justifiably so, due to the substance's lethality), and interprets their supposed fearfulness as evidence of their inability to perform simple tasks and their inadequacy as workers. According to Jacqueline Stewart, such characterizations are indeed a common trope in colonialist discourses about native populations.[130]

Newspaper descriptions of the characters also illustrate ambiguous ethnic/racial representations in the film. For example, Julanne Johnston, who played Sylvia (and had the previous year appeared as the female lead in *The Thief of Baghdad*), described the transformation of Gilda Gray into Aloma for the *Los Angeles Times* as follows: "She is brown and alluring, with dark hair in riotous curls, and a wind-blown grass skirt in the day-time, and she is blond, serene and smart in a different Paris gown every night."[131] Johnston's declarations reveal a view of the "native" as physically captivating but lacking in refinement. According to Johnston, the "real" (i.e., white) Gilda Gray was a proper, educated woman, while the Gilda Gray in "brownface" exuded untamed sexuality. The filmmakers' and stars' view of the "native" were, however, at odds with actual social development in Puerto Rico. Hence a photograph caption in the *Los Angeles Times* notes that "Porto Rico was too civilized for Gilda Gray—they say. The dancer, now making 'Aloma of the South Seas' for Paramount, had to import all the primitive atmosphere from the States, including her costume. This forms an enticing hint of what the South Seas mean to Gilda."[132] The image of the South Seas that *Aloma* sold appealed to prejudiced, ossified views among Americans about the tropics as underdeveloped. The filmmakers evidently felt that an orientalist representation of a generalized south would prove more appealing for movie audiences than a more faithful representation of what they encountered in the actual filming location of Puerto Rico, thus necessitating the use of admittedly inaccurate "South Seas" props.

Whatever else the makers of *Aloma* understood the tropics to encompass, they apparently considered dark skin coloring essential to representing the "native." Both Gray and Warner Baxter (who played Nuitane) used makeup to darken their skin as a key component in their transformation into "islanders." Another form in which the filmmakers used race to divide the "native" from the white involved the casting of extras. Maurice Tourneur, the film's director, requested "fifteen young ladies, all with tan skin," to form part of the production as "native" extras.[133] As one can perceive, Tourneur had to make the distinction of skin color when casting, revealing his awareness of the range of racialized bodies that inhabited Puerto Rico. His request also means that he had an artistic vision of the tropics as exclusively "tan," despite knowing that actual tropical locations like Puerto Rico had racially diverse populations. In addition, an article in the *Los Angeles Times* indicates that, "a troupe of Samoans, who have been touring in vaudeville were . . . sent along in case there are no dancing natives on the island."[134] The production's setting of Samoans and Puerto Ricans as interchangeable "tropical islanders" by virtue of their presumably tan skin—without regard to any sociocultural and even ethnic differences—further demonstrates the production's orientalist fantasy of the south.

In spite of the film's embedding in such racist ideologies, local Puerto Rican spectators found the project fascinating. The writer of an article in the local newspaper *El mundo* marveled at the attraction that San Juan inhabitants felt for the production, noting that "San Juan was left desolated and all its inhabitants that can afford not to work have gone to Cataño [the filming location for beach scene]."[135] Moreover, newspapers declared that *Aloma* was "an admirable cinematographic production," and that it offered local women cast as extras an opportunity to "find admirers in the north."[136]

Despite some U.S. trade press coverage of the film promulgating perspectives of hegemonic North Americans toward the South, some local filmmakers did benefit from the industrial aspect of production, even if not from its cultural representations. For instance, Juan Viguié, a local filmmaker and the focus of the next chapter, gained some professional opportunities through the production of *Aloma*, as he created some of the film's special effects.[137] Additionally, Mr. Bruno, the owner of the local Paramount Theater, the Cine Rialto, assisted Maurice Tourneur in casting the local women who served as extras, and received free advertisement for his theater through his association with the production.

Aloma received positive reviews from major American newspapers and became the top grossing film of 1926.[138] But an article in *Life* magazine offers a surprisingly different perspective. The playwright and screenwriter Robert E. Sherwood, then a film critic for *Life,* described the film as "the most effective mass of hokum that has been seen since 'Way Down East.' It possesses not an atom of truth, and almost no drama (artificially or otherwise)."[139] Sherwood had established a reputation as a highly professional and serious writer of film criticism, with his columns syndicated in magazines from *Photoplay* and *Movie Weekly* to *McCall's*.[140] Sherwood's *Life* review does not make clear if he disliked the film because of its melodramatic plot (as the comparison to Griffith's *Way Down East* suggests) or for its gratuitous use of the "exotic," as he also suggests later in the review, when he notes that the film's plot appears to be an excuse to showcase a beautiful setting.[141] However, he indisputably offers subtle criticism of the film's representation of race in his description of Warner Baxter in the role of a "nice Nordic Samoan."[142] The mildly sarcastic phrasing suggests that Sherwood viewed the appearance of white actors in "brownface" as problematic, if not for political reasons, then for their representational inaccuracy. Without asserting that the critic found the film racist, I would argue that he understood it to be fraught with representational problems. The Puerto Rican press's coverage of *Aloma* did not address those issues.

Beyond Fiction: Other Aspects of the Puerto Rican Film Industry in the 1920s

Even though it seems that no U.S. film company produced work in Puerto Rico later in the 1920s, nor during 1930–1950, the island still figured as the fictional setting of a number of Hollywood movies. In 1927, just one year after the release of *Aloma of the South Seas*, Warner Brothers released a film set in a fictionalized Puerto Rico entitled *The Climbers*, starring Irene Rich. In 1939 the first Hollywood "talkie" to feature fictional Puerto Rico came out; Twentieth-Century Fox released *Mr. Moto in Danger Island*, directed by Herbert I. Leeds and starring Peter Lorre. To my knowledge, this film stands as the only Hollywood film depicting Puerto Rico from the period of 1896–1950 extant.

The available records do not reveal what happened to the San Juan area studio after the *Aloma* crew left the island. It appears that no other U.S. production company came to film in Puerto Rico until the 1950s. An article in *Variety* does mention that sometime before 1950 the local government had negotiated with comedian Ed Gardner to bring business to the film studio: "Puerto Rican government is pinning its hopes—and publicity—for a revival there of feature film production on the contract under which Ed Gardner is now originating his 'Duffy Tavern' radio show from there. For Gardner to take advantage of the insular tax exemption, he must make a full-length film comedy, shorts for television and invest $250,000 of his own money in the projects. Once the film is produced, the government hopes it will call attention of the major Hollywood studios to the use of Puerto Rico for their foreign leasing."[143] Although no records indicate that Gardner actually made a film in Puerto Rico, this article does reveal that the government had taken control of the film studio at some point between 1925 and 1950.

Despite the fact that the number of fiction films produced in Puerto Rico by Puerto Ricans in the 1920s was smaller than that of (shorter) cinematic works produced in the 1910s, one cannot thereby conclude that the island's industry was completely inactive or strictly focused on U.S. investment during the period from 1917 to 1925. Although no Puerto Rican directors appear to have produced fictional films during the 1920s, I have found evidence that the local government sponsored the production of educational films. In effect, the departments of agriculture, sanitation, and education all used films as a method to communicate with and train the island's population.

An article in *Cinema* reveals that by 1923 the Department of Agriculture had produced films intended for the consumption of local farmers. Through these films the department "taught modern procedures for planting, and demonstrated other important industries."[144] The article also discloses that the Department of Sanitation, for its part, focused its film educational efforts on informing the public of "methods of prevention and treatment" of diseases. The article does not describe which particular diseases the department covered, but given the predominance of medical efforts concentrated on eradicating the hookworm during the first decades of the twentieth century, many of the department's films most likely focused on this subject.[145] Finally, *Cinema* describes a "campaign of objective education" that the Department of Education carried out through film production.[146] Although the meaning of the term "objective education" is not self-evident, it could refer to basic language or math instruction.

Under the auspices of the local government and international philanthropic organizations such as the Rockefeller Foundation, some filmmakers, such as Juan Viguié Cajas, gained from documentary filmmaking the necessary experience to delve into bigger, private film projects. In this way, the production of public nonfiction films also helped the growth and development of Puerto Rican cinema. Finally, in addition to these publicly funded educational films, local filmmakers evidently produced other nonfiction films in the form of actualities. For example, a film theater advertisement in

La correspondencia announces the projection of a sporting event pitting the "Dominican stars vs. Puerto Rico and Ponce."[147]

Despite the crucial turn that the Puerto Rican cinema industry took during the 1920s, attempting to attract U.S. investment for its development, local filmmakers continued to produce films with local capital. In addition, even when the feature films produced in the island during the 1920s espoused a U.S. point of view, local elites continued to view the films as promotions of Puerto Rican culture abroad. Nonetheless, a segment of the Puerto Rican film circle did start to appreciate film as more than culture on screen, moving toward a more business-centered perspective. The next chapter explores the strategies employed by Puerto Rican filmmakers to compete in a market controlled by Hollywood. Chapter 6 focuses on a director, Juan Viguié Cajas, and a producer, Rafael Ramos Cobián, to consider how they managed to balance local discourses regarding the educational/cultural purpose of film with economic practices inspired by the U.S. cinema industry.

6

Making the Nation Profitable

Industry-Centered Transnational Approaches to Filmmaking (1923–1940)

Although the construction of a film studio in San Juan in 1920 served as a catalyst for four U.S. studio productions on the island, by the end of the 1920s U.S.-based companies had stopped making films in Puerto Rico. Building on the infrastructure achieved by that point, Puerto Rican producers turned to new funding and distribution approaches to further develop the local film industry. The two figures who came to define Puerto Rican cinema during the 1930s, Juan Viguié Cajas and Rafael Ramos Cobián, emerged from different business backgrounds: Viguié was a veteran film industry employee, and Ramos Cobián a theater impresario. Perhaps because of their different qualifications, Puerto Rican film scholarship has discussed their careers in markedly different ways. Cinema scholars, many taking an auteurist approach to film history, have closely attended to and celebrated Viguié's artistic talent and business initiative, but have mentioned Ramos Cobián only somewhat in passing as a film industry financial backer. However, as I will demonstrate in this chapter, despite the differences in their credentials, both producers challenged the cultural–educational approach that had defined Puerto Rican cinema in the early decades of the twentieth century by moving to a more industry-conscious method of filmmaking. In this chapter I explain how both men sought artistic connections and business partners outside of Puerto Rico because they understood the necessity for transnational networks for the growth and development of national cultural products.

Remarkably, Viguié Cajas and Ramos Cobián achieved recognition in a deeply economically depressed market. Along with the collapse of the world market in the fall of 1929, Puerto Rico suffered two very widely destructive hurricanes, San Felipe in 1928 and San Ciprián in 1932, which decimated the agricultural industries on which the island's economy relied. The harsh economic reality also caused great social unrest as unemployment numbers grew and, unlike in the United States, the prices of goods increased (caused by shortages and import expenses).[1] Although the U.S. government intervened and aided in the process of recovery, it also tried to hold a tighter grip on Puerto Rican politics. Thus, in 1934 Franklin Roosevelt appointed Army General Blanton Winship as governor of Puerto Rico, who, according to historians Ayala and Bernabe, caused and witnessed "some of the bloodiest moments of a dramatic decade," including the Ponce Massacre.[2]

The economic and political turbulence, in turn, served as a stimulus for intellectual discussions about the nature of Puerto Rican identity. As mentioned in chapter 1, the "generación del treinta" (the thirties generation), as these thinkers are known, deeply concerned themselves with questions of collective identity, racial/ethnic makeup, and the influence of history in the formation of a distinct Puerto Rican people. Filmmakers Viguié and Ramos Cobián, however, went beyond the cultural–educational approach that dominated nationalist undertakings in the fields of literature and journalism and, as I showed in previous chapters, was also echoed in filmmaking practices up until that point. Their innovative filmmaking method strove to actually realize international distribution and financing by closely attending to audiences' tastes. More specifically, both contributed significantly to Puerto Rican cinema of the first half of the twentieth century through appropriating well-received generic formulations to produce modestly financially successful films.

In the 1930s, the introduction of sound to film also signaled a shift in the filmmaking endeavors of the previous decades. Since the successes of the 1927 Warner Brothers' partial "talkie" *The Jazz Singer* and full "talkie" *The Lights of New York* (1928), audiences reacted positively to the innovation of sound films, and film producers responded accordingly.[3] With the introduction of sound dialogues, producers recognized the necessity to adapt their products to the demands of multiple language markets, a task much more complex than the previous practice of translating intertitles. Even though, as Donald Crafton explains, the method and technology necessary for dubbing existed contemporaneously to the introduction of sound, "the techniques and equipment available in early 1930 were inadequate for large scale application [since] most sound tracks were still recorded with music, effects, and dialogues mixed together on the fly."[4] Hence, because of the technological constraints in the recording of sound, multiple language versions of the same film proved more appealing for both the public and film producers alike.

With their command of the Spanish language, Puerto Rican filmmakers and producers possessed a distinctive attribute sought after by U.S. producers looking to capture the Latin American market. Unabashedly, as Ginette Vincendeau argues, most U.S. studios quickly started to produce Spanish language films "because the Latin American Spanish Language market was clearly the most attractive, in terms both of audiences and number of theaters."[5] Given the new necessity for products tailored to specific international audiences, both Viguié and Ramos Cobián found themselves with an advantage unbeknownst to previous local filmmakers, and as I argue in this chapter, they both capitalize on this new industrial opportunity.

The Film Enthusiast: The Career of Juan E. Viguié Cajas

Previous historical accounts about the development of the film industry on the island, like those of Kino García and Juan Ortiz Jiménez, have asserted that Juan Viguié started his filmmaking career in 1912 with the production of a scenic film about the southern town of Ponce. Although a Joint Resolution of the Puerto Rican Legislature dated May 9, 1933, acclaims Viguié as "an expert cameraman who has practiced his profession since 1908," this court document does not reference him having produced a film in 1912.[6] In addition, a 1936 *Who's Who* publication edited by physician and public intellectual Conrado Asenjo mentions that Viguié worked as a film operator (i.e., projectionist) in Ponce from 1909 to 1914, and that from 1914 to 1917 he worked for the Universal Film Company in Fort Lee, New Jersey. Again, however, that source does not contain a reference to a 1912 film production.[7] The closest reference to this presumed 1912 actuality appears in another Asenjo publication, the 1923 film magazine *Cinema*. Because the vague and convoluted nature of the phrasing that the writer uses is important to determine chronology, I quote extensively from the 1923 article:

> Afterwards, this second failed company reorganizes itself. It emerges from its own ashes like the Phoenix, with the great experience of its failure, and taking advantage of its lavish studio, makes new attempts by importing scenarios, directors, and artists, and disguises our landscape to see if in this way it can open itself an easier access to the great markets of the North, which encompass all the markets of the world.
>
> At the same time, and isolated in our southern city, a spirit enthusiastic about film's graphic aspects, who relies on only his own efforts, Mr. Viguié, makes tests and more tests, filming and developing actualities, of technically great artistic merit, which are of even bigger historic value because they capture graphic memories of important events which will not stop being interesting tomorrow.[8]

The writer's reference in the first paragraph to the "second company" using actors and directors from the "North" is doubtless a reference to the Pathé/MacManus's collaboration with the studio erected by the Porto Rico Photoplays, the first Puerto Rican film company to engage directly with U.S. cinema producers and talent. The writer opens the second paragraph by using the phrase "at the same time," meaning the simultaneous nature of the events. The phrasing thus implies that Viguié, whom he does mention by name, produced actualities in Ponce (the southern city) contemporaneously to the Porto Rico Photoplays' projects, that is, in the 1920s. Since I have not found any evidence that Viguié actually made scenic films in 1912, I will not discuss his career as starting from that date, but, rather, will focus on his work in the 1920s and 1930s, for which one can find convincing documentation.

The historical records reveal that Juan Emilio Viguié Cajas was born on July 11, 1891, in the southern city of Ponce, as the son of a French man and an Ecuadorian woman.[9] No records exist detailing what happened to his parents, but the 1910 and 1920 U.S. Census reveal that he did not, at that time, live with them but instead with a man named Luis Caballer. According to José Artemio Torres, who interviewed Viguié's widow, before Viguié's birth, his father left Puerto Rico to work on the construction of the Panama Canal and died while working there. Further, soon after giving birth, his mother also died. However, historically, the French work in the Panama Canal had come to a stop by 1889, two years prior to Viguié's birth, which casts some doubt on the reasons for his father's disappearance. Torres further recounts that a local judge, Mr. Caballer, adopted and raised the orphan in Ponce.[10] Although the census records for both 1910 and 1920 list Juan Viguié Cajas as one of Luis Caballer's dependents, the records do not list Caballer as a judge or lawyer, but instead describe him, respectively, as an "*agente comisionario*" and "*agente corredor de mercancias*." That is, Caballer consistently reported himself as a finance-focused government agent rather than a judicial employee. Regardless of Viguié's childhood circumstances, both official records now available and previous historical accounts indicate that he started working as a camera operator in Ponce around 1909, at the age of seventeen or eighteen.

As noted earlier, a 1936 *Who's Who* asserts that Juan Viguié left Puerto Rico in 1914 to pursue a filmmaking career in the United States. The May 9, 1933, Joint Resolution of the Puerto Rican Legislature also mentioned earlier indicates that after 1914 Viguié pursued studies at the New York Institute of Photography, listed in the resolution as part of Columbia University.[11] An account appearing in 1926 in the *New York Times* notes that indeed Columbia University had offered filmmaking courses for a few terms, but that "the funds to pay for competent instructors were inadequate."[12] In addition, newspaper advertisements during 1915–1919 indicate that the New York Institute of Photography did exist by the date Viguié supposedly studied there, but that it was not affiliated with Columbia University. Instead, a man name Emile Brunel ran the institute located at 1269 Broadway Ave.[13] (In fact, the New York Institute of Photography still exists but only as a distance education program.[14]) Given the ambiguous writing in the Joint Resolution and the lack of archival evidence, it remains unclear when and where Juan Viguié Cajas learned the filmmaking trade. Nonetheless, all accounts indicate that he learned his trade in the United States, and most likely in New York.

Still, inconsistencies plague the historical accounts that might document the early career of Juan Viguié. For example, Conrado Asenjo asserted in 1936 that during the period 1917–1918, Viguié worked for Pathé in New Jersey, but his World War I registration card reveals him living in Ponce, Puerto Rico and holding the occupation of independent electrician.[15] Significantly, during the 1910s, the professional designation of "electrician" extended to include cinema operators.[16] In fact, Viguié's earliest connection to the United States that I have found comes in 1919 when the Ellis Island port records show him arriving in New York from San Juan.[17] Again, although Asenjo declares that Viguié worked for Universal and Pathé during 1914–1919, the earliest reference to a connection between Viguié and Pathé that I have found appears in 1925, when an article about *Aloma of the South Seas* refers to him as "a well-known cameraman for Pathé Frères."[18] I have found no evidence that he ever worked for Universal.

Although the aforementioned newspaper article declares that Viguié worked for Pathé as of 1925, an article circulated in both the Spanish newspaper *La correspondencia* and the New York–based magazine *Cine-Mundial* indicate that during the early 1920s he worked independently on the production of two films. In the article, the author declares that "soon a film which presents episodes from the life of the Antillean pirate Allan Cofresí will be exhibited in Puerto Rico" and that "the production is from a new Puerto Rican production company led by J. E. Viguié."[19] In addition, the article states that Viguié's company "was soon to release an educational film about the natural beauties of Puerto Rico, with the title *La isla maravillosa*, titled in English *The Treasure Island*."[20] Finally, the article also mentions that the company's headquarters were in Ponce and that the poet Felix Matos Bernier worked as a scriptwriter for the first project. The Puerto Rican press makes no mention of these projects, casting into doubt their completion (or that they even moved beyond the planning phase).

The evidence is firmer, however, in support of the claim that Juan Viguié produced and exhibited nonfiction films during the 1920s. As noted, Conrado Asenjo's 1923 film magazine *Cinema* asserted that Viguié produced actualities. In addition, Asenjo's 1936 *Who's Who in Puerto Rico* lists by title educational films shot and produced by Viguié. That publication mentions that he had worked for the departments of education and sanitation and names some films he worked on, as the following list of titles and credits reveals:

> *Combating the White Plague*, under the direction of Dr. Rodríguez Pastor, and *The Hookworm in Puerto Rico*, distributed by the Rockefeller Foundation.

> Actualities of different Sanitation Department activities, like *Child Care in Puerto Rico*; *Leprosy*, directed by the Jesuit Rev. Dr. Father Palacios de Borao. *The Life of the Malaria Mosquito*, photographing for the first time the complete life cycle of the anopheles mosquito, under the direction of Dr. Walter C. Earle of the Rockefeller Foundation. *Study of Bilharzia*, directed by Dr. W. H. Hoffman.... *The San Juan Carnival* made during the reign of Miss Josefina Guillermety, 1927. [In addition to the aforementioned film credits] because of his work, shot under imminent threat during the San Felipe hurricane in 1928, and the quickness with which it was sent to "Fox News," the name of Mr. Viguié was placed among the company's Honor Circle of Cameramen and he received a bonus.[21]

The Rockefeller Foundation films on which Viguié worked formed part of a health education campaign that worked to eliminate or reduce the incidence of diseases, including malaria, hookworm, and tuberculosis on the island, as the archives of the Rockefeller Foundation document. A letter from Dr. Walter C. Earle to the Rockefeller Foundation's Dr. H. H. Howard, discovered by medical historian Marianne P. Fedunkiw, reveals that Viguié's work for the Foundation ironically led to his contracting a disease he worked to eradicate. The letter reads: "I am enclosing a copy of the titles for the malaria picture we have been making here and I shall appreciate any criticism you may care to make. The pictures have all been taken and now we are waiting on Dr. Fernos for the Spanish translation. The day after we took the last picture, Viguie, the photographer, came down with malaria himself."[22] Despite this unfortunate event, Viguié continued to work on health-related materials, as a 1934 issue of the *Puerto Rico Journal of Public Health and Tropical Medicine* credits him with photographic work on *Bilharzia*, a film devoted to eradicating that other then common parasitic disease.[23]

Apart from medical projects, Viguié also worked in producing newsreels. As Ansejo declares, one of his films depicting the 1928 San Felipe Hurricane received noticeable attention in the United States. In fact, Fox's news division ran an advertisement in the *Exhibitors Daily Review* declaring Viguié's footage as unique and exceptional.[24] According to an article also published in the *Exhibitors Daily*, because of the quick arrival and brutal nature of the footage, Fox expected the film to prove financially successful for exhibitors. In addition, Fox's representatives declared that "this unusual feat of bringing actual motion pictures of a disaster to New York while the news was just trickling in by cable and wire was due in large measure to the courage of Juan E. Viguié, the Fox News cameraman stationed in San Juan."[25] These declarations disclose that Viguié apparently had a contract with Fox News, although there is also the possibility that Viguié simply sold the company this film and that Fox exaggerated the role of the filmmaker in the company to create the perception of having great international resources. Whatever his connections to Fox News, Viguié certainly built a productive career as a documentarist. Still, despite Viguié's extensive work in documentary filmmaking, film histories to date most enthusiastically discuss him as the director of the 1934 fictional sound film *Romance tropical*.

Romance tropical: Remaking the Dream

The archives conclusively document that *Romance tropical* was the first sound film both to be made by a Puerto Rican and to be shot in Puerto Rico. Indeed, the film has received so much local attention in academic circles likely because of its status as a "first." Although the film clearly belongs in the annals of Puerto Rican cinema history (directed by Juan Viguié, featuring a Puerto Rican cast, and shot on the island), a Latino filmmaker and entrepreneur from California, Frank Z. Clemente, also made important contributions as producer and distributor toward the success of the film.[26]

Clemente was born in San Francisco, California, on September 23, 1904, and later moved to Los Angeles to attend the University of Southern California.[27] It appears that after attending college, Clemente settled in Los Angeles and dedicated his professional life to the film industry. The *International Motion Picture Almanac* of 1940 declares that during the 1920s Clemente held positions in different leading film companies: working as assistant director for MGM's *Scaramouche* (1923), UA's *El Gaucho* (1924)—a Douglas Fairbanks production—and Fox's *Love of Carmen* (1924); as a technical adviser for Paramount's *The Spanish Dancer*; and as director of *Por Orden del Rey* (1929).[28] With the exception of *Scaramouche*, dealing with the French Revolution, the films Clemente worked on have Latinx or Spanish characters as their subjects. Perhaps because of his previous work experiences (and possibly his own background), in 1933 he started his own independent Spanish-language production company, Latin American Pictures Corporation, which produced pictures in Hollywood.[29] For his independent projects, Clemente worked with Tec-Art, a New York company that had recently moved to the West, which provided production facilities for independent producers.[30]

It seems that Clemente's Latin American Pictures Corp. did not succeed in Hollywood, as he quickly moved to New York in 1934 and established another independent film company, Latin Artists Pictures Corporation.[31] That company, had its headquarters in the RCA Building at 1250 Sixth Avenue in New York City.[32] Clemente worked with Viguié through his Latin Artists Pictures Corp. on the production of *Romance tropical*. The records do not show how Viguié established a relationship with Clemente's company, but ship manifests from August 1934 disclose that Viguié visited New York City in that month, possibly meeting with Clemente on that trip.[33] However they met, Viguié and Clemente's relationship proved fruitful, for Clemente's connections could guarantee the film's promotion and distribution in the Spanish-language market in the United States.

Perhaps because of a pre-established plan to cater to a U.S.-based audience, the plot of *Romance tropical* relies on established generic conceptions of Caribbean-themed Hollywood movies. Although I have not had the opportunity to see the recently discovered copy at UCLA, the archives of the New York State's Motion Picture Commission house a copy of the script, which I have consulted. That script reveals a story that revolves around Carlos (Jorge Rodríguez), a writer and musician, and his courting of an aristocratic woman named Margarita (Ernestina Canino). Margarita's father, Don Patricio (Sexto Cheummont), rejects Carlos as a suitor for his daughter on the grounds that Carlos is a penniless artist. When Don Patricio prevents the couple from meeting, Carlos, in despair, embarks on a transatlantic sailboat voyage with a physician friend, Dr. Hidalgo (Pedro Miranda). The action then flashes forward to a "savage" island (according to film reviewers, somewhere in Africa) called Mu, where Carlos teaches Spanish words to a native princess, Alura (Raquel Canino).[34] Alura shows Carlos a pearl necklace that she says belonged to her "white" mother, and Carlos marvels at the beauty of the necklace. Alura further reveals to him the existence of a water pit guarded by a shark god that houses even more beautiful pearls, and that only the tribe's medicine man can get past the shark. Carlos devises a plan to steal the medicine man's magic ointment to get to the underwater treasure, but tribal soldiers discover him in the process and he must flee the island with the treasure, a wounded Alura, and

Dr. Hidalgo. Meanwhile, in Puerto Rico, Margarita slowly deteriorates from heartache, and no doctor can cure her. Carlos's boat lands in Puerto Rico where Alura dies, first bequeathing the tribe's treasure to Carlos. Meanwhile, Don Patricio has searched frantically for Carlos as the only person who can save his daughter. Finally, Carlos, now with Don Patricio's approval for marriage, saves Margarita and gives her Alura's pearls.[35]

The film's script describes a tale remarkably similar to that of *Aloma of the South Seas* (discussed in the previous chapter), with an important genre elaboration: *Romance tropical* included musical numbers. Both films present a scorned white lover who sets sail for "savage" tropical islands. Both offer an alternative "uncivilized" love interest in a native princess (note the similar names, Aloma and Alura). Finally, both leading men eventually reunite with their original white lovers and return to their "civilized" lands. In addition, surviving stills from the films reveal that Alura and Aloma wore very similar costumes (flower crowns, bead necklaces, and revealing tops and skirts). The two films' similarities support other evidence that the filmmakers in both cases envisioned the United States as their primary market (although *Romance* clearly catered to a Spanish-language public), with Viguié and his collaborators aware of *Aloma*'s success. However, in contrast to *Aloma*, *Romance tropical* shows distinctive self-awareness about its fictitious nature, perhaps unsurprisingly, given both the deep Puerto Rican engagement in the original film and the new one's consciously derivative construction. Such self-awareness emerges in *Romance* through the use of a framing device, as documented in the script: Beginning at the opening of the film, Rosa (Cándida de Lorenzo), Margarita's grandmother, repeatedly reads to her granddaughter a fairy tale that mirrors the film's plot and provides flash-forwards of the film's action.

Thanks, probably in great part, to Frank Clemente's involvement, *Romance tropical* premiered on October 12, 1934, in New York City at the Campoamor Theater, located at the corner of Fifth Avenue and 116th Street.[36] Clemente's involvement and the location of the film's premiere, along with its Spanish dialogue, suggest that the filmmakers envisioned the audience of this film as Hispanics living in the United States, as opposed to *Aloma*'s more mainstream U.S. audience. The *New York Times* reviewed the film in largely positive terms. However, the reviewer did point to technical problems in the film, noting that "the photography of this highly sentimental screen effort is much better than the sound reproduction. Technical defects no doubt are responsible for imparting a grating note to the voices of some of the actors, especially the men."[37] Without mentioning any technical flaws, the *Film Daily* also reviewed the film positively, highlighting the film's "colorful native background."[38] Although *Variety* featured the film for more than nine months on its list of current releases, from November 1934 through September 1935, it carried no review but only a one-line description: "first picture made in Porto Rico."[39] In their reviews, *Film Daily* and the *New York Times* made similar claims about the film's status as a first, both stating that *Romance tropical* had been "labeled the first 100 percent Porto Rican production."[40] That both these publications use the word "labeled" suggests that promotional material from Puerto Rico or from Clemente deliberately used the "pioneering" stamp as an advertising strategy, despite everyone involved doubtless knowing full well that the film had predecessors.

Alongside its fairly positive reception by the *New York Times* and *Film Daily* critics, *Romance tropical* received an extremely negative review from the Spanish-language, Brooklyn-based newspaper *El curioso*. The writer for that publication, Tello Casiano, saw the film as a shameful degradation of Puerto Rican culture (in essence, a "sellout"):

> Whatever the feelings that Cubans felt after the insult perpetrated by a foreign company, their position is not as humiliating as that of Puerto Ricans after watching that caricature called "Romance Tropical." The humiliation is even more degrading in the Puerto Ricans' case because the film was not made by a foreign company, but instead by the first Puerto Rican filmmaking company. I went to the theater to see a "Tropical Romance" with Puerto Rican flavor, and instead I saw an "Anglo-Saxon Romance" with Hollywood flavor. . . . I saw the adultery of our customs and modalities, and I also witnessed the violation of our idiosyncrasies. The first Puerto Rican cinematographic production was a commercial triumph, but a patriotic failure. . . . Let's call the film NULLITY so as not to call it a BETRAYAL.[41]

Casiano's critique of the film focuses on the ideological–political implications of the filmmaker's alliance with a "Hollywood-esque," stereotype-filled plot. In the critic's view, the film does not offer an accurate representation of Puerto Ricanness and instead has consciously adhered to U.S. genre film conventions and colonialist representational tropes, making the film a wholly incompetent cultural ambassador. Nonetheless, Casiano also points out that the film attracted audiences (naming it a "commercial triumph").

As I mentioned earlier, given that *Romance tropical* was in Spanish, and that it premiered in a theater located in Spanish Harlem, it is very likely that the people who made this film a "success" were the same people that Casiano thought misrepresented. The disjuncture between the expectation of the critic and the apparent response of audiences calls into question the relationship between intellectual conceptions of the social role of film and lucrative practices in the entertainment business.

Writing in 2008 in Puerto Rico, filmmaker and scholar Roberto Ramos Perea in effect channels Tello Casiano in arguing that *Romance tropical* "lacked national perspective, and showcased instead a desire to be '*as good as them*.'"[42] Yet, whether the film deliberately appropriated Hollywood tropes or not, its likeness to other U.S. productions certainly did not mean that the film failed to culturally resonate with, nor even, in the Puerto Rican audience's perception, truthfully represent their nation and people. In fact, the film ran in Puerto Rico for over fifteen weeks, from its premiere in the Paramount Theater in San Juan on March 15, 1935, to its apparent last showing at the Estrella Theater in Hato Rey on June 26, 1935, the longest run for any Puerto Rican film up to that date.[43] In addition, the film toured outside of San Juan, with known presentations in Cataño, Arecibo, Ponce, and Bayamón.[44] Puerto Rican audiences clearly found the film appealing. Igor Kameneff, a critic writing for *El mundo* in 1935, even ventured to suggest that it was in fact the unoriginality of the script that resonated with Puerto Rican audiences: "Although not new, the plot of the film is interesting. It has been said that the plot is that of a feuilleton and that is perhaps the precise reason for [screenwriter] Luis Palés Matos' success. There have been very few men of letters who have been able to give the public what they want, and the writer who has not learned this lesson does not write for cinema."[45] It seems that for Viguié and his crew, giving the public what they wanted was not a question of nationalistic pride (as had been the case to at least some extent for previous filmmakers) but of good business sense.

Besides some local critics, advertisers certainly understood that the Puerto Rican production's strengths lay in its popular appeal rather than high art or cultural education. Adhering to standard business practice, theaters advertising the film defined its success by its box office draw, that is, by its sales, with one claiming that *Romance tropical* was "the first Puerto Rican film consecrated in the theater by the public" and another promoter exclaiming that the film enjoyed "a new success in every theater."[46] Although the claim of "audience approval" was not a new practice, when compared to previous advertising campaigns for Puerto Rican films, I find a change in the advertisers' perception of the power of the film to captivate audiences. Whereas promotional campaigns for previous films like *Un drama en Puerto Rico* or even *Tropical Love* sold them as a means of "seeing Puerto Rico on the screen," advertisers defined viewing *Romance tropical* as a fashionable social activity rather than an experience of island-internal tourism.

Local critics, like Igor Kameneff, described the film as a success based on apparent audience acceptance, even enthusiasm, both on the island and in the United States. However, despite the film's triumph on the island, the Puerto Rican critics consistently cite the positive U.S. *New York Times* review as evidence of the film's achievement, relying on outside perceptions for validation. For example, critic Carlos Carreras begins his review by stating that U.S. critics "praised the film's artists, and especially Raquel Canino," and goes on to explain that "the *New York Times* critic attributed the actress's appeal to the numerous close-ups of her character Alura."[47] Conflictingly though, Carreras himself affirms the film's Puerto Ricanness—specifically aspects of the island's geography—as a basis for the film's popularity, for he asserts that the "exciting panorama and our island's splendid light supported the work of the first-time actors to create an indisputable triumph."[48]

A critic going by the initials S.I.S. even more directly linked outside approval and local recognition of *Romance tropical* by translating into Spanish the full *New York Times* review for San Juan's *El mundo*. At the end of the translation, S.I.S. avers that after reading the U.S. newspaper's review, which she found "severe and impartial, [she] decided to see *Romance tropical* as soon as it was exhibited in San Juan."[49] For his part, Kameneff does not directly cite the *New York Times* but does refer to its comments about how the film's repeated close-up shots of Raquel Canino enhanced her appeal.[50] Although all the critics called the film a national achievement, they in large part defined that achievement by the consumption and support of the local product by "foreigners."

Conspicuously, none of the Puerto Rican reviewers cited Tello Casiano's review of the film, even though *El curioso* addressed Spanish speakers in New York City and would very likely have had a large Puerto Rican readership. Of course, the *New York Times* had printed a positive review and was a better known, well-established and highly respected publication, but should not the words of a fellow Hispanic have offered more advance

FIG. 6.1 The inhabitants of Mu Island (*Romance tropical*, 1934)

indication about how Puerto Rican audiences might receive the film? Apparently not, since in contrast to Casiano's warning of "humiliation," Puerto Rican audiences appeared to enjoy the film, and it seems that no one in Puerto Rico, at least publicly, acknowledged feeling a sense of betrayal or misrepresentation from *Romance tropical*.

The absence of documented objections in Puerto Rico to the film's stereotype-filled plot certainly does not mean that Casiano's denunciation was not fully warranted. The script and surviving stills validate his critique of its problematic representations, for the descriptions of settings and characters are replete with orientalist depictions of Africa and blackness. The filmmakers appear to have transferred all the stereotypes that Hollywood had promoted about the tropics onto black populations. The black inhabitants of Mu Island are superstitious, uncivilized, and very sensual, and only the mixed-race Alura can connect with and understand the ways of the civilized (white) Puerto Ricans. Still, even the sympathetic Alura dies toward the end of the film, ensuring a representation of Puerto Ricanness and civilization as whiteness (and hence Spanishness). The filmmakers' construction of Puerto Ricanness as European whiteness seems to follow the same pattern that Frantz Fanon described for Martiniquais racial identity in *Black Skin, White Masks*. Fanon explains that white colonial hegemony forces colonized subjects to shape their worldview in terms of a dichotomy of races, constructing whiteness, through the influence of popular culture, as all that is positive and desirable "because no black voice exists" to counter the claim.[51] The film's popular reception arguably bespeaks a 1930s Puerto Rican desire to be conceived as civilized or on par with the colonial metropolis, and hence, as equally white. In successfully emulating Hollywood tropes, the film in effect declared that Puerto Ricans were just like Americans, only speaking Spanish, a message that Puerto Rican audiences apparently found unproblematic.

Although the film found success in Puerto Rico as well as, by all evidence, among Spanish-speaking audiences in the United States, Viguié and his producer Frank Clemente did not make another film together. Moreover, the records suggest that Juan Viguié did not make another fictional film in his career. For his part, Frank Clemente continued working in the film industry. Reports in 1936 in *Variety* and the *Los Angeles Times* disclose that the producer hoped to recruit popular Brazilian actor Raul Roulien for a series of Spanish-language films.[52] By 1940, Clemente had moved from producing Spanish language films to creating his own independent New York–based company producing English language pictures.[53] In his 1952 account of Puerto Rican film history, Juan Ortiz Jiménez attributed the split between Clemente and Viguié and also Viguié's subsequent move away from fiction to a lawsuit over royalties brought about by *Romance*'s actresses.[54] Following Ortiz's lead, Kino García claims that due to the lawsuit, Viguié sold the rights to the film for $6,000 and then disengaged himself completely from the project and from fiction filmmaking.[55]

Whether or not the actresses sued Viguié (for which I have regrettably found no evidence), I believe that deep systemic problems can sufficiently account for his move away from feature filmmaking. First, the Puerto Rican exhibition market was too small to sustain the high costs of feature filmmaking (especially during the decade-plus-long Great Depression). Secondly, without a major production company backing the project, *Romance tropical* probably did not play in big U.S. markets, limiting its profits. In her work on Spanish-language movie theaters in New York City, Amy Beer found the following to be true: "From the mid-1930s to the mid-1980s, despite New York's relatively small *mexicano* population . . . the city's Spanish-language theaters played overwhelmingly popular, genre films imported from Mexico. Even on the most superficial cultural level, accordingly, these theaters were not initially primarily responding to new migrants' nostalgia for their culture of origin. Instead . . . Spanish-language film distributors, exhibitors and U.S. Latino audiences played a vital role for sectors of the Mexican and U.S. media industries."[56] Without the support of well-connected U.S. or Mexican distribution networks, Viguié's project, although extremely successful for Puerto Rican standards, probably did not achieve sufficiently wide or sustained circulation to cover its production costs. The tough feature-film market, in contrast to his previous positive and remunerative experiences with newsreel and documentary filmmaking, may have led Viguié to concentrate thereafter exclusively on nonfiction filmmaking. In fact, by the summer of 1935, the Puerto Rican Emergency Relief Administration had recruited Viguié to make four documentaries (*Servicio Social*, *Escuelas Maternales*, *Ingeniería*, and *Agricultura*). Additionally, a newspaper article, published just two months after the last known showing of *Romance tropical* in Puerto Rico, implied that Viguié had created a niche for himself as the "go-to-filmmaker" in the nonfiction market.[57] Even though he did not produce another fiction film, he continued to work for a number of years as a prolific and successful creator of documentaries and newsreels. Even in 1951, Viguié was regarded as the most important private nonfiction film producer in Puerto Rico.[58]

The Film Impresario: The Career of Rafael Ramos Cobián

Contrasting with Viguié who had produced documentaries before his venture into feature films, rather than as a filmmaker, Rafael Ramos Cobián first established himself as an entrepreneur in movie exhibition.[59] Although he made his name and fortune in San Juan, Rafael Ramos Cobián was born on March 19, 1904, in the southeastern town of Patillas, Puerto Rico.[60] His father, José Ramos Rodríguez, was a pharmacist, and his mother, Josefa Cobián Álvarez, a homemaker.[61] At some point before 1929, at about twenty-five years of age, Ramos Cobián moved to San Juan and established his own movie theater company called Empresas Ramos Cobián, with headquarters located at No. 4 San José Street.[62] Within five years, just as Viguié distributed *Romance tropical* in the United States and Puerto Rico (through winter 1934 and spring 1935), Ramos Cobián was in the process of becoming the president of the biggest theater chain on the island, United Theaters Incorporated.[63] By March 1935, United Theaters Inc. had gotten so large that Ramos Cobián had to fend off accusations of monopolizing film exhibition venues.[64]

Ramos Cobián's influence on Puerto Rican society extended beyond his involvement with the cinema industry. In 1936 he won the pro-independence Liberal Party's nomination for mayor of San Juan, although he lost to Carlos M. de Castro of the pro-statehood Republican Party in the general election.[65] In addition, years later, in 1956, he served as the Puerto Rican delegate to the Democratic National Convention held that year in Chicago, Illinois.[66] Nevertheless, for most of his professional life, Puerto Ricans knew Rafael Ramos Cobián primarily as a powerful theater promoter.

After at least ten years of working in the movie-house business, Ramos Cobián decided to try his hand at filmmaking. In January 1938 he joined Julio R. Bruno (another board member of United Theaters Inc.) to form a film production company under the name of Cobián Productions.[67] Apparently, before the company announced its articles of incorporation it had already made arrangements with Paramount and recruited talent. Both the *Film Daily* and the *New York Times* announced alongside the notice of its founding that the company would "produce three Spanish features starring Tito Guizar for distribution by Paramount in the world Spanish market."[68] Tito Guizar was a well-regarded Mexican folksinger who had recently gained movie fame by starring in Fernando de Fuentes's acclaimed film *Allá en el rancho grande* (Out on the big ranch, 1936).[69] U.S.-based Paramount showed interest in Ramos Cobián's plans to produce three films with Guizar, but committed to distributing only the first one, *Mis dos amores* (My two loves, 1938).[70]

Mis dos amores: The Union of Hollywood and Latin America

To produce his first film, Ramos Cobián named Lester P. Sussman (formerly with Paramount's foreign division) as production head.[71] In addition, he recruited the then fledgling Hollywood screenwriter Milton Raison to adapt for the screen the play *Sacrificio de una madre* (A mother's sacrifice), written by José A. Miranda, and negotiated a deal with Western Service

Studios in Hollywood for the shooting location of the film.[72] The movie initially had the original play's title as a working title but during production, in June 1938, the title changed to *Mis dos amores.*[73] Besides Tito Guizar as the film's male lead, the filmmakers cast as the female lead the Puerto Rican actress Blanca de Castejón. The actress had previously worked for Fox Film Corporation in *El Impostor* (The impostor, 1931), *Eran trece* (They were thirteen, 1931), and *Esclavas de la moda* (*Slaves to Love*, 1931); for Universal in *Resurrección* (Resurrection, 1931); and for MGM in *El carnaval del Diablo* (The Devil's carnival, 1937). The producers enlisted the Hollywood B-movie filmmaker Nick Grindé to direct.

Similar to *Romance tropical*, *Mis dos amores* was a musical melodrama about an artist (in this case a musician) and a disapproving father-in-law. Although no surviving copies of the film exist, the New York State Motion Picture Division archives contain a detailed screenplay (which include cinematographic cues).[74] According to the script, *Mis dos amores* is a melodrama that tells the story of the medical student and musician Julio (Guizar) and his love Rita (de Castejón), the daughter of a San Diego farmer, Antonio (Carlos Villaria). Antonio disapproves of Julio because he comes from a poor family with a drunken father, Rafael (Romualdo Tirado), so he sets up his daughter to marry a rich Puerto Rican coffee planter, Alfonso (Martin Garralaga). Rita does not want to marry Alfonso because she loves Julio, but also because Alfonso is her father's age. Nonetheless, in the middle of a party, Antonio announces (without consultation) his daughter's engagement to Alfonso. Distraught, Rita talks to Alfonso and he agrees to call off the engagement because she does not love him. The furious Antonio then declares that he will never let his daughter marry Julio. To try to win over Antonio and marry Rita, Julio drops out of medical school and moves to Hollywood to find a well-paying job as a singer. While in Hollywood, Julio meets Ana Celia (Carolina Segrera) and her daughter Anita (Evelyn del Rio), and they quickly become friends. Ana Celia finds Julio a job working as a singer at the cabaret where she dances, but the cabaret's owner, El Chato (Paul Ellis), quickly grows jealous of Julio's friendship with Ana Celia.

Meanwhile, back in San Diego, Rita awaits impatiently for news from Julio. She receives a letter that declares Julio's recruitment by a radio station to work as a live singer and that he will soon come back to marry her. Antonio, however, tells his daughter not to believe the letter, for he heard that Julio had taken a lover (Ana Celia). Rita does not accept her father's lies but agrees to visit Julio's cabaret to confront him. Once there, Rita, Antonio, and their lawyer friend José (Juan Torena) watch as Julio and Ana Celia perform together. Rita becomes so jealous while watching the duo that she quickly leaves. After they leave the stage, Ana Celia follows Julio backstage and declares her love for him. However, El Chato had followed them and starts a fight with Julio, during which El Chato fatally shoots Ana Celia. Just as Julio takes the gun away from El Chato's hand, people start pouring onto the scene. El Chato immediately screams that Julio killed Ana Celia and the police arrest Julio. Nonetheless, with her last breath, Ana Celia tells her daughter that it was El Chato who killed her.

José, a public prosecutor, asks Julio what really happened. Julio tells him that El Chato killed Ana Celia, but that he has no evidence to prove it. José tells Julio that there is nothing he can do for him, but agrees to send Anita to live with Julio's mother Mercedes (Emilia Leovali). Back in San Diego, Rita, Rafael, and Mercedes work to prove Julio's innocence, but the court sentences Julio to death. Anita accidentally sees a newspaper headline with a picture of her mother, Julio, and El Chato, and tells Julio's family about her mother's last words. Mercedes and Rita run to José's office to see if he can stop the execution. José says that he needs a confession from El Chato to change the ruling and sets a plan to obtain such a confession. José then lies to El Chato and tells him that the police already know that he killed Ana Celia and that in just a matter of minutes they will arrest him. When a fight ensues between the two, Rita calls the police, who arrive just as El Chato confesses that he accidentally killed Ana Celia.

In the final scene, Julio, Rita, Mercedes, and Anita gather at a radio station where Julio will perform. Rafael and Antonio arrive and also try to gain admittance, but the doorman stops them since the performance has already started. Antonio comments on how calm the previously often disorderly Rafael has remained; Julio's father responds that Anita has made him quit drinking. Both fathers hear the voice of Julio singing inside and the loud noise of the adoring crowd and comment on how much they *both* admire their son.

Given the story's emphasis on family life and enduring love, *Mis dos amores* seems to have targeted a socially traditionalist audience. However, a review in *Variety* written by a critic called Mr. Wear reveals that the film's visual construction offered a more complex audience address and appeal. Although the film's plot seems to criticize alcohol consumption, greed, and family negligence in trite and moralistic ways, Wear comments that "the romantic scenes and others in the café remind of the pre-Hays production code authority."[75] Wear's reference to pre-Hays representational practices indicates the film's, at least visual, sexual suggestiveness. Like other Hollywood productions of the 1930s, *Mis dos amores* appears to have couched an appeal to passionate fantasies under the guise of a family melodrama.

Not all critics found *Mis dos amores* a successful undertaking or even enjoyed it—with some speaking out against the film even in advance of its release. Writing for the San Antonio Spanish-language newspaper *La prensa*, Gabriel Navarro strongly criticized the project for having a "painfully mediocre script" and having dialogue "without ingenuity, without warmth, and without a trace of intelligence."[76] Significantly though, Navarro's major disappointment related to the film's casting: "The cast is already selected. And as we were expecting, apart from Tito Guizar, who is the film's main attraction and who will sell the film in Spanish America, there is not a single Mexican actor. There are Spanish, Cubans, South Americans, Filipinos, etc. Possibly the producers are under the impression that Mexicans 'do not know how to speak Spanish.'"[77] Navarro claimed that the Mexican press had also criticized the filmmakers, and Tito Guizar in particular, for the lack of Mexicans in the cast. In an interview with Navarro, Guizar claimed that he had tried to get the producers to cast more Mexicans but that he became "demoralized because the producers would not listen to [him]."[78]

It is unclear why Navarro and other critics expected the film to have a predominantly Mexican cast, and why they viewed a diverse Latinx cast as disrespectful to Mexicans. Certainly, besides the casting of the male lead, the film's setting in San Diego (which has a large Mexican-American population) and inclusion in the script of a party where everyone dresses like a Charro (i.e., Mariachi outfit) suggests that it may have targeted particularly Mexican audiences. However, as a powerful Puerto Rican film distributor, Ramos Cobián undoubtedly expected to exhibit the film not only in the United States and Mexico, but also in Puerto Rico and elsewhere in Latin America. Likely the casting of Blanca de Castejón as the female lead aimed to please Puerto Rican audiences. Fascinatingly, because it had a diverse cast, had crew and audience appeal, was a Puerto Rican production, was filmed in Hollywood, and starred a Mexican actor, it became simultaneously a Puerto Rican and a Mexican production, and even an American one if we consider its distribution company, Paramount.

Nevertheless, despite Ramos's multinational commercial vision, *Mis dos amores* received little newspaper coverage in the United States and Latin

America after the initial production period. Wear's review in *Variety*, however, gave the film a glowing evaluation, praising everything from Guizar's performance to the "excellent taste" of the director and producer.[79] Similarly, *Cine-Mundial* praised Guizar (commenting that he "confirmed his excellent qualities for the cinema") and Grindé (for "directing with perfect command").[80] Although the *Los Angeles Times* did not review the film, it reported in the news columns that "there were shouts of joy at the preview of all-Spanish picture 'My Two Loves.'"[81] The *Los Angeles Times* also interviewed Ramos Cobián for a special feature focused on Hollywood's shift in targeting films for Latin America, and away from the "dwindling European market."[82] In that feature, Ramos Cobián expresses the view that "Hollywood at last has hit upon a happy combination: American technique supervised by Latins who understand the people and the market."[83]

In Puerto Rico, the premiere of *Mis dos amores* on October 4, 1938, proved the social event of the year. San Juan newspapers reported heavily on the "Hollywood style" premiere of the film, calling it a "true act of artistic and social significance," and "a luxurious social event."[84] The film's premiere was so opulent that Ramos Cobián even requested the services of Juan Viguié to take footage of the event, and later exhibited the footage in theaters for the general public to see.[85] In addition, according to *La democracia*, although the actors were not present for the premiere, Blanca de Castejón sent a recorded message from Hollywood to play during the presentation.[86]

After the premiere, *El mundo*, *La democracia*, and *La correspondencia* all carried very positive reviews of *Mis dos amores*, particularly highlighting the performances of the two Puerto Rican actresses, Blanca de Castejón and the child Evelyn del Río.[87] Writing about the technical aspects of the film for *La correspondencia*, Conde Danilo declared, "The technique is perfect, the script is very well written and the scenes skillfully edited, the songs are beautiful, the music gracious, and the dialogue short and interesting."[88] In its review, the magazine *Puerto Rico ilustrado* looked beyond the Puerto Rican border to proclaim that the film "[had] caused much hype in all Spanish-speaking countries."[89] Remarkably, none of the press reports on the island make reference to the film's evidently sexualized content or the Mexican public's apparent disapproval.

Still, notwithstanding the good press the completed film received in Puerto Rico and parts of the United States, some newspaper accounts point to problems during the film's production. Cándido Arreche, reporting for *El mundo*, commented that the film had to "overcome many obstacles to get to the screen."[90] Similarly, Navarro declared that *Mis dos amores* had given Ramos Cobián "many headaches."[91] The sources do not describe the exact problems that the production faced, but these problems do not appear to have been catastrophic since just one month after filming *Mis dos amores* (just as the film was released in the United States) in August 1938, the *Film Daily* reported that Twentieth Century-Fox had made a distribution agreement with Ramos Cobián for "a minimum of four class A Spanish pictures a year."[92]

Los hijos mandan: The Separation of Hollywood and Latin America

The records do not explain why Ramos Cobián left Paramount to work with Fox, although it looks as if he may have received a better contract from the latter. The female star of *Mis dos amores*, Blanca de Castejón, also left Paramount to join Cobián in the production of his second film, *Los hijos mandan* (*The Son's Command*, 1939) but Guizar did not follow him. According to the *Film Daily*, by January 1939 Ramos Cobián had signed five popular Mexican stars to join his cast: Fernando and Julian Soler, Arturo de Córdova, Jorge Negrete, and Carmen Mora.[93] For *Los hijos mandan* Ramos Cobián also cast his own son Rudy Ramos Santiago, who went by the stage name of Rudy Cobián.[94]

Previous historical accounts of Ramos Cobián's projects neglect to mention the important role that Blanca de Castejón played in the making of Cobián's U.S.-based productions. Aside from working as the leading actress in both *Mis dos amores* and *Los hijos mandan*, de Castejón also served as the main scriptwriter for the latter movie. It seems that the producers deemed her participation as integral to the project: the film's script (housed at the archives of the New York State's Motion Picture Commission) features her name prominently alongside Ramos Cobián's and that of the director Gabriel Soria. In addition, a major promotional article for the film that appeared in the popular Puerto Rican magazine *Puerto Rico ilustrado* focuses exclusively on de Castejón's script-writing method.[95] These incidents, coupled with the fact that de Castejón left Paramount to join Ramos Cobián at Fox (which Tito Guizar did not do), suggest her deep involvement in the creative process and advertisement of Ramos Cobián's productions.

Markedly different from *Mis dos amores, Los hijos mandan* was a tragic melodrama about female sacrifice with a disheartening ending. Based on José López Pinillos's 1921 play *El caudal de los hijos* (The flow of children), *Los hijos mandan* tells the story of Francisca (Blanca de Castejón), a young beauty from Valencia, Spain, whose father Raimundo (Antonio Sandoval) squandered the family's fortune.[96] Francisca is in love with Miguel (Arturo de Córdova), a young Mexican sculptor who leaves for France to make a name as an artist to enable their marriage. While Miguel is away, the Duke of Montesino (Fernando Soler) asks for Francisca's hand in marriage. Because the family is destitute, Francisca agrees to marry the duke. The story moves forward ten years; the couple has a child, Alfonsito (Rudy Cobián), and seems to have a happy family life. The family's peace is disturbed when, after achieving success in France, Miguel returns to Valencia and seeks to reunite with Francisca. Francisca plans to run away with Miguel but the duke stops her by threatening to separate her from her child and by reminding her that if she were to leave, she would tarnish Alfonsito's reputation.

The film moves forward ten more years as Alfonso (now played by Julian Soler) leaves for college in Oxford. While on an academic break from his English school, Alfonso and his friends go to France, where Alfonso falls in love with a cabaret singer, Ivonne (Carmen Mora). Ivonne has a boyfriend, Andre (Paul Ellis), but decides to leave him to marry the wealthy and charming Alfonso. After marrying and living in France for a couple of months, the couple goes to Valencia because the duke learned about Alfonso leaving college and threatens to discontinue economic support if Alfonso does not return home. Alfonso obeys but surprises the family with the news that he married Ivonne. The duke, outraged by the news, wants to disinherit Alfonso, but Francisca convinces him that she can transform Ivonne into a proper lady.

The film moves forward a couple of years; Ivonne and Alfonso have a baby, but Ivonne is extremely unhappy with her family life. Alfonso engages in many aristocratic activities like hunting and horseback riding, often leaving Ivonne alone. In addition, Francisca forbids Ivonne from taking care of her child because she deems it unbecoming for a lady to care for a baby when a servant can do the job. Out of misery Ivonne writes a letter to her former lover, Andre, imploring him to take her away from her aristocratic jail. Andre comes to Valencia and writes to Ivonne to set up a meeting time.

Francisca then finds Andre's letter and confronts Ivonne on the night of her planned escape. On that night, Francisca reveals to Ivonne that she once too thought of leaving her family to join her lover, but that her son and his future kept her from leaving. In the speech that finally convinces Ivonne not to leave, Francisca declares, "People say that men rule, but don't believe it Ivonne; in reality it is the sons. Our lives belong to them." After realizing that Ivonne will not leave, Andre enters the house and declares that if he cannot have Ivonne no one will, and he shoots at her. However, Francisca steps in front of Ivonne and the bullet hits her, and the terrified Andre flees the scene. Because of the noise generated by the incident, the duke and Alfonso come downstairs and find Ivonne holding the dying Francisca. With her last breath, Francisca looks lovingly at Ivonne and declares that a burglar has shot her.

Whereas Ramos Cobián's previous film *Mis dos amores* had made use of California as its setting, *Los hijos mandan*, despite having a mostly Mexican and Puerto Rican cast, takes place in Spain. Even though the literary source adapted into the film's script is a Spanish play, the filmmakers' decision to retain the setting in Spain, the common "ancestor" of Hispanic America, may also have had economic motivations. First, the conservative, traditional, arguably even Madonna-inspired plot as well as the setting of the film in the Hispanic "motherland" suggests an interest in catering to a diverse (transglobal) Spanish-speaking audience. Simultaneously, as I discussed in chapter 1, certainly in the first half of the twentieth century, Spain signified high culture, at least in the Puerto Rican imaginary (even amidst the then ongoing civil war, a popular republican cause among artistic circles). Ramos Cobián and scriptwriter de Castejón may well have considered the setting as well as other associations with the Spanish-source play a means of imbuing the film with an artistic aura.

The international elements of the production of *Los hijos mandan* precluded any singular assignment of nationality to the finished film, as was the case for *Mis dos amores*. As noted, the original source for *Los hijos mandan* and the film's setting were Spanish; three of its main actors and the director were Mexican; two of the main actors, the screenwriter (Blanca de Castejón) and the producer were Puerto Rican; and a North American production company financed and distributed the film. Critics ascribe the film to U.S., Mexican, and Puerto Rican national traditions. The American Film Institute categorizes the film as American, while recognizing its production for the Hispanic market.[97] The Texas-borderland, Mexican-American newspapers *La prensa* (San Antonio) and *El heraldo de Brownsville* ran articles at the time of the film's release proclaiming it a Mexican production.[98] However, although the aforementioned publications recognized the film as Mexican, some Mexican publications saw the production as a Hollywood plot to destroy Mexican cinema by stealing its directors and actors.[99] Those accusations ignored Ramos Cobián's identity as a Puerto Rican and in essence transformed him into a powerful *American* film producer.

In Puerto Rico, reporters categorized the film as a "true Puerto Rican success" and highlighted Ramos Cobián as the real genius behind the film.[100] The filmmakers further emphasized the production's Puerto Ricanness through the staging of the film's world premiere in San Juan on September 4, 1939.[101] Puerto Rican reviewers again focused on the Puerto Rican actress Blanca de Castejón as the key figure making the film brilliant. For example, writing for *Puerto Rico ilustrado*, Edna Coll describes the film and in particular de Castejón's performance as follows: "[The film] is a perfect portrayal of our mother, just as she is, the perfect example of sacrifice. And of course, the abnegation of the mother who sacrifices herself for her son, stupendously portrayed by Blanca de Castejón, moves us in such a way that we frequently find tears in our eyes . . . and that is why our public, which is very emotional, will enjoy this film, which will without a doubt awaken the most intense sensations of the heart."[102] In her article, Coll ties the appeal of the film to supposed Puerto Rican conceptions of motherhood and to de Castejón's accurate representation of these cultural values. Putting aside the accuracy of Coll's cultural claims, her appropriation of a Spanish source and characters as speaking directly to Puerto Ricans signals the tie to "Spanishness" that cultural producers and intellectuals had construed as part of Puerto Rican identity.

In addition, other Puerto Rican reporters also commented on the sensitivity of the Puerto Rican public, not as a mark of an overly emotional people, but rather as a sign of empathic intelligence and appreciation of powerful art. Hence an anonymous reviewer for *El mundo* declares that the local public would like *Los hijos mandan* because it was an example of how "the cinema spoken in our language follows an ascending trend, climbing to new heights until it reaches the climax of success, propelled by its moving scenes of indispensable tragic value."[103] Similarly, another (or possibly the same) anonymous reviewer writing for *El mundo* describes the film as reaching the pinnacle of emotional and artistic value for any Spanish-language film: "if you want to know how far Spanish-language cinema has progressed, attend a showing of *Los hijos mandan*."[104] As I previously showed, the Puerto Rican press did tend to grant hyperbolic praise to any production with a trace of Puerto Ricanness. However, Emilio Escalante, writing for the San Antonio newspaper *La prensa* (which had predominantly Mexican-American readers), also categorized the film as "the most interesting and exciting film that has been filmed in Hollywood."[105]

In his book *Hollywood and the Foreign Touch*, film historian Harry Waldman tells a very different story from the Puerto Rican and Hispanic American critics who praised the film so highly. Waldman recounts problems from the start of the production of *Los hijos mandan*. The Mexican actors, whom Fox rather than Ramos Cobián chose, disliked Blanca de Castejón's script and demanded changes.[106] For example, Arturo de Córdova "refus[ed] to act out his role as a dancer from Spain" and instead "recast himself as a painter from Mexico."[107] Waldman also reports that Twentieth Century Fox demanded script changes and that Ramos Cobián ended up going over budget by $20,000.[108] Finally, Waldman notes that *Los hijos mandan* did not play very well in Mexico, where he recounts the film ran for only one week.[109] The *Film Daily* also informs that *Los hijos mandan* exceeded its budget, but they offer the higher figure of $26,000.[110] Still, this *Film Daily* article also reports that Ramos Cobián had already started to work on a second project for Fox; nonetheless, that second project was never released.[111] The reason for the subsequent separation of Ramos Cobián and Fox remains elusive, but the records seem to indicate that it must have been tied to the exhibition of *Los hijos mandan* rather than to issues in the production process itself. That is, even if it did well in Puerto Rico and some Hispanic markets in the United States, the film appears to have flopped in other Spanish-speaking markets, prompting Fox to sever ties with Ramos Cobián.

Responding during this period to the outbreak of war in Europe, which caused reductions in distribution outlets for U.S.-made films, and also, more positively, by the spirit of (and U.S. government support for) the Good Neighbor policy, major Hollywood studios like Twentieth Century Fox began to turn to Latin America as an untapped, potentially lucrative market. Despite their interest in capitalizing on Spanish language film markets, U.S film companies tended to homogenize the region without considering specific national audiences' tastes and needs.[112] The different fates of *Mis dos amores* and *Los hijos mandan* seem to indicate the centrality of Mexicans as an economically powerful Spanish-language film audience that could make or break a project. In fact, as Amy Beer explains, by the mid-1930s the U.S. government actively promoted the importation of Mexican films above all other Spanish-speaking markets, even "brokering an exclusive deal between the most productive Mexican studios and a prominent New York exhibitor for the best Mexican films . . . [which] limited the possibilities for distribution of Spanish-language films to U.S. audiences by firms independent of Mexican studios."[113] Even Blanca de Castejón based her rather successful career subsequent to her involvement with Ramos Cobián in Mexico.[114] It looks like, in the end, despite the advantages of working in Spanish, other cultural markers (like accents, costumes, or stars) proved very important for different Spanish-language audiences, and thus bigger markets like Mexico dictated what other smaller Latin American markets made and consumed. Puerto Rico, as a market for local independent, Spanish-language foreign films and especially Hollywood productions, was simply too small to support on its own a Puerto Rican–centered film industry.

After *Los hijos mandan*, Ramos Cobián made no further films for more than two decades, finally returning to production in 1961 with *The Fiend of Dope Island* (dir. Nate Watt). In the meantime he continued his career as a movie theater entrepreneur, even expanding his business to Cuba in December 1944.[115] Although he did not make films during the 1940s and 1950s, he continued to influence local audiences' tastes and desires by controlling what films played (and for how long) in Puerto Rico's biggest theater chain, United Theaters.

The End of an Era: The Local Government as Producer

Influenced by the presence of U.S. companies on the island during the 1920s, Puerto Rican producers had recognized the need to see the filmmaking craft as a transnational business. Both Juan Viguié and Rafael Ramos Cobián perceived that in order to make profitable films they had to reach both local Puerto Rican and other Latinx audiences (mainly from the United States) and capitalize on the film industry's newfound necessity to produce in local languages. Even if they ultimately failed to establish a feature film production industry on the island, they in effect significantly tested and ultimately exposed the economic limitations encountered by independent producers working in a small market. Still, both Viguié and

Ramos Cobián also made evident that feature filmmaking was not the only existing route to develop a national cinema industry. Ramos Cobián's story showcases the potential power of exhibitors to mold audiences' desires and expectations and thus, to some degree, to decide who portrays the nation and how (to the extent that films that played in theaters depicted or dealt with Puerto Rico, if at all). Juan Viguié, for his part, demonstrated that Puerto Rican newsreel and documentary filmmaking need not suffer the same fate as inadequately circulated fiction films, but rather could prove to be a locally self-sustaining and even profitable form of filmmaking.

By the beginning of the 1940s, through the work of different national and foreign filmmakers and producers, the Puerto Rican cinema industry had established businesses of distribution and exhibition, trained technicians such as cinematographers and editors as well as lighting and sound experts, and had even, from the outset, helped build the necessary infrastructure in the form of a film studio in San Juan (Hato Rey). All of these developments made it possible for the local government to recognize film as a powerful tool for educational and economic development. Nonetheless, although past independent filmmakers had played a crucial role in the creation of the Puerto Rican government's filmmaking division, the sociopolitical volatility during the years of the Great Depression, coupled with the allocation of vast funds from relief programs (such as the Puerto Rican Emergency Relief Administration and the Puerto Rican Relief Administration) gave rise to a very appealing nativist, populist political discourse. This populist discourse shaped the educational and economic development the island underwent between the 1940s and 1960s, and from which, as Catherine Marsh explains, the Division of Community Education (DIVEDCO, for its Spanish acronym), the most prolific (public) film production unit in Puerto Rico, came into existence.[116]

A key turn in Puerto Rican politics, the rise of the Popular Democratic Party (PPD, for its Spanish acronym) defined 1940s Puerto Rico. Particularly important for cinema, the PPD had a populist vision and a friendly relationship with Franklin Roosevelt's government, which ensured the allocation of funds for national cultural projects.[117] According to Marsh, DIVEDCO arose from the desire of the PPD, and its leader Luis Muñoz Marín in particular, to promote both democratic, popular education, and the institutionalization of culture.[118] DIVEDCO made both fiction and documentary films, but as the name of the division suggests, all its projects had the aim of educating the masses, particularly the rural populations (the *jíbaros,* discussed in chapter 3 in relation to Rafael Colorado's early film work).

Although the formation of DIVEDCO marked a stark change from the pattern of independent film production that had characterized Puerto Rican cinema until 1940, in many ways it also greatly resembled previous efforts. With its emphasis on the rural peasant as the embodiment of Puerto Rican identity, the division followed the trope realized in the projects of both Rafael Colorado and the Tropical Film Company. DIVEDCO's prolific production of documentary films also signaled recognition not only of the form's educational potential but also of its previous success as a self-sustaining medium.[119] Yet, by choosing to focus on intellectuals' vision of cinema as cultural promotion and education, rather than on cinema as industrial development, DIVEDCO also hindered or even supplanted the business-centered movement that had started to emerge on the island in the 1920s and 1930s. Once again, propelled by DIVEDCO's mission, critics and commentators understood Puerto Rican national cinema principally as a means of defending and promoting national culture over fostering any film industrial development. That vision remains the primary focus of Puerto Rican filmmaking to this day, notwithstanding the many and varied contributions both Viguié Cajas and Ramos Cobián made in the 1930s toward building a commercially viable Puerto Rican cinema.

Conclusion

Early Puerto Rican Cinema and Stateless Nation Building

Early Puerto Rican filmmakers and film critics' deliberations about the role of the national in cinema paved the way for the government to perceive film's nation-building potential. After many years of autonomous entrepreneurial filmmaking, in 1949 the Puerto Rican government formally created a state sanctioned and supported film division within the project named the División de Educación a la Comunidad/Division of Community Education (DIVEDCO). This government program became the official and most prolific filmmaking entity in the island until its disbandment in 1989.

Although the creation of DIVEDCO would not have been possible without the aid provided by the New Deal policies, its efforts did deliver a broad distribution (throughout the island) of a state-sanctioned version of national culture. Regardless of DIVEDCO's productiveness (in both creation and distribution of material), the structures, problems, failures, and successes that had defined Puerto Rican filmmaking before 1949 continued. Even if entrepreneurial filmmaking, the principal form of filmmaking that existed on the island until that point, now played a secondary role, DIVEDCO engaged in many of the same cross-cultural, transnational patterns that defined the initial decades of cinema history in Puerto Rico. That is to say, although DIVEDCO was clearly a Puerto Rican agency that promoted Puerto Rican culture, its policies, methodologies, and even personnel were transnational.

Thus, foreigners and Americans like Jack and Irene Delano (photography, printmaking, and film), Edwin Rosskam (photography and film), Benjamin Doniger (film), and Willard Van Dyke (photography and film), among others, became important and even defining figures—as is particularly the case with the Delanos—of Puerto Rican visual culture.[1] In addition, DIVEDCO's close ties with previous New Deal programs, such as the Works Projects Organization and the Farm Security Administration, inscribe it inside a trans-American network of economic aid and artistic and educational endeavors. In fact, DIVEDCO worked along with and similarly to the New Deal project of government-sponsored documentary films like those of Pare Lorentz. In addition, U.S. institutions helped to make DIVEDCO's local work visible internationally through the distribution networks of the United States Information Agency and the United Nations Educational, Scientific, and Cultural Organization.[2] Furthermore, although DIVEDCO's primary goal was education (and not directly economic development), it also underscored popular themes and iconography present in previous independent film productions—particularly with its emphasis on rural people and settings.

Even though DIVEDCO was the island's main film producer well into the 1980s, with the works of Fernando Cortés, Juan Orol, Amílcar Tirado, and Orestes Trucco, among others, by the 1980s, the autonomous entrepreneurial filmmakers again became major filmmaking agents in Puerto Rico. These private producers, and the many that have followed them (e.g., Marcos Zurinaga, Jacobo Morales, Luis Molina Casanova), have made use of business tactics and nationalist discourses remarkably similar to the ones I identified in the early years of Puerto Rican filmmaking. With the exception of a few business-driven projects like *Una aventura llamada Menudo* (1982) or *Talento de barrio* (2008), film producers and critics alike continue to rhetorically heighten nationalist ideals and desires and downplay transnational influences in local productions. In other words, despite years of border crossing, political–cultural negotiations, and industrial development, little has changed in how local elites envision the role of cinema in the process of nation building.

The colonial circumstances in both early twentieth-century and present-day Puerto Rico have triggered a strategy of defining the nation and national cultural productions as pure, unadulterated, and natural as a defense mechanism against U.S. acculturation. As Jorge Duany eloquently states, "During the twentieth century, Puerto Rican intellectuals developed a nationalist discourse based on the celebration of a unique cultural identity, the moral regeneration of the people, and the rejection of outside influences, particularly from the United States. As a result of their control over powerful cultural institutions such as the university, the intellectuals' discourse has become the official version of Puerto Ricanness."[3] As I have argued, this nativist, nationalist position negates the importance of cross-cultural, transnational exchanges for the development of Puerto Rican national culture (or any national culture for that matter), and, more importantly, does not fit the evidence. I propose instead that we understand the nation as a mediation among contradictory discourses. Obviously the Puerto Rican nation could not be what it is today if it were not for its colonial relationships with the United States and Spain; thus discourses generated in these metropolitan localities that directly or indirectly address(ed) Puerto Rico are also essential for understanding the island's process of nation building.

Although I understand and even sympathize with the resistance among scholars and critics to accept U.S. products, producers, and capital as part of the Puerto Rican nation, the transnational exchange between these two places has undeniably marked Puerto Rico's cultural productions. As, for example, the transnational figure of Rafael Colorado discussed in chapter 3 reveals, accepting and appropriating foreign or colonial influence does not have to mean a denial of an autonomous national culture. Accepting the foreign as an intrinsic element of the national can lead us away from the dire nationalistic future that scholars like Arjun Appadurai foretell in which "the politicization [of culture] is often the emotional fuel for more explicitly violent politics of identity."[4]

As the island's colonial status continues to prevail, and more and more Puerto Ricans move back and forth between the island and the United States, an awareness of the long-standing nature of these cultural exchanges can help ease concerns that territorial dislocations will spell doom for the existence of an independent national culture. Consequently, instead of ignoring and knowingly misrepresenting the transcultural reality imbedded in the process of nation building in Puerto Rico, we should embrace the potential of historical knowledge to enhance our understanding of the present. By isolating Puerto Rico and its cultural producers from a historical reality of transnational trade, and by stubbornly adhering to conservative conceptions of the nation and identity formation, we have misinterpreted, ignored, and lost valuable cultural knowledge. Conversely, considering transnational connections as part of the island's rich cultural history can deepen our understanding of the discourses that have long structured our perceptions of the nation and our identity as Puerto Ricans.

Finding the National in the Transnational

Throughout this book I have attempted to explain the intricacies of filmmaking in colonial contexts. I have also shown how conceptions of the national have long arisen in relation to transnational networks and trends. From its beginnings, Puerto Rican cinema, like other world cinemas, negotiated local interests and means with global trends and markets. Puerto Rico's colonial position, however, also propelled national political discourses to appropriate local productions as strategies for asserting an autonomous and sovereign national culture. In the absence of international recognition of their nation as an independent cultural entity, local elites—particularly critics—saw cultural productions as nation-building tools that could also have economic benefits. The island's colonial position also entailed the introduction of cinema into the political battles over who gets to represent and define Puerto Rico (and its citizens) in an international context. More than a defense of the local industry and market amidst the threats of globalizing forces like Hollywood, discourses that celebrated the island's cinema and criticized U.S. films aimed to situate Puerto Rico positively vis-à-vis global politics.

Despite elites' strong desire to differentiate Puerto Rico from the United States, the colonial reality, coupled with the island's small size, forced local filmmakers to actively engage with U.S. and other international markets and resources in transnational exchanges of capital, products, and even creative ideas. In addition, the relative ease with which Puerto Ricans could cross borders among different parts of the Caribbean and the United States created strong cultural and migratory links that helped to construct the island as fundamentally a transnation. That is, Puerto Rican culture appropriated elements from conflicting transnational discourses about the island's social position in the Caribbean, Spanish America, and the United States, which became the de facto measure of who belonged (or not) to the nation. Filmmaking as both a cultural and business enterprise thus fluctuated between addressing local identity issues (the national) and promoting itself as both a global ambassador and a consumer product (the transnational).

Beyond a historiographic study of Puerto Rican film, with this book I have attempted to demonstrate that (post)colonial cultural products often appropriate transnational influences, capital, and even individuals as cornerstones of national identity. In other words, as the case of early Puerto Rican film production and consumption illustrates, the constant circulation and adoption of outside products and ideas is an intrinsic part of the colonial condition. Instead of the transnational emanating out of the national, in the Puerto Rican case, the national emanated from both rejecting and embracing different transnational discourses about the island's image and place in the world.

However distinct Puerto Rico's colonial history might have been (or continues to be) many of its transnational developments were not unique to the island. For example, discussing the relationship between Mexican audiences and their consumption of U.S. silent films, Laura Isabel Serna argues that, just like in Puerto Rico, these early audiences incorporated U.S. products and the discourses that circulated around them into their conception of a unique Mexican cultural space, which she calls "Cinelandia." According to Serna, in this constructed space, Mexican spectators could see both foreign and local productions as validations of the nation and a national identity.[5] Similarly, both Puerto Rican filmmakers and critics integrated outside products and discourses into their conception of what a national cinema meant. More than mere recipients or victims of the globalizing power of American culture, Puerto Rican cultural producers and consumers derived their own understanding of what it meant to be Puerto Rican from a negotiation of cultural, educational, political, and business appeals relating to cinema and other cultural products that circulated transnationally.

Considering the contradictory forces that help to shape (post)colonial nations, Philip Rosen describes the particularity of postcolonialism (and diasporas) as "an awareness of the unavoidability *and yet* the artificiality of identity."[6] After all, one must remember that despite how emotionally definitive it might feel, cultural identity is not a natural or essential phenomenon but instead a social construct. When considering the historical cinema experience of colonized nations, like Puerto Rico, one notices how this artificiality that Rosen refers to plays out in our understanding of what the nation and the state mean as individual terms and in relation to each other. Therefore, "nation" and "state" cannot stand as self-evident terms that come about "organically," but rather they are defined (and redefined) through constant negotiations among power, exposure, and identity occurring at both the local and the global level. Thus one must recognize, as this book has demonstrated in detail, that, paradoxically, national identity is necessarily a transnational phenomenon.

Acknowledgments

I could not have completed this work without the help and support of many people. Although I cannot mention everybody in this brief space, I hope you all know that I greatly appreciate you and all that you have given me. First, I would like to recognize Ramona Curry, whose unconditional support, careful feedback, and meticulous proofreading gave me the confidence to push forward. Ramona, you made me a better scholar and person, and for that you have my eternal gratitude.

To editors Greg Clingham and Aníbal González, thank you for taking this project on with such rousing enthusiasm. To Managing Editor Pamelia Dailey, thank you for your patience! I also want to acknowledge Anustup Basu, Manisha Basu, and Dara E. Goldman at the University of Illinois for asking challenging questions and offering guidance that led to the betterment of my research. To Cory J. Provence, I really value your detective work; thank you for making my life easier. I want to give special recognition to my Puerto Rican collaborators Joaquín "Kino" García, Mónica Felix, and Rose Marie Bernier for eagerly sharing their wonderful work with me. We are all fortunate to have such great film scholars working in Puerto Rico.

I want to thank Dr. Reza Malek-Madani and the Naval Academy Research Council for the grants that made the completion of this book possible. I also thank all my colleagues and friends at USNA for their emotional and intellectual support, especially Mike Parker, Charlie Nolan, Audrey Wu Clark, Calina Ciobanu, Megan Geigner, Thomas Ward, Karyn Sproles, Noah Comet, and my marvelous writing partner, Greg Melville. Lastly, to the brilliant Jill Fitzgerald, the yang to my yin, thank you for poking me when I needed to be poked.

I am particularly grateful to my husband, Marcos Cerdeira, for always saying yes, even when he really, really wants to say no. Thank you for your patience; I love you. Finally, I thank my family, who taught me the great value of an education. To my parents, Radamés and Kathleen, and my sister, Katia, you are the inspiration for everything I do.

Notes

Introduction

1 Although I refer to Puerto Rico as "the island" it is in fact an archipelago encompassing the "big island" Puerto Rico, as well as Culebra, Vieques, and La Mona (and smaller keys).

2 Given that celluloid is an extremely flammable compound, the Library of Congress estimates that only about 25 percent of early films are still extant. Since there appears to have been little interest in preserving Puerto Rican films, only one film from the early period, *Romance tropical* (1936), is known to still exist (in the UCLA film archives).

3 Although historians usually refer to this war simply as the Spanish-American War the name is extremely controversial. Politically, I feel it should be referred to as the Spanish-American-Cuban-Filipino War and not the Spanish-American War because the latter ignores the great amount of local involvement in the war and perpetuates colonial definitions of alignment. Hence, despite the convoluted name I will continue to refer to this war as the Spanish-American-Cuban-Filipino War.

4 In his book, *Breve historia del cine puertorriqueño*, Kino García argues that despite having elements and aspirations, Puerto Rico does not have a national cinema. García proposes that two major factors contribute to the lack of a proper Puerto Rican national cinema: first, historically there has been no continuous production, and second, a great number of the films produced in/about Puerto Rico do not, in his view, represent and/or correspond to the interests of the Puerto Rican nation.

Though García declares that geography, language, and even the nationality of directors are not necessarily central to deciding what is and what is not national, he does have very specific criteria for how to define the national cultural industry. For him the two most important aspects to decide what does or does not belong to the nation's cinema are, first, the film's approach to the national subject, and second, the values espoused and represented in the work. In his estimation, for a group of films to be considered Puerto Rican national cinema, their producers must aim for them to be thus understood, and the films must be made in the context of a marked historical project. Joaquín "Kino" García, *Breve historia del cine puertorriqueño* (San Juan: Cine-gráfica, 1984), 3–8.

5 Marcos Zurinaga, "Marcos Zurinaga: Cine de proyección internacional," in *Dominio de la imagen; hacia una industria de cine en Puerto Rico*, ed. Raúl Ríos Díaz and Francisco González (San Juan: Librería Editorial Ateneo, 2000), 26. All translations from the Spanish are my own unless otherwise noted.

6 Carlos Pabón, *Nación postmortem: Ensayos sobre los tiempos de insoportable ambigüedad* (San Juan: Ediciones Callejón, 2003), 19.

7 See, for example, Roberto Ramos Perea, *Cinelibre* (San Juan: Editions Le Provincial, 2008), 54: "How can we talk about a Puerto Rican cinema, about a national cinema, if a great percent of its creators do not live and breathe in San Juan, but in Hollywood and Beverly Hills?"; Luis Molina, "Luis Molina: un nuevo modelo de cine educativo," in *Dominio de la imagen; hacia una industria de cine en Puerto Rico*, ed. Raúl Ríos Díaz and Francisco González (San Juan: Librería Editorial Ateneo, 2000), 39; Francisco González, "La gran ilusión: La industria de cine en Puerto Rico," in *Dominio de la imagen; hacia una industria de cine en Puerto Rico*, ed. Raúl Ríos Díaz and Francisco González (San Juan: Librería Editorial Ateneo, 2000), 8.

8 Although other national/ethnic identities form a part of the Puerto Rican society (Cuban, Venezuelan, Virgin Islanders, just to name a few), Dominicans are by far the most numerous and influential.

9 I note these three actors as clear examples of conflicts with the aforementioned definition of Puerto Rican cinema, but there are more complex instances like that of filmmakers Poli Marichal and Frances Negrón Muntaner, both of whom were born and raised in Puerto Rico but are currently working in the United States in productions that address the diasporic Puerto Rican community.

10 Legally, as of 2007, anyone born in Puerto Rico, or who has a parent born in Puerto Rico, or who is an American citizen living in Puerto Rico for more than a year is entitled to Puerto Rican citizenship. Despite the supposed independence of Puerto Rican citizenship from American citizenship, clearly this recently created citizenship depends on U.S. definitions of what is Puerto Rico and who can be Puerto Rican as a basis for granting the exclusively locally recognized citizenship. That is, essentially, you must first be defined as an American citizen to qualify for subsequent categorization as a Puerto Rican citizen. Even though Puerto Rican citizenship might be a source of national pride for a considerable group of people, it is impractical, because it is not internationally recognized and hence is extremely problematic when traveling abroad. Puerto Rico Supreme Court case *Miriam J. Ramírez de Ferrer v. Juan Mari Brás* (1997) ratified in *Miriam J. Ramírez de Ferrer v. Juan Mari Brás II* (2006).

11 The 2016 U.S. congressional imposition of a Fiscal Control Board to oversee Puerto Rico's tax and spending decisions has further blurred the island's rights to self-government and solidified its status as a colony.

12 Pheng Chea, *Spectral Nationality: Passages of Freedom from Kant to Postcolonial Literatures of Liberation* (New York: Columbia University Press, 2003), 359.

13 I use the term "rhizomatic" as defined by Gilles Deleuze and Félix Guattari in their book *A Thousand Plateaus: Capitalism and Schizophrenia* (Minneapolis: University of Minnesota Press, 1980).

14 Chris Berry, "What is Transnational Cinema? Thinking from the Chinese Situation," *Transnational Cinemas* 1, no. 2 (2010): 124.
15 For some case studies of early transnational production and distribution, see, for example, Ramona Curry, "Benjamin Brodsky (1877–1960): The Transpacific American Film Entrepreneur—Part One, Making *A Trip Thru China*," *Journal of American-East Asian Relations* 18, no. 1 (2011): 58–94; Laura Isabel Serna, "Exhibition in Mexico during the Early 1920s: Nationalist Discourses and Transnational Capital," in *Convergence Media History*, ed. Janet Staiger and Sabine Hake (New York, Routledge, 2009), 69–80; Kim Fahlstedt, "Marketing Rebellion: The Chinese Revolution Reconsidered," *Film History* 26, no. 1 (2014): 80–107.
16 Will Higbee and Song Hwee Lim, "Concepts of Transnational Cinema: Towards a Critical Transnationalism in Film Studies," *Transnational Cinemas* 1, no. 1 (2010): 18.
17 Andrew Higson, "The Concept of National Cinema," *Screen* 30, no. 4 (1989): 36.
18 Eric J. Hobsbawm, *Nations and Nationalism since 1780: Programme, Myth, Reality* (New York: Cambridge University Press, 1990).
19 Wayne Norman, *Negotiating Nationalism: Nation-Building, Federalism, and Secession in the Multinational State* (New York: Oxford University Press, 2006), 25–26.
20 Giuliana Bruno coined the term "absent presence" to refer to gaps in historical archives that through their absence reveal sociocultural values and institutional priorities. See, *Streetwalking on a Ruined Map: Cultural Theory and the City Films of Elvira Notari* (Princeton, NJ: Princeton University Press, 1993).

Chapter 1 Contexts for a National Cinema

1 Rubén Ríos Ávila, *La raza cómica del sujeto en Puerto Rico* (San Juan: Ediciones Callejón, 2002), 23. All translations from the Spanish, unless otherwise noted, are my own.
2 Carlos Pabón, "De Albizu a Madonna: Para armar y desarmar la nacionalidad," *Bordes* 1 (1995): 22–40.
3 Fernando Picó, *Historia general de Puerto Rico* (San Juan: Huracán, 1986); Francisco Scarano, *Puerto Rico: Cinco Siglos de Historia* (México D.F.: McGraw-Hill, 2008); Carmelo Rosario Natal, *Puerto Rico y la crisis de la Guerra Hispanoamericana* (San Juan: Ramallo Brothers Printing, 1975).
4 Richard Gott, *Cuba: A New History* (New Haven, CT: Yale University Press, 2005), 73.
5 The Puerto Rican and the Cuban revolts were supposed to take place at the same time; however, the Spanish force uncovered the Puerto Rican plot, and the revolutionaries were forced to move their strike ahead.
6 To this day an idealized vision of this connection between particularly Cuba and Puerto Rico circulates, especially among the pro-independence groups in Puerto Rico. Lola Rodríguez de Tió's famous verses "Cuba y Puerto Rico son / de un pájaro las dos alas / reciben flores y balas / sobre el mismo corazón" (Cuba and Puerto Rico are from a bird the two wings, they receive flowers and bullets on the same heart) are still cited as evidence of this connection. Furthermore, the Puerto Rican left values Hostos's thoughts so much that one of the leading pro-independence groups carries his name (Movimiento Independentista Nacional Hostosiano).

7 Rosario Natal, *Puerto Rico y la crisis de la Guerra Hispanoamericana*, 8–9.
8 The Venezuelan Crisis of 1895 came about because of a dispute between Venezuela and British Guiana (present-day Guyana) over the territory of Essequibo. The United States intervened, citing the Monroe Doctrine as grounds for jurisdiction, and finally drew up a resolution that gave the United Kingdom 90 percent of the disputed territory without providing any factual reasons for the decision.
9 Rosario Natal, *Puerto Rico y la crisis de la Guerra Hispanoamericana*, 21.
10 This idealized vision of a united Cuba and Puerto Rico comes from the involvement of key Puerto Rican figures in the PRC (Partido Revolucionario Cubano). This involvement included participation of the Puerto Rican members in Cuba's wars of independence and the creation of the current-day Puerto Rican flag, made to mimic the Cuban flag as a sign of support.

When I use the term "turn-of-the-century," I am using it in its most common understanding: the last years of the nineteenth century and the initial years of the twentieth century.
11 Scarano, *Puerto Rico*, 368.
12 Scarano.
13 On Spain's colonial censorship of the Puerto Rican press, see Rosario Natal, *Puerto Rico y la crisis de la Guerra Hispanoamericana*, 50.
14 Fernando Picó, *1898: La Guerra después de la Guerra* (San Juan: Ediciones Huracán, 1987).
15 Luce López Baralt and Mercedes López Baralt, "La crónica del 98 de Esteban López Giménez," in *Un cambio de siglo 1898: España, Cuba, Puerto Rico, Filipinas y Estados Unidos*, ed. José Girón (Oviedo, Spain: Universidad de Oviedo, 2008), 329.
16 "Seva" is a short story that narrates the resistance to the American invasion of a fictional town in the east coast of Puerto Rico named Seva, and its subsequent genocidal erasure by the American authorities as a plot to deprive Puerto Ricans of a history of defiance.
17 Picó, *Historia*, 200–204.
18 Scarano, *Puerto Rico*, 451–452.
19 Scarano, 457.
20 For an example on this "betrayal" position, see Rubén Berríos Martínez, "Puerto Rico's Decolonization," *Foreign Affairs* 76, no. 6 (1997): 100–114.
21 Picó, *1898*, 167–170.
22 For more on the emergence of Latin American nationalism, see Benedict Anderson, *Imagined Communities*, rev. ed. (New York: Verso, 2006), 48–53.
23 Picó, *Historia*, 248.
24 Luis E Agrait, "Estampas del 98 en Puerto Rico," in *Un cambio de siglo 1898: España, Cuba, Puerto Rico, Filipinas y Estados Unidos*, ed. José Girón (Oviedo, Spain: Universidad de Oviedo, 2008), 306.
25 The "ñ" is the only Spanish letter that is completely absent from the English alphabet, and the word "coño" is a very common swear word in Puerto Rico, perhaps equivalent in use to "damn" in the United States.
26 The campaign's slogan can be translated to "defective language, defective thought," and it included examples like "do not say 'size,' say 'talla' or 'tamaño,'" or "Tuna is the one that sings, in Spanish we eat 'atún.'" Furthermore the campaign proclaimed that "language is the blood of the spirit, speak it well, proudly."

27 For a deeper analysis on the position of Puerto Ricans in the United States see Jorge Duany, *The Puerto Rican Nation on the Move: Identities on the Island and in the United States* (Chapel Hill: University of North Carolina Press, 2002).

28 Although technically other industries were also active, such as tobacco and needlework, sugar was by far the biggest industry and monopolized the majority of the arable land.

29 Scarano, *Puerto Rico*, 476–477.

30 César J. Ayala and Rafael Bernabe, *Puerto Rico in the American Century: A History since 1898* (Chapel Hill: University of North Carolina Press, 2007), 38.

31 César J. Ayala, *American Sugar Kingdom: The Plantation Economy of the Spanish Caribbean 1898–1934* (Chapel Hill: University of North Carolina Press, 1999), 178–182.

32 Ayala, *American Sugar Kingdom*, 127–128.

33 The Resident Commissioner to this day has the right to sit in and comment on the proceedings of the U.S. House of Representatives but does not have a vote.

34 For more on the problematic definition of the Puerto Rican citizenship, see U.S. Supreme Court case *González v. Williams* (1904).

35 For further explanations on the relationship between the Jones Act and World War I, see Picó, *Historia*.

36 The phrase means, basically, "the art of dealing"; however, due to its multiplicity of nuanced meanings, the term resists full or even adequate translation. See Arcadio Díaz Quiñones, *El arte de bregar* (San Juan: Ediciones Callejón, 2000).

37 Luis Felipe Díaz, *La na(rra)ción en la literatura puertorriqueña* (San Juan: Ediciones Huracán, 2008), 129.

38 Díaz Quiñones, *El arte de bregar*, 99.

39 René Marqués, *El puertorriqueño dócil y otros ensayos* (San Juan: Editorial Antillana, 1993); José Luis González, *El país de cuatro pisos y otros ensayos* (San Juan: Ediciones Huracán, 1980).

40 Juan Flores, *Insularismo e ideología burguesa* (San Juan: Ediciones Huracán, 1979), 67.

41 Flores, *Insularismo e ideología burguesa*, 115.

42 Ayala and Bernabe, *Puerto Rico in the American Century*, 105.

43 Ayala and Bernabe, 107.

44 Díaz Quiñonez, *El arte de bregar*, 94.

45 The Ponce Massacre was the culmination of a series of violent exchanges between the Winship government and the Nationalist Party. The series of events started with the killing of four nationalists at the University of Puerto Rico in Rio Piedras in 1934 (the Rio Piedras Massacre), which in turn led to the assassination of police colonel Elisha Francis Riggs by nationalist cadets Hiram Rosado and Elías Beauchamp. The police captured Rosado and Beauchamp and executed them while in custody, and later the police also imprisoned other leaders of the Nationalist Party, among them Albizu Campos, for supposed ties with the event. Then, on Palm Sunday in 1937, the Ponce Massacre occurred when police met a Nationalist march commemorating the abolition of slavery and protesting the imprisonment of Albizu Campos with extreme violence, resulting in twenty-one deaths and the wounding of hundreds of nationalists and passers-by.

46 Díaz Quiñones, *El arte de bregar*, 88.

47 Ayala and Bernabe, *Puerto Rico in the American Century*, 144.
48 The appropriation of lands from big farmers was not actually a new idea but instead the initiative proposed the real implementation of an existing law that limited the size of farms to 500 acres, a law the government rarely enforced because of economic pressures from big sugar plantations.
49 In Puerto Rico I have heard many colleagues melancholically say that if only the Plan Chardón had actually been implemented, our history as a nation would have been so different. There is no denying that history would have been different (since something would have been done differently) but there is no guarantee that the plan would have been successful or that it produced the desired outcomes that later generations assign to it.
50 Ayala and Bernabe, *Puerto Rico in the American Century*, 151.
51 Ayala and Bernabe, 151.
52 Since its foundation in 1967 the PNP (New Progressive Party) has been one of the two leading parties in Puerto Rico along with the PPD. It advocates for the inclusion of Puerto Rico into the American Union through statehood. Also, notice the emphasis on development evidenced in the term "progressive" in the party's name.
53 This type of "progress in the future" rhetoric provides an interesting contrast to the American fascination with the glories of the past, like the forefathers and the Constitution.
54 For a complete list of DIVEDCO film titles see: https://www.archivoicp.com/divedco/.
55 These colonial concerns are best exemplified by the political obsession with Puerto Rico's political status. For example, political parties are divided based on their beliefs about state status rather than on social issues. Furthermore, since 1993 Puerto Rico has had three referendums regarding political status.

Chapter 2 Cinema Comes to Puerto Rico

1 Juan Ortiz Jiménez, "40 años de cinematografía puertorriqueña," *Puerto Rico ilustrado* (San Juan), February 16, 1952, 42.
2 Ortiz Jiménez, "40 años de cinematografía puertorriqueña," 38–40.
3 Joaquin "Kino" García, *Breve historia del cine puertorriqueño* (San Juan: Cinegráfica, 1984). For another example of how historians have built on Ortiz Jiménez's work see José Artemio Torres, "Apaga Musiú: Los primeros pasos de cine puertorriqueño," in *Idilio tropical: La aventura del cine puertorriqueño*, ed. Marta Aponte Alsina (San Juan: Banco Popular, 1994).
4 Although scholars have revealed that most of the supposed "battle footage" of the war was re-created on sets in the United States, the Library of Congress has identified footage shot by Biograph cameramen Billy Bitzer and Arthur Marvin as well as Edison's William Paley as actually shot on the coast of Cuba. The available "real" footage of the war in the Philippines was in fact shot after 1900 by the Biograph Co. of the subsequent Philippine Revolution, but the Edison Manufacturing Film Co. did make re-creations of the 1898 events. For a list of the available footage, see the Library of Congress's collection *The Spanish-American War in Motion Pictures* available online at: http://memory.loc.gov/ammem/sawhtml/sawhome.html. See also Charles Musser, *Before the Nickelodeon: Edwin S. Porter*

and the Edison Manufacturing Company (Berkeley: University of California Press, 1991), 126–142.

5 Giuliana Bruno, *Streetwalking on a Ruined Map: Cultural Theory and the City Films of Elvira Notari* (Princeton: Princeton University Press, 1993), 3.

6 Bruno, *Streetwalking on a Ruined Map*, 150.

7 Ana M. López, "Early Cinema and Modernity in Latin America," *Cinema Journal* 40, no. 1 (2000): 50.

8 López, "Early Cinema and Modernity in Latin America,".

9 See, for example, García, *Breve historia del cine puertorriqueño*.

10 "Cinematógrafo," *Boletín mercantil* (San Juan), July 5, 1901, 3.

11 For example, see Torres, "Apaga Musiú."

12 For Hervet's travel, *La Bretagne* Manifest number 82522. http://www.germanimmigrants1890s.com/index.php?id=1570027. For Edison's Kinetoscope see, Musser, *Before the Nickelodeon*, 35.

13 For evidence of Hervet's presence in Mexico City in 1896, see "Letter List," *Mexican Herald* (Mexico City, Mexico) February 12, 1896, 7; and in 1898, see Luis Recillas Enecoiz, "Atisbo al cine mudo en Toluca, 1896–1905 (Primera parte: 1896–1900)," *El ojo que piensa*, last modified July 1, 2011, http://www.elojoquepiensa.net/elojoquepiensa/index.php/articulos/148#citas

14 Cinematógrafo Hervet, Advertisement, *Boletín mercantil*, July 5, 1901,1. All translations from the original Spanish are my own unless otherwise noted.

15 "El cinematógrafo de Payret," *Diario de la Marina* (Havana), January 29, 1900, 4.

16 Empresa E. Hervet, Advertisement, *Estado de São Paulo* (Brazil), April 11, 1905, 4.

17 U.S. National Archives, available via Ancestry.com [database on-line]. Provo, UT, USA: Ancestry.com Operations, Inc., 2010 (henceforth NARA/Ancestry.com), *New York Passengers List 1820–1957*; Microfilm Serial: 15; Roll: T715_377.

18 Rose Marie Bernier, "Las rutas del cine en el Viejo San Juan: Memoria y planificación," (master's thesis, University of Puerto Rico, 2011), 49.

19 "Anoche," *La correspondencia* (San Juan), May 10, 1897, 2.

20 "El cinematógrafo," *Boletín mercantil*, May 12, 1897, 3.

21 "Para esta noche," *La correspondencia*, May 9, 1897, 3.

22 Bernier, "Las rutas del cine en el Viejo San Juan," 49–50.

23 "Anoche hizo su primera exhibición," *La correspondencia* (San Juan), May 10, 1897, 2.

24 I myself interviewed Dr. Sánchez Longo, born in 1926, by telephone on December 4, 2012.

25 *The Dolorita Passion Dance*, advertised as part of Luis Pío's exhibition, had been censored in Atlantic City because of its sexually suggestive material, but as *La correspondencia* declares, not only did the film make it to Puerto Rico but it was also one of the most popular parts of the show (although as Bernier comments the film was deemed inappropriate for female audiences). On the film's censorship see John E. Semonche, *Censoring Sex: A Historical Journey through American Media* (Lanham, MA: Rowman and Littlefield Publishing Group, 2007), 98. On Pío's show see "Los cuadros que exhibió anoche," *La correspondencia* (San Juan), May 14, 1897, 3. On female audiences see Bernier, "Las rutas del cine en el Viejo San Juan,"57.

26 American Film Institute, "The Dolorita Passion Dance," accessed January 23, 2012, http://www.afi.com/members/catalog/DetailView.aspx?s=&Movie=41263. The

Vitascope was the Edison Manufacturing Company's first commercially available film projector, complementing (and later replacing) the personal Kinetoscope in April 1896: Deac Rossell, *Living Pictures: The Origins of the Movies* (Albany: State University of New York, 1998), 146.

27 Sánchez Longo, Luis Pío, phone interview by author, Providence, December 4, 2012.

28 For the relationship between Sanchez Longo and Sanchez Rivera, NARA/Ancestry.com, 1910 U.S. Census, Comerio, Puerto Rico, Roll:T625_2053; NARA/Ancestry.com, 1940 U.S. Census, Comerio, Puerto Rico, Roll: T627_4635; Sánchez Longo, phone interview by author, December 4, 2012. Monserrate Rivera Vásquez, from the town of Comerío and mother of Luis Muñoz Rivera, was the sister of Soledad Rivera Vásquez, mother of Luis Pío Sánchez Rivera, making them maternal cousins. For more on Monserrate see A. W. Maldonado, *Luis Muñoz Marín: Puerto Rico's Democratic Revolution* (San Juan: Editorial de la Universidad de Puerto Rico, 2006), 16.

29 NARA/Ancestry.com, 1910 U.S. Census, Comerio, Puerto Rico, Roll:T625_2053.

30 James H. McLeary, *First Annual Register of Porto Rico* (San Juan: Press of the San Juan News, 1901), 276.

31 William H. Hunt, *Third Annual Report of the Governor of Porto Rico* (Washington DC: Government Printing Office, 1903), 206.

32 "Un empresario inglés," *La democracia* (Ponce), August 6, 1897, 3. Although San Juan is located on the northeast part of the island, Ponce is located at almost the diametrically opposite point on the southwest part of the island. In 1897 residents of these two cities, then the largest on the island, would have constituted a significant segment of the population, particularly the educated and political elite.

33 César J. Ayala and Rafael Bernabe, *Puerto Rico in the American Century: A History since 1898* (Chapel Hill: University of North Carolina Press, 2007), 19.

34 On the Englishman's exhibition see "Un empresario ingles," 3. On the Vitascope see Rossell, *Living Pictures*, 146.

35 "El aparato," *La democracia* (Ponce), August 7, 1897, 3.

36 As Musser explains, "although Blair's semi-opaque product had been excellent, the emulsion peeled away from the base of its clear stock." Musser, *Before the Nickelodeon*, 87.

37 "Cinematógrafo Lumier," *Boletín mercantil*, March 4, 1898, 3.

38 Salvador Negra traveled in February 1897 to New York from Curaçao. Venezuela ship manifest; Batch number: P00320-5; Page Ref. Number: 168. http://www.ellisisland.org/search/FormatPassRec.asp?ID=103205020491&BN=P00320-5&sship=Venezuela&lineshipid=3880.

39 "Cinematógrafo Lumier," *Boletín mercantil*, March 6, 1898, 3; "El cinematógrafo," *Boletín mercantil*, March 9, 1898, 4.

40 As Charles Musser argues for the United States, the initial novelty appeal of cinema as technological novelty "quickly lost its value," and shows relied more and more on editing and other cinematic techniques to attract customers. Musser, *Before the Nickelodeon*, 100.

41 For examples of accounts of the Spanish-American War in Puerto Rican film historiography, see Torres, "Apaga Musiú" or Roberto Ramos Perea, *Cinelibre* (San Juan: Editions Le Provincial, 2008).

42 On the capacity of some projectors to also shoot film, see Richard Abel, *Encyclope-*

dia of Early Cinema (New York: Routledge, 2005), 182. See also Rossell, *Living Pictures*, 120 and 129.

43 "Free Exhibition of War Pictures," *Trenton State Gazette*, December 15, 1898, 5.

44 "Free Exhibition of War Pictures," 5, and J. B. Vandegrift and Company, *Handbook of the United States Tariff Containing the Tariff Act of 1909* (New York: J. B. Vandegrift and Company, 1909), 71.

45 "Free Exhibition of War Pictures," 5.

46 On Sampson, see Francisco A. Scarano, *Puerto Rico: Cinco Siglos de Historia* (San Juan: McGraw Hill, 2008), 444.

47 "Photography That Is Perilous," *Atlanta Constitution*, August 13, 1899, A4. In *Harper's Pictorial History of the War with Spain* (1899), one can find multiple pictures and paintings of San Juan and its subsequent bombardment by the U.S. Navy in May 1898. Although it has no references to film cameras, the book does demonstrate that "reporters" were present during the conflict.

48 Joseph P. Eckhardt, *The King of the Movies: Film Pioneer Siegmund Lubin* (Cranbury, NJ: Associated University Presses, 1997), 28.

49 S. Lubin Manufacturing Optician, Advertisement, *New York Clipper*, January 21, 1899, 802.

50 Eckhardt, *The King of the Movies*, 28. Charles Musser, *The Emergence of Cinema: The American Screen to 1907* (Berkeley: University of California Press, 1990), 257–258.

51 L. M. Martin's Cineograph, Advertisement, *Omaha World Herald*, April 14, 1900, 3. On the cineograph, Eckhardt, *The King of the Movies*, 21; Musser, *The Emergence of Cinema*,168–169.

52 L. M. Martin's Cineograph, 3.

53 Kyle Evered, "Fostering Puerto Rico: Representations of Empire and Orphaned Territories during the Spanish-American War," *Historical Geography* 34 (2006): 110.

54 American Film Institute, *American Film Institute Catalog of Motion Pictures Produced in the United States: Film Beginnings, 1893–1910* (New York: Bowker, 1971), 1162.

55 American Film Institute, *American Film Institute Catalog of Motion Pictures Produced in the United States*.

56 Just for the year of 1899 I have discerned on the WorldCat at least twenty-five commercially published U.S. publications dealing in part or in full with Puerto Rico. Some of the titles include *The Philippines and New Possessions* (R. H. Woodward Co.), *Everything about Our New Possessions* (Fenno), and *The Story of Our Wonderful Victories Told by Dewey, Schley, Wheeler, and Other Heroes* (American Book and Bible House).

57 L. M. Martin's Cineograph, Advertisement, 3; "Free Exhibition of War Pictures," *Trenton State Gazette*, December 15, 1898, 5; S. Lubin Manufacturing Optician, Advertisement, *New York Clipper*, January 21, 1899, 802.

58 The Superior Board of Health, *Report of the Military Governor of Porto Rico from October 18, 1898, to April 30, 1900* (Washington, DC: Government Printing Office, 1901), 69.

59 Superior Board of Health.

60 For more on the link between hygiene and imperialism in Puerto Rico see Laura Briggs, *Reproducing Empire: Race, Sex, Science and U.S. Imperialism in Puerto Rico* (Berkeley: University of California Press, 2002).

61 Dominick LaCapra, *History and Memory after Auschwitz* (Ithaca: Cornell University Press, 1998), 10.
62 José B. Capino, "Cinema and the Spectacle of Colonialism: American Documentary Film and (Post) Colonial Philippines, 1898–1989" (PhD diss., Northwestern University, 2002), 9.
63 Stephen Crane, "Burial at Ponce," *Boston Daily Globe*, August 15, 1898, 3.
64 Edward W. Said, *Culture and Imperialism* (New York: Vintage Books, 1994), 31.
65 See note 57.
66 Alison Griffiths, *Wondrous Difference: Cinema, Anthropology, and Turn-of-the-Century Visual Culture* (New York: Columbia University Press, 2002), 204–205.
67 Evered, "Fostering Puerto Rico," 112.
68 On travel literature see Jeanne-Maris Warzeski, "Mapping the Unknown: Gendered Spaces and the Oriental Other in Travelogues of Egypt by U.S. Women, 1854–1914," *History and Anthropology* 13, no. 4 (2002): 301–317. On travel film see Griffiths, *Wondrous Difference*.
69 Griffiths, *Wondrous Difference*, 326.
70 American Film Institute, *American Film Institute Catalog of Motion Pictures Produced in the United States*, 494.
71 You can find a copy of the film's poster in Deems Taylor, *A Pictorial History of the Movies* (New York: Simon and Schuster Inc, 1943), 4.
72 "The New York Theater," *New York Daily Tribune*, July 12, 1854, 5.
73 Most of the articles discussing Puerto Rican woman were written by anonymous authors and mainly address the "backward" courtship practices that reveal the deep problems embedded in Spanish law. The references for the two articles mentioned: "Willing Slave to the Men Are Our Puerto Rican Sisters," *Cincinnati Enquirer*, August 13, 1899, 25; "Courtship in Porto Rico," *Washington Post*, August 28, 1899, 7.
74 Carpenter's article was published in at least seven large-circulation newspapers: *Atlanta Constitution* (July 23, 1899), Washington, D.C.'s *Evening Star* (July 29, 1899), *Kansas City Journal* (July 30, 1899), *Omaha Daily Bee* (July 30, 1899), *St. Paul Globe* (July 30, 1899), *Boston Daily Globe* (July 30, 1899), and *Los Angeles Times* (July 30, 1899).
75 Frank G. Carpenter, "Pretty Porto Girls," *St. Paul Globe* (Minn.), July 30, 1899, 24.
76 Carpenter, "Pretty Porto Girls."
77 Jorge Duany, *The Puerto Rican Nation on the Move: Identities on the Island and in the United States* (Chapel Hill: University of North Carolina Press, 2002), 54–55.
78 Scarano, *Puerto Rico*, 449.
79 Warwick Anderson, *Colonial Pathologies: American Tropical Medicine, Race, and Hygiene in the Philippines* (Durham, NC: Duke University Press, 2006).
80 "El cinematógrafo Vargas," *Boletín mercantil* (San Juan), January 23, 1906, 1; Rose Marie Bernier, "El comienzo de los cines carpas," *Cine movida*, accessed March 4, 2013, http://cinemovida.net/historia_del_cine_en_puerto_rico
81 Bernier, "El comienzo."

Chapter 3 Stateless Nationhood, Transnationalism, and the Difficulties of Assigning Nationality

1 "SUAGM celebra 100 años de cine puertorriqueño," last modified September 12, 2011, http://www.suagm.edu/news02.asp?cnt_id=701. All translations from the original Spanish are my own unless specified otherwise.

2 See, for example, an entry in the blog of the theater chain Caribbean Cinemas, http://caribbeancinemas.blogspot.com/2011/08/celebrar-los-100-anos-del-cine.html.

3 An auteurist understanding of cinema contends that a film reflects its director's particular and personal vision and aesthetic style; such an approach in film studies thus heavily emphasizes directors' contributions as a basis for understanding and cataloging cinematic productions.

4 Colorado identified strongly as a Spaniard throughout his life. In his sixties, in 1930, in an attempt to honor the Spanish King, he set sail to retrace Columbus's route from the "New World" to Spain and bring good tidings to the Spanish nation (although he did not make it past the Bahamas). "Sails Columbus Route," *New York Times*, August 4, 1930, 4.

5 Roberto Ramos Perea, *Cinelibre: Historia desconocida y manifiesto por un cine puertorriqueño independiente y libre* (San Juan: Editions Le Provincial, 2008), 4–5. Francisco González, "La gran ilusión: La industria de cine en Puerto Rico," *Dominio de la imagen: Hacia una industria de cine en Puerto Rico*, ed. Raúl Ríos-Díaz and Francisco González (San Juan: Librería Editorial Ateneo, 2000), 8.

6 Conrado Asenjo, *Quién es quién en Puerto Rico*, 2nd ed. (San Juan: Real Hermanos Inc, 1936), 191.

7 Juan Ortiz Jiménez, "40 años de cinematografía puertorriqueña," *Puerto Rico ilustrado*, February 16, 1952, 38–40.

8 Rafael Colorado, "Nostalgia . . . de tiempos viejos," *El mundo* (San Juan), February 21, 1959, SS2.

9 Colorado, "Nostalgia . . . de tiempos viejos."

10 Colorado.

11 Ángel Rivero Méndez, *Crónica de la Guerra Hispanoamericana en Puerto Rico* (Madrid: Sucesores de Rivadeneyra, 1922), VIII and 192.

12 Rivero Méndez, *Crónica de la Guerra Hispanoamericana en Puerto Rico*, VIII.

13 Rivero Méndez, 625.

14 See, for example, Joaquín "Kino" García, *Breve historia del cine puertorriqueño* (San Juan: Cine-gráfica, 1984), 23; José Artemio Torres, "Apaga Musiú: Los primeros pasos de cine puertorriqueño," *Idilio tropical: La aventura del cine puertorriqueño*, ed. Marta Aponte Alsina (San Juan: Banco Popular, 1994), 12.

15 Ramos Perea, *Cinelibre*, 6.

16 Cine Puerto Rico, Advertisement, *Gráfico* (San Juan), July 14, 1912. I should note that Colorado was the general administrator of *Gráfico*, which had also previously been called *El Carnaval* when Colorado ran the magazine in Ponce. Antonio Salvador Pedreira, *El periodismo en Puerto Rico* (San Juan: Editorial Edil, 1982), 457.

17 Cine Puerto Rico, Advertisement, *Gráfico* (San Juan), July 14, 1912.

18 "Bou v. Colorado," *Porto Rico Reports Volume 24: Cases Adjudge in the Supreme Court of Porto Rico from May 30, 1916 to March 15, 1917* (San Juan: Bureau of

Supplies, Printing and Transportation, 1917), 125–130. The case discussed at the high court involved unpaid rent to the theater's owner Rafael Bou by the theater managers Ramón Bosch and Luis Ferreras. Colorado had cosigned the initial agreement between Bou, Bosch, and Ferreras and was thus involved in the lawsuit.

19 "Bou v. Colorado."

20 Simpler, Advertisement, *Gráfico* (San Juan), September 6, 1913.

21 For Colorado travel records see, for example, *Carolina Ship Manifest*, July 13, 1914, page 0259, manifest line number 0004; *Caracas Ship Manifest*, December 22, 1916, page 0615, manifest line number 0005; *San Juan Ship Manifest*, July 29, 1919, page 0501, manifest line number 0005.

22 Gran establecimiento fotográfico de Rafael Colorado, Advertisement, *Gráfico* (San Juan), November 10, 1912.

23 "San Juan y la isla," *La democracia* (San Juan), May 28, 1912, 1.

24 "San Juan y la isla," 1.

25 "El arte cinematográfico en Puerto Rico," *Puerto Rico ilustrado*, June 1, 1912, n.p.

26 "Las tres banderas," *La correspondencia*, May 28, 1912, n.p.

27 "Las tres banderas," *La correspondencia*, May 25, 1912, n.p.; "El cine Versalles" *La correspondencia*, May 30, 1912, 8.

28 "La empresa del cine," *La correspondencia*, May 29, 1912, n.p.; "Las tres banderas," *La correspondencia*, May 25, 1912, n.p. You can find a picture (not from the film) of Rosita Realí here: http://vintagek2.com/vintage/cuple/cuple.html. For more on the *Porto Rico Provisional Regiment of Infantry* see Héctor Andrés Negroni, *Historia militar de Puerto Rico* (Madrid: Sociedad Estatal Quinto Centenario, 1992).

29 "El arte de la cinematografía en Puerto Rico," *Gráfico* (San Juan), August 9, 1913.

30 "El arte de la cinematografía en Puerto Rico." Notice that "America" does not necessarily mean the United States but refers to the hemisphere generally and likely more specifically to Latin America.

31 "El arte de la cinematografía en Puerto Rico." What the writer means by "foreign" is not clear, but the term most likely refers to U.S. productions and perhaps French as well.

32 "Cine 'Las Tres Banderas,'" *Gráfico* (San Juan), April 5, 1913, n.p.

33 "Cine 'Las Tres Banderas,'" *Gráfico* (San Juan), May 17, 1913, n.p.

34 Bill Route, "The Emergence of Australian Film," in *The Oxford History of World Cinema*, ed. Geoffrey Nowell-Smith (New York: Oxford University Press, 1997), 423.

35 Kevin Rockett, "History, Politics and Irish Cinema," in *Cinema and Ireland*, ed. Kevin Rockett, Luke Gibbons, and John Hill (New York: Routledge, 1987), 7.

36 José de la Torre Muñiz, "De Puerto Rico," *Cine mundial*, November, 1916, 477.

37 De la Torre Muñiz, "De Puerto Rico."

38 José Luis Sáez, *Historia de un sueño importado: Ensayos sobre el cine en Santo Domingo* (Santo Domingo: Ediciones Siboney, 1982), 42–43.

39 Hugo, "Cine Ideal," *La correspondencia*, July 28, 1916, 8; "Cine Ideal," *La democracia* (San Juan), July 25, 1916, 8.

40 Hugo, "Cine Ideal."

41 Cine Luna, Advertisement, *La democracia* (San Juan), August 24, 1916, 8.

42 In this speech before the U.S. House of Representatives in May 1916, Muñoz Rivera declared that assigning American nationality to Puerto Ricans under the proposed

Jones Act would mean "to make Puerto Ricans pariahs in their own country." See Antonio Fernós, *¡Ser nosotros mismos!: La angustiosa lucha del pueblo puertorriqueño por su soberanía nacional* (San Juan: Editorial de la Universidad de Puerto Rico, 2003), 58.

43 "Éxito de la cinematografía," *La democracia* (San Juan), September 25, 1916, 8.

44 César J. Ayala and Rafael Bernabe, *Puerto Rico in the American Century: A History since 1898* (Chapel Hill: University of North Carolina Press, 2007), 57–58.

45 Ayala and Bernabe, *Puerto Rico in the American Century*, 57.

46 "Éxito de la cinematografía," 8.

47 "Éxito de la cinematografía."

48 Ayala and Bernabe, *Puerto Rico in the American Century*, 66.

49 Rafael Colorado Jr., "Impresiones," *Gráfico* (San Juan), September 20, 1913, n.p.

50 Ortiz Jiménez, "40 años de cinematografía puertorriqueña," 40–42.

51 "Por la hembra y por el gallo," *La correspondencia*, September 20, 1916, 7.

52 Geoffrey Nowell-Smith, "The Heyday of the Silents," in *The Oxford History of World Cinema*, ed. Geoffrey Nowell-Smith (New York: Oxford University Press, 1997), 195.

53 For more on the transition of melodrama from U.S. stage to cinema, see Ben Brewster and Lea Jacobs, *Theater to Cinema: Stage Pictorialism and the Early Feature Film* (New York: Oxford University Press, 1997). For more on U.S. film melodrama, see Linda Williams, "Melodrama Revised," in *Refiguring American Film Genres: History and Theory*, ed. Nick Browne (Berkeley: University of California Press, 1998), 42–88.

54 On *The Birth of a Nation*, Norman King, "The Sound of Silents," in *Silent Film*, ed. Richard Abel (New Brunswick, NJ: Rutgers University Press, 1995), 31; On Lyda Borelli, Paolo Cherchi Usai, "Italy: Spectacle and Melodrama," in *The Oxford History of World Cinema*, ed. Geoffrey Nowell-Smith (New York: Oxford University Press, 1996), 129.

55 For a discussion of melodrama in Pathé films see Richard Abel, *The Ciné Goes to Town: 1896–1914* (Berkeley: University of California Press, 1994), 130.

56 The U.S. census for 1910 and 1920 (as well as later) provides details about Colorado's residence in San Juan. NARA/Ancestry.com, 1910 U.S. Census, San Juan, Puerto Rico, Roll: T624-1778; NARA/Ancestry.com, 1920 U.S. Census, San Juan, Puerto Rico, Roll: T625-2069.

57 Francisco Scarano, "The Jíbaro Masquerade and the Subaltern Politics of Creole Identity Formation in Puerto Rico, 1745–1823," *American Historical Review* 101, no. 4 (1996): 1404.

58 Scarano, "The Jíbaro Masquerade and the Subaltern Politics of Creole Identity Formation in Puerto Rico, 1745–1823," 1430.

59 Ortiz Jiménez, "40 años de cinematografía puertorriqueña," 42.

60 For separation from Capella see NARA/Ancestry.com, 1920 U.S. Census, San Juan, Puerto Rico, Roll: T625-2069; for divorce and new marriage see NARA/Ancestry.com, 1930 U.S. Census, San Juan, Puerto Rico, Roll: 2661.

61 Homi K. Bhabha, "DissemiNation: Time, Narrative, and the Margins of the Modern Nation," in *Nation and Narration*, ed. Homi K. Bhabha (New York: Routledge,1990), 300.

62 Carlos Pabón, *Nación postmortem: Ensayos sobre los tiempos de insoportable ambigüedad* (San Juan: Ediciones Callejón, 2003), 38.

63 For more on Operation Serenity: Soraya Serra Collazo, *Explorando la Operación Serenidad* (San Juan: Editorial de la Fundación Luis Muñoz Marín, 2011).

Chapter 4 In the Company of the Elites

1 M. Román, Advertisement, *Juan Bobo*, July 1, 1916, 15; "Espectáculos," *El mundo* (San Juan), September 6, 1919, n.p.

2 I refer to the Tropical Film Company as the first indisputably "native" film company because, although Colorado's Cine Puerto Rico Company was the first to incorporate in Puerto Rico, Colorado's nationality is somewhat ambiguous, as discussed in the previous chapter. By contrast, Canales and Lloréns were born on the island and are universally recognized as Puerto Rican.

3 Lys Amencio, "Notas cinematográficas," *Juan Bobo*, February 24, 1917, 29.

4 1910 U.S. Census, U.S. National Archives and Records Administration, available by individual subscription to the genealogical databases of Ancestry.com (henceforth NARA/Ancestry.com).

5 Cine Luna, Advertisement, *La democracia*, December 7, 1916, 8.

6 Tropical Film Company, Advertisement, *Juan Bobo*, December 23, 1916, 28. All translations from the original Spanish are my own.

7 As noted in chapter 1, the Grito de Lares was a failed revolt against the Spanish government in 1868, in which the town of Lares was proclaimed the Republic of Puerto Rico for a few hours.

8 "El arte de la cinematografía en Puerto Rico," *Gráfico*, August 9, 1913, 21.

9 Joaquín García Morales, *Breve Historia del cine puertorriqueño* (San Juan: Cinegráfica, 1984), 16.

10 Joaquín García Morales, "Puerto Rico: Towards a National Cinema," *Sargasso* 8 (1992): 74.

11 García Morales, *Breve Historia*, 5.

12 Juan Ortiz Jiménez, "40 años de cinematografía puertorriqueña," *Puerto Rico ilustrado* (San Juan), February 16, 1952, 35.

13 Ortiz Jiménez, 42.

14 Roberto Ramos Perea, *Cinelibre* (San Juan: Editions Le Provincial, 2008), 3.

15 Ramos Perea, *Cinelibre*, 7.

16 Ramos Perea, 5.

17 Amencio, "Notas cinematográficas," 30; Tropical Film Company, December 23, 1916, 28.

18 Arcadio Díaz Quiñones, Preface to *Luis Lloréns Torres: Antología, verso y prosa*, by Luis Lloréns Torres (San Juan: Ediciones Huracán, 1996), 9.

19 An article in the *New York Times* (April 26, 1916, p. 11) states that *United States Marines under Fire in Haiti* had a private showing for high-ranking military officials, signaling that the U.S. military sanctioned the film. Pryer continued to work for the U.S. military, making the recruitment film *The Peacemakers* (1916), and eventually in 1935 becoming the U.S. consul to Haiti. On *The Peacemakers* see U.S. Marine Corps, "'Reel' Recruiting," *Recruiter's Bulletin* November 1916: 12. For information about Pryer's role as consul, see "The Foreign Service," *New York Times*, March 31, 1935: N10.

20 NARA/Ancestry.com, U.S. World War I Draft Registration Cards, 1917–1918, Roll: 2022240.

21 NARA/Ancestry.com, *New York, Passenger Lists, 1820–1957*, Microfilm Serial:

T715; Microfilm Roll: 2444; NARA/Ancestry.com, *New York, Passenger Lists, 1820–1957*, Microfilm Serial: T715; Microfilm Roll: 2420.

22 NARA/Ancestry.com, 1910 U.S. Census, Roll: T624_1027; NARA/Ancestry.com, World War I Draft Registration Card, Roll: 2022240.

23 See note 19.

24 NARA/Ancestry.com, *Passport Applications, January 2, 1906–March 31, 1925*, Collection Number: ARC Identifier 583830/MLR Number A1 534; "New Reel Photographer Makes Sound Pictures in City," *Daily News* (St. Thomas, U.S. Virgin Islands), July 11, 1933, 1.

25 American Film Institute, *Following the Flag in Mexico*, Accessed January 23, 2014, http://www.afi.com/members/catalog/DetailView.aspx?s=&Movie=1854.

26 American Film Institute, *Marines under Fire in Haiti*, Accessed January 23, 2014, http://www.afi.com/members/catalog/DetailView.aspx?s=&Movie=14405.

27 "Marines in Haiti in Film," *New York Times*, April 26, 1916, 11; "Uncle Sam Planning Movie Campaign for Recruiting Marines," *Salt Lake Telegram*, August 26, 1916, 9.

28 Cinemovida Entertainment Inc., "Biografías," *Cinemovida*, July 2, 2011, http://www.cinemovida.net/historia_del_cine_en_puerto_rico/biografias.

29 December 6, 1916, New York Ship's arrival records, available from NARA/Ancestry.com, *New York, Passenger Lists, 1820–1957*, Microfilm Serial: T715; Microfilm Roll: 2507.

30 For Colorado see: S.S. Caracas ship's manifest, December 16, 1916, NARA/Ancestry.com, *Passenger and Crew List of Vessels Arriving at New York, New York, 1897–1957*, Microfilm T715; for Pryer see: Emergency Passport Application, 8 September 1919, NARA/Ancestry.com, *Emergency Passport Applications Argentina through Venezuela, 1906–1925*, ARC Identifier 1244183/MLR Number A1 544.

31 Amencio, "Notas cinematográficas," 29.

32 Tropical Film Company, December 23, 1916, 28.

33 Arcadio Díaz Quiñones, Introduction to *Luis Lloréns Torres: Antología, verso y prosa* by Luis Lloréns Torres (San Juan: Ediciones Huracán, 1996), 30.

34 Lys Amencio is probably Nemesio Canales's (or possibly Luis Lloréns's) pseudonym. I come to this conclusion because the two writers were the main contributors to this magazine, and the name is very strange and unlike any Puerto Rican name, in addition to having all the letters necessary to be an anagram for Canales's given name. Amencio, "Notas Cinematográficas," 29.

35 Amencio, "Notas Cinematográficas."

36 Luis Trelles Plazaola, *Ante el lente extranjero: Puerto Rico visto por cineastas de afuera* (San Juan: Editorial de la Universidad de Puerto Rico, 2000), 2.

37 Don Panchito, "La estética en el cine," *Juan Bobo*, July 8, 1916, 5.

38 To my knowledge, no study of early film audiences in Puerto Rico exists to date. I am extrapolating the trends seen in the United States to the Puerto Rican case. However, the fact that the writers of *Juan Bobo* (as seen above) describe films as "vulgar" suggests that the early low cultural status of films observed in the United States did apply at least in part in Puerto Rico. For a discussion of early American film audiences, see, for example, Steven J. Ross, *Working-Class Hollywood: Silent Film and the Shaping of Class in America* (Princeton: Princeton University Press, 1998), 15–16; J. A. Lindstrom, "Where Development Has Just Begun: Nickelodeon Location, Moving Picture Audiences, and Neighborhood Development in

Chicago," in *American Cinema's Transitional Era: Audiences, Institutions, Practices*, ed. Charlie Keil and Shelley Stamp (Berkeley: University of California Press, 2004), 217–238.

39 The Union Party's main focus was to repeal the Foraker Law (which postulated that local officials would be appointed by the U.S. president) with the purpose of gaining more control over local politics by creating a local government elected by Puerto Ricans. Other notable members of the Union Party (Partido Unión) were Luis Muñoz Rivera, José de Diego, Rosendo Matienzo Cintrón, Manuel Zeno Gandía, and Antonio R. Barceló, among others. Fernando Picó, *Historia General de Puerto Rico* (San Juan: Ediciones Huracán, 1986), 235–236.

40 Servando Montaña Peláez, Preface to *Antología de Nemesio Canales* by Nemesio Canales (San Juan: Editorial de la Universidad de Puerto Rico, 2000), 6.

41 César Borgia, "El secretario y los cines," *Juan Bobo*, April 1, 1916. It is worth noting that Martín Travieso was also a member of the Union Party. Also, given that César (or Cesare) Borgia was a famous fifteenth-century Italian papal military leader, it is very likely that this is a penname for either Canales or Lloréns.

42 Borgia, "El secretario y los cines."

43 Francisco González, "La gran ilusión: La industria de cine en Puerto Rico," *Cuadernos del Ateneo: Serie de Cine* 2 (2000): 4.

44 "Tropical Film Company," December 23, 1916, 28.

45 Amencio, "Notas cinematográficas," 30. James Beauchamp "Champ" Clark, a Democratic representative from Missouri and speaker of the U.S. House of Representatives from 1911 to 1919, was an outspoken supporter of Manifest Destiny and the acquisition of former Spanish colonies following the Spanish-American War.

46 Amencio, "Notas cinematográficas."

47 Nemesio Canales, "Querido Mr. Wilson," in *Antología de Nemesio Canales*, ed. Servando Montaña Peláez (San Juan: Editorial de la Universidad de Puerto Rico, 2000), 140.

48 "De Puerto Rico," *Cine mundial*, May 1917, 245.

49 García Morales, "Towards," 71.

50 "El arte de la cinematografía en Puerto Rico," 21.

51 Silvia Alvarez Curbelo, "A Passion for Film," in *Idilio tropical: La aventura del cine puertorriqueño* (San Juan: Banco Popular, 1994), 3.

52 Alvarez, "A Passion for Film," 5.

53 Cine Luna, Advertisement, *La democracia*, December 7, 1916, 8.

54 Picó, *Historia General de Puerto Rico*, 235.

55 Cine Luna, Advertisement, 8.

56 The right to have a local Congress was granted the following year (1917) under the Jones Act.

57 For a discussion on silent film speed see Richard Koszarski, *An Evening's Entertainment: The Age of the Silent Feature Picture, 1915–1928* (Berkeley: University of California Press, 1994), 56.

58 "Un gran acontecimiento," *La correspondencia* (San Juan), December 8, 1916, 2.

59 "Éxito de la cinematografía," *La democracia* (San Juan), September 25, 1916, 8.

60 "La semana," *Juan Bobo*, December 16, 1916.

61 "Un gran acontecimiento," 2.

62 "Un gran acontecimiento."

63 “Un gran acontecimiento.”

64 Amencio, “Notas Cinematográficas,” 29. The title literally means “Dove of the hill”; however, Paloma is a woman’s name and del Monte is a surname, so the title probably referred metaphorically to the main character’s nature.

65 Amencio. Aquiles Zorda, accompanied by his wife Amelia and daughter Clara, was the director of a theatrical troupe that came on tour to Puerto Rico and was apparently recruited by the Tropical Film Company to act in its productions. However, the Zordas did not fully settle in Puerto Rico, as one can find references to the family appearing in the theaters of Santo Domingo, Dominican Republic, in the 1920s. Margarita Vallejo de Paredes and Lilia Portalatín Sosa, *Antología literaria dominicana: Teatro* (Santo Domingo: Instituto tecnológico de Santo Domingo, 1981), 20.

66 Amencio, “Notas cinematográficas,” 30.

67 Lys Amencio, “Lloréns Torres y Paloma del monte,” *Juan Bobo*, February 10, 1917, 14.

68 “Gabriel Tejel,” *Juan Bobo*, March 3, 1917, 25.

69 “Gabriel Tejel.”

70 Alvarez Curbelo, “A Passion for Film,” 2.

71 Amencio, “Notas cinematográficas,” 29.

72 Amencio, 30.

73 Paula Amad, “Between the ‘Familiar Text’ and the ‘Book of the World’: Touring the Ambivalent Context of Travel Film,” in *Virtual Voyages: Cinema and Travel*, ed. Jeffrey Ruoff (Durham, Duke University Press, 2006), 105.

74 Fredrick B. Pike, *The United States and Latin America: Myths and Stereotypes of Civilization and Nature* (Austin: University of Texas Press, 1992), 188.

75 “Rasgo jíbaro,” *Juan Bobo*, March 3, 1917, 25.

76 “Rasgo jíbaro.”

77 “Rasgo íbaro.” The jíbaro’s dialogue reads, “Agualde un momento compae; es de veldá o de ajugando?”

78 Roberto Cofresí (1791–1825) was a Puerto Rican pirate born in the town of Cabo Rojo of an Austrian father (Franz von Kupferschein) and a Puerto Rican mother (María Germana Ramírez de Arellano). Cofresí’s importance in the Puerto Rican national myth stems from the belief that as a pirate he initially targeted only U.S. ships because of a particular dislike toward that nation. Cofresí also allegedly sympathized with a separatist faction that condemned the Spanish government as oppressive. Cofresí was executed in Puerto Rico by firing squad after being captured following a fight with a U.S. vessel commanded by Captain Sloat. It is popularly believed that Cofresí’s last words were a curse on Capt. Sloat and his vessel. Roberto Fernández Valledor, *El mito de Cofresí en la narrativa antillana* (San Juan: Editorial de la Universidad de Puerto Rico, 1978).

79 Tropical Film Company, Advertisement, *Juan Bobo*, February 10, 1917.

80 Amencio, “Notas cinematográficas,” 30.

81 Amencio.

82 Ortiz Jiménez, 42.

83 Amencio, “Notas cinematográficas,” 31.

84 Amencio, 29.

85 Amencio.

86 Amencio; "Película cómica," *Juan Bobo*, March 3, 1917, 27.
87 "Película cómica," 27.
88 "Película cómica."
89 Ortiz Jiménez, 42; García Morales, *Breve Historia*, 118.
90 José Artemio Torres, "Apaga Musiú: Los primeros pasos de cine puertorriqueño," *Idilio tropical: La aventura del cine puertorriqueño*, ed. Marta Aponte Alsina (San Juan: Banco Popular, 1994), 16.
91 William Uricchio, "The First World War and the Crisis in Europe," in *The Oxford History of World Cinema*, ed. Geoffrey Nowell-Smith (New York: Oxford University Press, 1996), 62–70.
92 César J. Ayala and Rafael Bernabe, *Puerto Rico in the American Century: A History since 1898* (Chapel Hill: University of North Carolina Press, 2007), 80.
93 Ayala and Bernabe, *Puerto Rico in the American Century*, 83.
94 Osvaldo García, *Fotografías para la historia de Puerto Rico 1844–1952* (San Juan: Editorial de la Universidad de Puerto Rico, 1989), 246.

Chapter 5 Perilous Paradise

1 María E. Ordóñez, "La ciudad y los cines," *Cinema*, January 7, 1923, 1.
2 Roy Armes, *Third World Filmmaking and the West* (Berkeley: University of California Press, 1987), 47.
3 *Aloma of the South Seas* (Famous Players-Lasky/Paramount, Dir. Maurice Tourneur) was the top grossing film made in the United States in 1926, earning three million dollars in revenue. Terry Christensen and Peter J. Haas, *Projecting Politics: Political Messages in American Film* (New York: M.E. Sharpe, 2005), 326.
4 Andrew Higson, "The Limiting Imagination of National Cinema," in *Cinema and Nation*, ed. Mette Hjort and Scott MacKenzie (London: Routledge, 2000), 69.
5 Higson, "The Limiting Imagination of National Cinema."
6 Jacqueline Najuma Stewart, *Migrating to the Movies: Cinema and Black Urban Modernity* (Berkeley: University of California Press, 2005), 25.
7 On U.S.–Latin America diplomacy in the 1920s and 1930s, see Thomas S. Skidmore and Peter H. Smith, *Modern Latin America* (New York: Oxford University Press, 2005) and Dennis Merrill, *Negotiating Paradise: U.S Tourism and Empire in Twentieth-Century Latin America* (Chapel Hill: University of North Carolina Press, 2009).
8 Skidmore and Smith, *Modern Latin America*, 406.
9 Skidmore and Smith.
10 John Charles Chasteen, *Born in Blood and Fire: A Concise History of Latin America* (New York: W. W. Norton and Company, 2006), 206.
11 Theodore Roosevelt, "Puerto Rico: Our Link with Latin America," *Foreign Affairs* 12, no. 2 (1934): 280.
12 Merrill, *Negotiating Paradise*, 31.
13 Philip Swanson, "Going Down on Good Neighbours: Imagining América in Hollywood Movies of the 1930s and 1940s (*Flying Down to Rio* and *Down Argentine Way*)," *Bulletin of Latin American Research* 29, no. 1 (2010): 72.
14 American Film Institute, *The American Film Institute Catalog of Motion Pictures Produced in the United State: Feature Films, 1911–1920* (New York: Bowker, 1971), 369.

15 For more on Theda Bara as "vamp" see, Gaylyn Studlar, "Theda Bara: Orientalism, Sexual Anarchy, and the Jewish Star," in *Flickers of Desire: Movie Stars of the 1910s*, ed. Jennifer M. Bean (New Brunswick, NJ: Rutgers University Press, 2011), 113–136.

16 The Transvaal, though controlled by the English after 1877, was populated primarily by Boers (Dutch Settlers) as well as local African peoples. In 1880 the Boers rebelled against the English government and by 1881 successfully achieved independence (along with the Orange Free State) through the start of the Second Anglo-Boer War in 1899. For more on the Anglo-Boer Wars, see Martin Meredith, *Diamonds, Gold and War: The British, the Boers, and the Making of South Africa* (New York: Public Affairs, 2007).

17 The novel's critique of the Boers can be appreciated in Bessie's declarations, when she says, "I am sick to death of hearing about the Boers and all their got-up talk. I know what it is; it is just an excuse for them to go away from their farms and wives and children and idle about at these great meetings, and drink 'square-face' with their mouths full of big words," and "I don't like your going at all among all those wild Boers. You are an English officer, and if they find you out they will shoot you. You don't know what brutes some of them are when they think it safe to be so." The author also criticizes the British's final withdrawal from the conflict as represented in the novel, when Bessie's Uncle Silas declares, "This morning I would have said that my country would avenge me; I cannot say that now, for England has deserted us, and I have no country." J. Ridder Haggard, *Jess* (N.P.: n.p., 1887), *Project Gutenberg*, Web. June 10, 2013, http://www.gutenberg.org/files/5898/5898-h/5898-h.htm.

18 "New Theda Bara Drama Four Days at Strand," *Atlanta Constitution*, May 20, 1917, C6.

19 American Film Institute, Catalog, 369; "Heart and Soul," *Variety*, May 25, 1917, 22; "New Theda Bara Drama Four Days at Strand." C6; "Coming to the Theaters," *Washington Post*, July 5, 1917, 9.

20 "Heart and Soul," 22.

21 "Photoplays," *Indianapolis Star*, November 5, 1917, 8. My emphasis.

22 Studlar, "Theda Bara," 118.

23 "Heart and Soul," 22.

24 Jorge Duany, *The Puerto Rican Nation on the Move: Identities on the Island and in the United States* (Chapel Hill: University of North Carolina Press, 2002), 54.

25 César J. Ayala and Rafael Bernabe, *Puerto Rico in the American Century: A History Since 1898* (Chapel Hill: University of North Carolina Press, 2007), 32.

26 I do not mean to imply that the "nonwhite" population in Puerto Rico was minimal. Instead, I wish to suggest that had the whole Puerto Rican population been "nonwhite," the colonization process would have taken a different route, perhaps more akin to what happened in the Philippines.

27 Juan F. Perea, "Fulfilling Manifest Destiny: Conquest, Race, and the *Insular Cases*," in *Foreign in a Domestic Sense: Puerto Rico, American Expansion, and the Constitution*, ed. Christina Duffy Burnett and Burke Marshall (Durham: Duke University Press, 2001), 160.

28 "Forty Thousand Babies Die Daily," *El Paso Herald*, September 25, 1912, 7.

29 "Lazy Bug Gets Porto Ricans," *Detroit Free Press*, March 7, 1920, C5; "Fighting the Porto Rican Microbe of Laziness," *Washington Times*, August 7, 1904, 7.

30 B. Yorkton Hogg, "General Wood's Future," *New York Tribune*, July 11, 1920, II.8.
31 Studlar, "Theda Bara," 128.
32 On the studio location, see "Four New Fox Films Are Now Announced," *Baltimore Sun*, August 11, 1918, CA11; on the film's length, see "Virginia Pearson Tonight," *Bemidji Daily Pioneer* (Minn.), August 24, 1918, 3.
33 "The Liar," *Variety*, September 13, 1918, 44.
34 "The Liar."
35 Ann Laura Stoler, "Making Empire Respectable: The Politics of Race and Sexual Morality in Twentieth-Century Colonial Cultures," in *Dangerous Liaisons: Gender, Nation, and Postcolonial Perspectives*, ed. Anne McClintock, Aamir Mufti, and Ella Shohat (Minneapolis: University of Minnesota Press, 1997), 345.
36 Stoler, "Making Empire Respectable."
37 Stoler.
38 Stuart Hall, "Cultural Identity and Cinematic Representation," *Framework* 36 (1989), 76.
39 Vega does not offer the name of the film but based on the date of his narrative, which takes place during 1917–1918, he must be referring to one of these two films (the only two from these years to feature Puerto Rico as their setting). Bernardo Vega, *Memoir of Bernardo Vega: A Contribution to the History of the Puerto Rican Community in New York* (New York: Monthly Review Press, 1984), 33–34.
40 Duany, *The Puerto Rican Nation on the Move*, 89.
41 Ayala and Bernabe, *Puerto Rico in the American Century*, 77–79.
42 Douglas Gomery, "The Rise of Hollywood," in *The Oxford History of World Cinema*, ed. Geoffrey Nowell-Smith (New York: Oxford University Press, 1996), 43–45.
43 "Puerto Rico ofrece un gran campo para el cinematógrafo," *El mundo* (San Juan), September 8, 1919, 3. All translations from the original Spanish are my own unless otherwise noted.
44 "Puerto Rico ofrece un gran campo para el cinematógrafo."
45 On the Mastercraft company, see Anthony Slide, *American Racist: The Life and Films of Thomas Dixon* (Lexington: University Press of Kentucky, 2004), 124. On Farnsworth's work as a travel lecturer, see "Farnsworth Travel Talks," *Washington Times*, January 8, 1911, 9; "Farnsworth's Lectures," *New York Tribune*, March 5, 1911, C6; "Ex-king Kleagle of Klan in Maine Dead," *Boston Daily Globe*, March 15, 1926, A3.
46 "Ex-king Kleagle of Klan in Maine Dead," A3.
47 "Ex-king Kleagle of Klan in Maine Dead," A3.; "Dead on Stage," *Boston Daily Globe*, May 17, 1901, 1.
48 "F. E. Farnsworth, Ex-Kleagle, Dies," *Boston Daily Globe*, March 16, 1926, 11.
49 Slide, *American Racist*, 126.
50 "Ex-king Kleagle of Klan in Maine Dead," A3.
51 "King Kleagle of Maine Quits," *Boston Daily Globe*, April 25, 1924, 14.
52 "King Kleagle of Maine Quits," 14.
53 "Puerto Rico ofrece un gran campo para el cinematógrafo," 3.
54 "Farnsworth on Panama," *Washington Post*, January 28, 1911, 3; "Tells of Canal Zone," *Boston Daily Globe*, February 18, 1911, 4. U.S. National Archives, available via Ancestry.com [database on-line]. Provo, UT, USA: Ancestry.com Operations, Inc.,

2010 (henceforth NARA/Ancestry.com), *New York Passengers List 1820–1957*; Microfilm Serial: T715; Roll: 1116. NARA/Ancestry.com, *New York Passengers List 1820–1957*; Microfilm Serial: T715; Roll: 1422.

55 A "cuerda" measures 3,930.39 square meters, an acre measures 4,046.856 square meters. "Puerto Rico ofrece un gran campo para el cinematógrafo," 3.

56 "Porto Rico Is Ideal for Movie Studios," *Washington Herald*, June 1, 1919, 7; "Porto Rico Future Movie Studio Home," *Bisbee Daily Review* (Ariz.), June 1, 1919, 6.

57 "Industria que beneficiará grandemente a Puerto Rico," *El mundo* (San Juan), October 11, 1919, 3.

58 "Industria que beneficiará grandemente a Puerto Rico," 3.

59 Jesús M. Amadeo, "La cinematografía en Puerto Rico, el patriotismo y el dólar: Asunto de dignidad," *El mundo* (San Juan), October 10, 1919, 10.

60 Amadeo, "La cinematografía en Puerto Rico, el patriotismo y el dólar."

61 "La Porto Rico Photoplays, Inc," *Cine mundial*, January 1921, 85; "Industria que beneficiará grandemente a Puerto Rico," 3.

62 "El estudio cinematográfico se abrirá en breve," *El mundo* (San Juan), September 4, 1920, 1.

63 "El estudio cinematográfico se abrirá en breve."

64 "Puerto Rico ofrece un gran campo para el cinematógrafo," 3; "El estudio cinematográfico se abrirá en breve," 1.

65 According to the American Film Institute's film catalog the film was based on Guy McConnell's short story "Peaks of Gold," and it consisted of five reels (running approximately 60 minutes). American Film Institute, "Tropical Love," accessed May 17, 2013, http://www.afi.com/members/catalog/DetailView.aspx?s=&Movie=12852.

66 Film historian Anthony Slide reports that Reginald Barker, the director of the sole film production (*The One Woman*) of the Mastercraft production company, of which Farnsworth was president, had "previously associated with producer Thomas H. Ince" during Barker's years at the New York Motion Pictures Company. Especially given Farnsworth's evident drive to make show business connections, he may have parlayed his acquaintance with Barker into an introduction to Thomas H. Ince or perhaps met or at least known of his brother Ralph and that man's own interest in moviemaking. See Anthony Slide, *Silent Players: A Biographical and Autobiographical Study of 100 Silent Film Actors and Actresses* (Lexington: University Press of Kentucky, 2002), 124.

67 I have found little information regarding Playgoers, but, according to the American Film Institute, the company produced eight films in 1921–1922. I should note that no Playgoers director or actor worked in more than one production, suggesting that the firm did not rely on star popularity as attraction to their product. American Film Institute, "Playgoers Pictures," accessed May 17, 2013, http://www.afi.com/members/catalog/SearchResult.aspx?s=&Type=PR&ID=5549.

68 "La Porto Rico Photoplays, Inc," *Cine mundial*, January 1921, 8.

69 For evidence of the film's U.S. promotion, see, "Tropical Love at the Elko Theater Saturday," *Bemidji Daily Pioneer* (Minn.), September 8, 1922, 4; "Tropical Love," *Bisbee Daily Review* (Ariz.), July 23, 1922, 6. On the film's circulation in India, see "Bombay Amusements," *Times of India*, December 23, 1922, 23.

70 New York State Archives, *Tropical Love* Motion Picture Case File, File-Box# 16897-2839.

71 "Amor Tropical," *El mundo* (San Juan), October 25, 1921, 5.
72 Obdulia C. de Lázaro, "Amor Tropical," *La correspondencia* (San Juan), October 24, 1921, 1.
73 "Amor Tropical," *El mundo* (San Juan), October 25, 1921: 5; "Amor Tropical," *La correspondencia* (San Juan), October 25, 1921, 8.
74 "Amor Tropical," *La correspondencia* (San Juan), October 25, 1921, 8.
75 De Lázaro, 1; "Amor Tropical," *El mundo* (San Juan), October 27, 1921, 3.
76 De Lázaro, 1; "Amor tropical," 3.
77 De Lázaro, 1; "Amor tropical," 3.
78 "Amor Tropical," *El mundo* (San Juan), October 27, 1921, 3; De Lázaro, 1.
79 Although Ruth Clifford's character is named Rosario (a "Latina-sounding" name), as the plot develops it emerges that she is American. American Film Institute, "Tropical Love," accessed May 17, 2013, http://www.afi.com/members/catalog/DetailView.aspx?s=&Movie=12852.
80 American Film Institute, "Tropical Love"; "Tropical Love," *Pullman Herald* (Washington), March 24, 1922, 2.
81 "Tropical Love at the Elko Theater Saturday," *Bemidji Daily Pioneer* (Minnesota), September 8, 1922, 4.
82 "Tropical Love," *Coconino Sun* (Ariz.), January 13, 1922, 2.
83 "Tropical Love," *Pullman Herald* (Wash. State), March 24, 1922, 2.
84 American Film Institute, "Tropical Love."
85 "La casa 'Pathé' ha hecho proposiciones a la 'Photoplays,'" *El mundo* (San Juan), October 28, 1921, 6.
86 NARA/Ancestry.com, *New York Passengers List 1820–1957, December 27, 1922*, Microfilm Serial: T715; Roll: 3236. The Statue of Liberty–Ellis Island Foundation, *San Lorenzo Ship Manifest*, March 28, 1921, Manifest Line: 0025;The Statue of Liberty–Ellis Island Foundation, *San Lorenzo Ship Manifest*, April 10, 1922, Manifest Line: 0026; "King Kleagle of Maine Quits," *Boston Daily Globe*, April 25, 1924, 14.
87 "Inside Stuff- Pictures," *Variety*, February 15, 1950, 16.
88 Juan Ortiz Jiménez, "40 años de cinematografía puertorriqueña," *Puerto Rico ilustrado,* February 23, 1952, 36.
89 "Ruth Clifford Demanda," *Cine mundo,* August 1921, 572. Worth mentioning, Clifford later became (1944–1952) the voice of Disney's "Minnie Mouse."
90 "Ruth Clifford Demanda."
91 "La casa Pathé ha hecho proposiciones a la Photoplays," 6.
92 David Harley Mould, *American Newsfilm, 1914–1919: The Unexposed War* (New York: Garland Publishing, 1983), 38; Louis Pizzitola, *Hearst over Hollywood: Power, Passion, and Propaganda in the Movies* (New York: Columbia University Press, 2002), 102.
93 "Blackton Again Heads Trade Board," *Moving Picture World*, February 26, 1916, 1275; W. H. Leffingwell, *Making the Office Pay* (New York: A. W. Shaw Company, 1918), 372; "Edward A. MacManus Makes Industrial Film," *Printers' Ink*, April 3, 1919, 170.
94 American Film Institute, "Edward A. MacManus," accessed June 23, 2013, http://www.afi.com/members/catalog/SearchResult.aspx?s=&retailCheck=&Type=PN&CatID=DATABIN_PRODUCER&ID=45110&AN_ID=&searchedFor=Edward_A._MacManus_.
95 "Shadows on the Screen," *New York Tribune*, April 23, 1922, 4; "Porto Rican Films," *Film*

Daily, April 15, 1922, 1. On Pathé's relationship to Associated Exhibitors see, "Brunet Promises Broader Pathé Aims," *Motion Picture News*, November 22, 1919, 3724.

96 "Porto Rican Films," 1.

97 "Porto Rican Films," 1.

98 "Cine Puerto Rico," *La correspondencia* (San Juan), November 18, 1922, 1; "Cine Puerto Rico," *La democracia* (San Juan), November 18, 1922, 1.

99 "Rare Art Treasure Used in Film Made in Porto Rico," *Washington Post*, February 4, 1923, 60.

100 "Last Night's Openings at Local Theaters," *Washington Post*, February 6, 1923, 9.

101 "May Allison Comes to the America in Latest Film Play," *Colorado Springs Gazette*, December 31, 1922, 31.

102 American Film Institute, "The Woman Who Fooled Herself," accessed May 25, 2013, http://www.afi.com/members/catalog/DetailView.aspx?s=&Movie=13447.

103 "Northwestern District," *Baltimore Sun*, January 21, 1923, MA10.

104 Studlar, "Theda Bara," 121.

105 Ana M. López, "Are All Latins from Manhattan? Hollywood, Ethnography, and Cultural Colonialism," in *Unspeakable Images: Ethnicity and the American Cinema*, ed. Lester D. Friedman (Urbana: University of Illinois Press, 1991), 404–424.

106 American Film Institute, "The Lost Battalion," accessed July 2, 2013, http://www.afi.com/members/catalog/DetailView.aspx?s=&Movie=2031.

107 American Film Institute, "Charles A. Logue," accessed July 2, 2013, http://www.afi.com/members/catalog/SearchResult.aspx?s=&TBL=PN&Type=WP&ID=190293&pName=%20%20Charles%20A.%20Logue.

108 Mae Tinée, "Where Rodolf Loses Some of His Laurels," *Chicago Daily Tribune*, July 14, 1923, 19.

109 "Sheiks Again Busy in 'Tents of Allah,'" *Los Angeles Times*, April 3, 1923, II11.

110 American Film Institute, "The Tents of Allah," accessed November 18, 2011, http://www.afi.com/members/catalog/DetailView.aspx?s=&Movie=12579.

111 "El hijo del desierto," Advertisement, *La democracia* (San Juan), January 18, 1923, 8; "El hijo del desierto," Advertisement, *El mundo* (San Juan), January 20, 1923, 9.

112 American Film Institute, "The Tents of Allah."

113 New York State Archives, *The Tent of Allah* Motion Picture Case File, File-Box # 15788-2816.

114 "El hijo del desierto," *La democracia* (San Juan), January 18, 1923, 8; "El hijo del desierto," *El mundo* (San Juan), January 20, 1923, 9.

115 "El hijo del desierto," *Cinema* (San Juan), January 21, 1923.

116 Despite sharing last names with famous politician Luis Muñoz Rivera, articles make no references to a family relation between the actress, who was possibly a child, and the politician. As to the unexpected name of Mary Thurman for a Spanish language reviewer in Puerto Rico, Rob King describes the critic as the daughter of wealthy Danish Mormons living in Utah who had been hired by the Keystone Film Company as a comedic actress in 1916. That biography, however, does not account for her presence or engagement in film journalism on the island. Rob King, *The Fun Factory: The Keystone Film Company and the Emergence of Mass Culture* (Berkeley: University of California Press, 2008), 235.

117 "El hijo del desierto," *Cinema* (San Juan), January 21, 1923.

118 Ruth Vasey, *The World According to Hollywood, 1918–1939* (Madison: University of Wisconsin Press, 1997), 163.
119 "'Tents of Allah' Made in Tropics," *Los Angeles Times*, March 29, 1923, I17.
120 "Heat in Porto Rico Nearly Ruins Films for Photoplay," *Boston Daily Globe*, July 22, 1923, 54.
121 New York State Archives, *Picturesque Porto Rico* Motion Picture Case File, File-Box # 11266-2742.
122 "Rialto," *La correspondencia* (San Juan), January 27, 1923, 1.
123 "Porto Rico Bidding," *Variety*, July 12, 1923, 22.
124 Slide, *American Racist*, 163.
125 Mordaunt Hall, "Farce-Comedy Serves as Antidote to Adroitly Directed Melodrama," *New York Times*, May 23, 1926, X2.
126 R. E. Sherwood, "The Silent Drama," *Life*, June 3, 1926, 26; "In the Wake of the Camera," *Los Angeles Times*, November 15, 1925, J4.
127 American Film Institute, *Catalog of Motion Pictures Produced in the United States: Feature Films 1921–1930* (New York: Bowker, 1971), 16. Though a 1941 Paramount production with the same title also exists (and copies are available) based on the 1926 description the two films appear to be significantly different since in the 1941 version there is only one American character (in a secondary role), and the other characters appear to be Samoans or other Pacific Islanders.
128 Duany, *The Puerto Rican Nation on the Move*, 50–54.
129 "Trees Rain Cocoanuts," *Washington Post*, November 14, 1926, F5.
130 Stewart, *Migrating to the Movies*, 72.
131 Julanne Johnston, "Flashes," *Los Angeles Times*, December 5, 1925, 7.
132 "Fresh from the Busy Film Mart," *Los Angeles Times*, December 20, 1925, I3.
133 "Quince portorriqueñas trabajaran con Gilda Gray," *El mundo* (San Juan), October 13, 1925, 2.
134 "Gilda Departs," *Los Angeles Times*, October 11, 1925, 27.
135 "Cataño la Meca de los curiosos," *El mundo* (San Juan), October 24, 1925, 16.
136 "Un grupo de notables artistas de la pantalla se encuentra aquí para hacer una admirable producción cinematográfica," *La democracia* (San Juan), October 14, 1925, 1; "Los artistas cinematográficos que llegaron ayer en el 'Puerto Rico' a filmar una película," *La correspondencia* (San Juan), October 14, 1925, 2.
137 "Un grupo de notables artistas," 1.
138 Hall, "Farce-Comedy Serves as Antidote, X2; "Gilda Gray Film Feature At Palace," *Washington Post*, November 14, 1926, F1. For *Aloma*'s earnings see note 2.
139 R. E. Sherwood, "Aloma of the South Seas," *Life*, June 3, 1926, 26.
140 Harriet Hyman Alonso, *Robert E. Sherwood: The Playwright in Peace and War* (Amherst: University of Massachusetts Press, 2007), 75.
141 Sherwood, "Aloma," 26.
142 Sherwood, "Aloma," 26.
143 "Inside Stuff-Pictures," 16.
144 "El cine en el gobierno," *Cinema*, January 21, 1923, 1.
145 Francisco A. Scarano, *Puerto Rico Cinco Siglos de Historia* (San Juan: McGraw-Hill, 2008), 488.
146 "El cine en el gobierno," 1.
147 "Monte Carlo y Real," *La correspondencia* (San Juan), November 7, 1922.

Chapter 6 Making the Nation Profitable

1 César J. Ayala and Rafael Bernabe, *Puerto Rico in the American Century: A History since 1898* (Chapel Hill: University of North Carolina Press, 2007), 96–97; James L Dietz, *Economic History of Puerto Rico: Institutional Change and Capitalist Development* (Princeton, NJ: Princeton University Press, 1986), 139.

2 Ayala and Bernabe, *Puerto Rico in the American Century*, 97.

3 Donald Crafton, *The Talkies: American Cinema's Transition to Sound, 1926–1931* (Berkeley: University of California Press, 1999), 265, 277, and 517.

4 Crafton, *The Talkies*, 425.

5 Ginette Vincendeau, "Hollywood Babel: The Coming of Sound and the Multiple Language Version," in *The Classical Hollywood Reader*, ed. Stephen Neale (New York: Routledge, 2012), 140.

6 *Acts and Resolutions of the Fourth and Fifth Special Sessions of the Twelfth Legislature of Puerto Rico and of the First Regular Session of the Thirteenth Legislature of Puerto Rico* (San Juan: Bureau of Supplies, Printing and Transportation, 1933), 704.

7 Conrado Asenjo, *Quién es quién en Puerto Rico* (San Juan: Real Hermanos, 1936), 191.

8 "La industria del cine en Puerto Rico," *Cinema* (San Juan), February 25, 1923, 1–2. All translations from the original Spanish are my own.

9 NARA, *World War I Selective Service System Draft Registration Cards, 1917–1918,* Microfilm M1509; NARA/Ancestry.com, 1920 U.S. census.

10 José Artemio Torres, "Apaga Musiú: Los primeros pasos de cine puertorriqueño," *Idilio tropical: La aventura del cine puertorriqueño*, ed. Marta Aponte Alsina (San Juan: Banco Popular, 1994), 13. Torres cites an interview with the filmmaker's widow as the source of this information. Further information gathered from the U.S. Census of 1910 and 1920 indicates that the full names of Viguié's adoptive parents are Luis Caballer (S)Otero and Virginia Arenas de Caballer (NARA/Ancestry.com, 1910 U.S. census; NARA/Ancestry.com, 1920 U.S. census).

11 *Acts and Resolutions of the Fourth and Fifth Special Sessions of the Twelfth Legislature of Puerto Rico*, 704.

12 Carl Louis Gregory, "Camera Study in the Movies," *New York Times*, October 24, 1926, X6. Gregory (1882–1951), the author of the item was himself a cinematographer and director associated most closely with the New York–based Thanhouser Company (1909–1918).

13 "Learn Photography," *New York Times*, October 10, 1915, 113; "E Brunel," *New York Times*, March 2, 1919, 38.

14 I attempted to search the records of the NY Institute of Photography but learned that the institution no longer possesses any files that predate the 1960s. An article published in *El mundo*, August 16, 1935, 4 ("Juan Emilio Viguié") declares that Viguié graduated from the "New York Institute of Photographers," operating in Columbia University, with a title of "cameraman and cinematographer," but it does not mention the year. The article also declares that he was the main cameraman for *Aloma of the South Seas*, but none of the 1925 publicity of the film mentions him has having done any camera work (only special effects). In addition, his name does not appear on the film's credits.

15 Conrado Asenjo, *Quién es quién en Puerto Rico*, 191; NARA, *World War I Selective Service System Draft Registration Cards, 1917–1918,* Microfilm M1509.

16 See for instance Harry D. Brown, "The Importance of the Studio Electrician," *American Cinematographer*, August 1922, 7.

17 The Ellis Island Foundation, "USS Philadelphia Ship Records," August 29, 1919, Manifest Line Number 0005.

18 "Un grupo de notables artistas," *La democracia* (San Juan), October 14, 1925, 1.

19 "Por esos mundos," *La correspondencia* (Madrid), July 2, 1921, 3; "Cofresí, el pirata del Caribe," *Cine mundial*, June 1921, 433. Interestingly, the Tropical Film Company had advertised the making of a film about Cofresí back in 1917. Viguié perhaps worked or saw this production and was himself inspired to work on the same subject if not even rework some of the footage available from the past production.

20 "Cofresí," 433.

21 Asenjo, *Quién es quién*, 191.

22 Marianne P. Fedunkiw, "The Rockefeller Foundation's 1925 *Malaria* Film," (presentation, Quinnipiac/Rockefeller Archive Center Workshop, November 2003). See also: Marina Dahlquist, "Unhooking the Hookworm: The Rockefeller Foundation and Mediated Health," *Rockefeller Archive Center Research Reports* (Sleepy Hollow, NY: Rockefeller Archive Center, 2012).

23 Ernest Carroll Faust, Charles A. Jones, and William A. Hoffman, "Studies on *Schistosomiasis mansoni* in Puerto Rico," *Puerto Rico Journal of Public Health and Tropical Medicine* 10, no. 2 (December 1934): 143.

24 Fox News, Advertisement, *Exhibitors Daily Review*, September 19, 1928, 4.

25 "Fox Scoops Newsreels on Hurricane Pictures," *Exhibitors Daily Review*, September 19, 1928, 2.

26 "Frank Z. Clemente," in *1940–41 International Motion Picture Almanac*, ed. Terry Ramsaye and Ernest A. Rovelstad (New York: Quigley Publishing Company, 1941), 110; "Romance Tropical," *The 1935 Film Daily Yearbook of Motion Pictures*, ed. Jack Alicoate (New York: The Film Daily, 1935), 185.

27 "Frank Z. Clemente," 110.

28 "Frank Z. Clemente," 110.

29 "Frank Z. Clemente," 110.

30 "Frank Z. Clemente," 110; Richard Koszarski, *Hollywood on the Hudson: Film and Television in New York from Griffith to Sarnoff* (New Brunswick, NJ: Rutgers University Press, 2010), 78–79.

31 "Frank Z. Clemente," 110.

32 "Frank Z. Clemente," Advertisement, *The 1936 Film Daily Yearbook*, ed. Jack Alicoate (New York: The Film Daily, 1936), 232. The RCA building, now called the GE building, is located in what is now called Rockefeller Center.

33 NARA/Ancestry.com, *New York Passenger Lists, 1820–1957*; Microfilm Serial: T715; Roll: T715_5528.

34 Carlos Carreras, "Una película portorriqueña, Romance Tropical," *El mundo* (San Juan), March 14, 1935, 4.

35 The NY State Archives houses a bilingual copy of *Romance*'s script because it had to be translated into English for the purpose of passing the New York State film licensing and censor board. New York State Archives, *Romance Tropical* Motion Picture Case File, File-Box #: 28117-324.

36 "Romance Tropical at Campoamor," *Film Daily*, October 12, 1934, 2.

37 H.T.S., "Film from Puerto Rico," *New York Times*, October 15, 1934, 20. H.T.S. were

the initials of Harry T. Smith, a *New York Times* critic in charge of foreign publications and films. Elmer Davis, *History of the New York Times 1851–1921* (New York: New York Times, 1921), 412.

38 "Reviews of the New Films: Foreign," *Film Daily*, October 16, 1934, 9.

39 "Calendar of Current Releases," *Variety*, November 6, 1934, 38; "Calendar of Current Releases," *Variety*, September 25, 1935, 37.

40 "Reviews of the New Films: Foreign," 9; H.T.S., "Film from Puerto Rico," 20.

41 Tello Casiano, "¡Pan pan . . . Vino vino!" *El Curioso* (Brooklyn), March 16, 1935, 2. (Emphasis in the original).

42 Roberto Ramos Perea, *Cinelibre* (San Juan: Editions Le Provincial, 2008), 10. (Emphasis in the original).

43 Paramount, Advertisement, *El mundo* (San Juan), March 15, 1935, 4; "Espectáculos," *El mundo* (San Juan), June 26, 1935, 4.

44 Rex (Cataño), Advertisement, *El mundo,* March 27, 1935, 5; Teatro Oliver (Arecibo), Advertisement, *El mundo* (San Juan), April 3, 1935, 4; Fox-Delicias (Ponce), Advertisement, *El mundo* (San Juan), April 4, 1935, 4; Variedades (Bayamón), Advertisement, *El mundo* (San Juan), May 4, 1935, 4.

45 Igor Kameneff, "Los últimos estrenos: *Romance tropical*," *El mundo* (San Juan), March 19, 1935, 4.

46 Rialto Theater, Advertisement, *El mundo*, March 20, 1935, 4. Eureka, Advertisement, *El mundo*, April 23, 1935, 5.

47 Carlos Carreras, "Una película portorriqueña, Romance Tropical," 4.

48 Carreras, 4.

49 S.I.S., "El cinema portorriqueño: Lo que dice el 'Times' de 'Romance Tropical,'" *El mundo* (San Juan), March 23, 1935, 6.

50 Kameneff, "Los últimos estrenos," 4.

51 Frantz Fanon, *Black Skin, White Masks* (New York: Grove Press, 1967), 152–153.

52 "Clements on Dicker for Roulien, Par Release," *Variety*, March 23, 1936, 2; "Roulien to Aid Spanish Revival," *Los Angeles Times*, March 19, 1936, 11.

53 "Frank Z. Clemente," 110.

54 Juan Ortiz Jiménez, "40 años de cinematografía puertorriqueña," *Puerto Rico ilustrado*, February 23, 1952, 37.

55 Joaquín "Kino" García, *Historia del Cine Puertorriqueño (1900–1999): Un siglo de cine en Puerto Rico* (San Juan: Editorial de la Universidad de Puerto Rico, 2000), 34–35.

56 Amy Beer, "From the Bronx to Brooklyn: Spanish-Language Movie Theaters and Their Audiences in New York City, 1930–1999," (PhD diss., Northwestern University, 2001), 8.

57 Fernando Bermejo, "Juan Emilio Viguié," *El mundo* (San Juan), August 16, 1935, 4, 10.

58 Nicolás Kanellos, *Hispanic Firsts: 500 Years of Extraordinary Achievements* (New York: Visible Ink Press, 1997), 62; "New Export Firm Will Produce in Puerto Rico," *Billboard*, March 27, 1954, 7.

59 Although Ramos is Rafael Ramos Cobián's paternal last name, and Cobián his maternal one, U.S. publications referred to him as Mr. Cobián probably because of ignorance of Spanish naming customs, although he also used Cobián as the name for the companies he established, perhaps because Cobián is a more memorable last

name than the very common Ramos (such as the cases of Marquez for García Marquez, or Lorca for García Lorca).

60 Social Security Administration/Ancestry.com, *Social Security Death Index*, Puerto Rico, Number: 581-07-5594.

61 NARA/Ancestry.com, *1910 U.S. Census*, Patillas, Puerto Rico, Roll:T624_1773.

62 "Ramos Cobian," in *The 1929 Film Daily Yearbook*, ed. Jack Alicoate (New York: The Film Daily, 1929), 1040.

63 "Acquires Major Product for Porto Rico Circuit," *Film Daily*, August 15, 1935, 2.

64 Rafael Ramos Cobián, "Nosotros no somos monopolizadores del negocio," *El mundo* (San Juan), March 15, 1935, 5.

65 "Theater Man Candidate," *Film Daily*, September 11, 1936, 14.

66 United States Democratic Party, *Official Report of the Proceedings of the Democratic National Convention, Chicago, Illinois August 13 through August 17, 1956* (Boston: Beacon Press, 1956), 75.

67 "Cobian's Spanish Plans," *Film Daily*, January 13, 1938, 3.

68 "Cobian Will Produce for Spanish Speaking Market," *Film Daily*, March 4, 1938, 1 and 8; "Of Local Origin," *New York Times*, January 14, 1938, 20.

69 Eduardo de la Vega Alfaro, "Allá en el rancho grande," in *The Cinema of Latin America*, ed. Alberto Elena and Marina Díaz López (New York: Columbia University Press, 2003), 28–33.

70 "Paramount Signs Cobian," *Motion Picture Daily*, April 21, 1938, 7; "R. Cobian to Coast Today to Start Spanish Picture," *Film Daily*, April 25, 1938, 2.

71 "Cobian Will Produce for Spanish-Speaking Markets," *Film Daily*, March 4, 1938, 1–2.

72 "Cobian to Make Spanish Pix for Para. on Coast," *Film Daily*, April 21, 1938, 2. "Mis dos amores," *Mensajero Paramount*, July 1938, 9. Although I have not been able to ascertain who José A. Miranda was, a play by the name of *Sacrificio de una madre* ran in Spain during the period of October to December of 1850. Dionisio Hidalgo, "Sacrificio de una madre," *Boletín Bibliográfico Español y Extranjero* 1, no. 20–24 (1850): 317.

73 "Cobian to Make Spanish Pix," 2; "Mis dos amores," 9.

74 New York State Archives, *Mis dos amores* Motion Picture Case File, File-Box # 39915-851.

75 Wear, "Mis dos amores," *Variety*, August 17, 1938, 23.

76 Gabriel Navarro, "Mal principio lleva la película *Mis dos amores,* con Tito Guizar de estrella," *La Prensa* (San Antonio), June 19, 1938, 10.

77 Navarro.

78 Gabriel Navarro, "Habla Tito Guizar sobre las películas en español que se hacen en Hollywood," *La prensa* (San Antonio), July 31, 1938, 2.

79 Navarro, "Mal principio lleva la película *Mis dos amores*, con Tito Guizar de Estrella."

80 Pego, "Mis dos amores," *Cine mundial,* October 1938, 512.

81 Hedda Hopper, "Hedda Hopper's Hollywood," *Los Angeles Times*, August 17, 1938, 12.

82 Philip K. Scheuer, "Producers Turning to Latin Countries," *Los Angeles Times*, August 21, 1938, C3.

83 Scheuer, "Producers Turning to Latin Countries."

84 Conde Danilo, "La premier de Mis dos amores en el Paramount," *La democracia*

(San Juan), October 8, 1938, 6; "La premier de 'Mis dos amores' en el teatro Paramount," *El mundo* (San Juan), October 6, 1938, 6.

85 "'Mis dos amores' se estrena hoy en el teatro Paramount," *El mundo* (San Juan), October 4, 1938, 6.

86 "Mis dos amores' se estrena hoy en el teatro Paramount."

87 "La premier de 'Mis dos amores' en el teatro Paramount," *El mundo* (San Juan), October 6, 1938, 6; Conde Danilo, "La premier de Mis dos amores en el Paramount," *La democracia* (San Juan), October 8, 1938, 6; Conde Danilo, "La 'premier' de 'Mis dos amores' constituyó un acontecimiento social," *La correspondencia* (San Juan), October 8, 1938, 3.

88 Conde Danilo, "La 'premier' de 'Mis dos amores' constituyó un acontecimiento social," 3.

89 "Mis dos amores," *Puerto Rico ilustrado*, October 8, 1938, 49.

90 Cándido Arreche, "Mis dos amores," *El mundo* (San Juan), October 1, 1938, 6.

91 Gabriel Navarro, "La embajada artística de México en Hollywood," *La prensa* (San Antonio), January 29, 1939, 9.

92 "Cobian to Make Four 'A's' in Spanish for 20th-Fox," *Film Daily*, August 12, 1938, 2.

93 "Cobian Signs Mexican Stars," *Film Daily*, January 27, 1939, 13. The article wrongly refers to Julian Soler as Domingo Soler and to Carmen Mora as Margarita Mora.

94 Cronista, "Hoy llegará el productor portorriqueño Ramos Cobián," *El mundo* (San Juan), September 4, 1939, 6.

95 Edna Coll, "Los hijos mandan," *Puerto Rico ilustrado*, September 2, 1939, 11 and 56.

96 I base the description of *Los hijos manadan*'s plot on a copy of the film's script housed in the archives of the New York State Motion Picture Division. According to the American Film Institute there is a surviving print of the film, but I have not been able to locate it. For the script: New York State Archives, *Los hijos mandan* Motion Picture Case File, File-Box# 37430-733. For the American Film Institute: AFI, "Los hijos mandan," accessed April 7, 2014, http://www.afi.com/members/catalog/DetailView.aspx?s=&Movie=1233.

97 American Film Institute, "Los hijos mandan," accessed April 11, 2014, http://www.afi.com/members/catalog/DetailView.aspx?s=&Movie=1233.

98 Navarro, "La embajada artística de México en Hollywood," 9; "Los hijos mandan," *El heraldo de Brownsville* (Texas), November 3, 1939, 2.

99 Navarro, "La embajada artística de México en Hollywood," 9.

100 Edna Coll, "Los hijos mandan," *Puerto Rico ilustrado*, September 2, 1939, 11 and 56; "Hoy llegará el productor portorriqueño Ramos Cobián," *El mundo* (San Juan), September 4, 1939, 6.

101 Teatro Paramount, Advertisement, *El mundo* (San Juan), September 4, 1939, 6.

102 Coll, "Los hijos mandan," 56.

103 "La nueva producción de Ramos Cobián estrenará aquí," *El mundo*, September 2, 1939, 7.

104 "Hoy llegará el productor portorriqueño Ramos Cobián," 6.

105 Emilio Escalante, "La película: Los hijos mandan," *La prensa* (San Antonio), April 9, 1939, 11.

106 Harry Waldman, *Hollywood and the Foreign Touch* (Lanham, MD: Scarecrow Press, 1996), 135–136.

107 Waldman, *Hollywood and the Foreign Touch*.

108 Waldman.
109 Waldman.
110 "Cobian to Start His Second for 20th-Fox in Three Weeks," *Film Daily*, March 9, 1939, 5.
111 "Cobian to Start."
112 Scheuer, "Producers Turning to Latin Countries," C3; "20-Fox Latin-Amer, Expansion Policy," *Film Daily*, April 20, 1939, 1 and 6.
113 Beer, "From the Bronx to Brooklyn," 57.
114 Miluka Rivera, "Blanca de Castejón," in *Legado puertorriqueño en Hollywood: Famosos y olvidados*, ed. Miluka Rivera (Burbank: Kumaras Center for the Arts & Etiquette, 2010), 59–60.
115 Although Ramos Cobián acquired the Cuban Theater company "Smith" in December 1944, he quickly sold his shares to Paramount in November 1945. Nonetheless by May 1946 he came back to Cuba to start a new theater chain. Mary Louise Blanco, "Cobian Out of Cuban Circuit," *Film Daily*, November 5, 1945, 1; "Cobian Planning New Cuban Theater Chain," *Film Daily*, May 16, 1946, 1.
116 Francisco A. Scarano, *Puerto Rico: Cinco siglos de historia* (México D.F.: McGraw Hill, 2008), 570–572. Catherine Marsh, "La negociación de la cultura en una nación sin estado: La producción cultural de la División de Educación de la Comunidad del Estado Libre Asociado de Puerto Rico (1948–1968)," (PhD diss., University of California, Berkeley, 2001), 20–23. The PRERA (Puerto Rican Emergency Relief Administration) and PRRA (Puerto Rican Relief Administration) were two New Deal programs focused on providing emergency food and housing, as well as developing infrastructure and industries in Puerto Rico.
117 Ayala and Bernabe, *Puerto Rico in the American Century*, 136–144.
118 Marsh, "La negociación de la cultura en una nación sin estado," 49–50.
119 The Archivo de Imágenes en Movimiento (Moving Images Archive) of the Archivo General de Puerto Rico (General Archive of Puerto Rico) houses 112 films produced by DIVEDCO, most of which are documentaries.

Conclusion

1 Marimar Benítez, "La década de los cincuenta: afirmación y reacción," in *Puerto Rico arte e identidad*, ed. Hermandad de artistas gráficos de Puerto Rico (San Juan: Editorial de la Universidad de Puerto Rico, 1998), 116–123; See also the catalog for the University of Puerto Rico museum exposition *Irene y Jack Delano en Puerto Rico* (San Juan: Afirmación cultural, 1981). Some of the films made by Delano, Rosskam, Doniger, and Van Dyke include *Una gota de agua* (Jack Delano and Edwin Rosskam, 1947), *Los peloteros* (Jack Delano and Edwin Rosskam, 1951), *Modesta* (Benjamin Doniger, 1955), and *El de los cabos blancos* (Willard Van Dyke, 1955), among many others.
2 Alyosha Goldstein, "The Attributes of Sovereignty: The Cold War, Colonialism, and Community Education in Puerto Rico," in *Imagining Our Americas: Towards a Transnational Frame*, ed. Sandhya Shukla, Heidi Tinsman (Durham, NC: Duke University Press, 2007), 323.
3 Jorge Duany, *The Puerto Rican Nation on the Move: Identities on the Island and in the United States* (Chapel Hill: University of North Carolina Press, 2002), 35.

4 Arjun Appadurai, *Modernity at Large: Cultural Dimensions of Globalization* (Minneapolis: University of Minnesota Press, 1996), 44.
5 Laura Isabel Serna, *Making Cinelandia: American Films and Mexican Film Culture before the Golden Age* (Durham, NC: Duke University Press, 2014), 222.
6 Philip Rosen, "Nation and Anti-Nation: Concepts of National Cinema in the 'New' Media Era," *Diaspora* 5, no. 3 (1996): 397. Emphasis in the original.

Bibliography

Books and Articles (Secondary Sources)

Abel, Richard. *The Ciné Goes to Town: 1896–1914*. Berkeley: University of California Press, 1994.

———. *Encyclopedia of Early Cinema*. New York: Routledge, 2005.

Agrait, Luis E. "Estampas del 98 en Puerto Rico." In *Un cambio de siglo 1898: España, Cuba, Puerto Rico, Filipinas y Estados Unidos*, edited by José Girón, 299–306. Oviedo, Spain: Universidad de Oviedo, 2008.

Alonso, Harriet Hyman. *Robert E. Sherwood: The Playwright in Peace and War*. Amherst: University of Massachusetts Press, 2007.

Alvarez Curbelo, Silvia. "A Passion for Film." In *Idilio tropical: La aventura del cine puertorriqueño*, 1–9. San Juan: Banco Popular, 1994.

Amad, Paula. "Between the 'Familiar Text' and the 'Book of the World': Touring the Ambivalent Context of Travel Film." In *Virtual Voyages: Cinema and Travel*, edited by Jeffrey Ruoff, 99–116. Durham, NC: Duke University Press, 2006.

American Film Institute. *Catalog of Motion Pictures Produced in the United State: Feature Films, 1911–1920*. New York: Bowker, 1971.

———. *Catalog of Motion Pictures Produced in the United States: Feature Films, 1921–1930*. New York: Bowker, 1971.

———. *Catalog of Motion Pictures Produced in the United States: Film Beginnings, 1893–1910*. New York: Bowker, 1971.

———. "Charles A. Logue." Accessed July 2, 2013. http://www.afi.com/members/catalog/SearchResult.aspx?s=&TBL=PN&Type=WP&ID=190293&pName=%20%20Charles%20A.%20Logue.

———. "The Dolorita Passion Dance." Accessed January 23, 2012. http://www.afi.com/members/catalog/DetailView.aspx?s=&Movie=41263.

———. "Edward A. MacManus." Accessed June 23, 2013. http://www.afi.com/members/catalog/SearchResult.aspx?s=&retailCheck=&Type=PN&CatID=DATABIN_PRODUCER&ID=45110&AN_ID=&searchedFor=Edward_A._MacManus_.

———. "Following the Flag in Mexico." Accessed January 23, 2014. http://www.afi.com/members/catalog/DetailView.aspx?s=&Movie=1854.

———. "Los Hijos Mandan." Accessed April 11, 2014. http://www.afi.com/members/catalog/DetailView.aspx?s=&Movie=1233.

———. "The Lost Battalion." Accessed July 2, 2013. http://www.afi.com/members/catalog/DetailView.aspx?s=&Movie=2031.

———. "Marines under Fire in Haiti." Accessed January 23, 2014. http://www.afi.com/members/catalog/DetailView.aspx?s=&Movie=14405.

———. "Playgoers Pictures." Accessed May 17, 2013. http://www.afi.com/members/catalog/SearchResult.aspx?s=&Type=PR&ID=5549.

———. "The Tents of Allah." Accessed November 18, 2011. http://www.afi.com/members/catalog/DetailView.aspx?s=&Movie=12579.

———. "Tropical Love." Accessed May 17, 2013. http://www.afi.com/members/catalog/DetailView.aspx?s=&Movie=12852.

———. "The Woman Who Fooled Herself." Accessed May 25, 2013. http://www.afi.com/members/catalog/DetailView.aspx?s=&Movie=13447.

Anderson, Benedict. *Imagined Communities*. Rev. ed. New York: Verso, 2006.

Anderson, Warwick. *Colonial Pathologies: American Tropical Medicine, Race, and Hygiene in the Philippines.* Durham, NC: Duke University Press, 2006.

Appadurai, Arjun. *Modernity at Large: Cultural Dimensions of Globalization*. Minneapolis: University of Minnesota Press, 1996.

Armes, Roy. *Third World Filmmaking and the West*. Berkeley: University of California Press, 1987.

Ayala, César J. *American Sugar Kingdom: The Plantation Economy of the Spanish Caribbean 1898–1934*. Chapel Hill: University of North Carolina Press, 1999.

Ayala, César J., and Rafael Bernabe. *Puerto Rico in the American Century: A History since 1898.* Chapel Hill: University of North Carolina Press, 2007.

Beer, Amy. "From the Bronx to Brooklyn: Spanish-Language Movie Theaters and Their Audiences in New York City, 1930–1999." PhD diss., Northwestern University, 2001.

Benítez, Marimar. "La década de los cincuenta: Afirmación y reacción." In *Puerto Rico arte e identidad*, edited by Hermandad de artistas gráficos de Puerto Rico, 116–123. San Juan: Editorial de la Universidad de Puerto Rico, 1998.

Bernier, Rose Marie. "El comienzo de los cines carpas." Cine Movida. Accessed March 4, 2013. http://cinemovida.net/historia_del_cine_en_puerto_rico.

———. "Las rutas del cine en el Viejo San Juan: Memoria y planificación." Master's thesis, University of Puerto Rico, 2011.

Berry, Chris. "What Is Transnational Cinema? Thinking from the Chinese Situation." *Transnational Cinemas* 1, no. 2 (2010): 111–127.

Bhabha, Homi K. "DissemiNation: Time, Narrative, and the Margins of the Modern Nation." In *Nation and Narration*, edited by Homi K. Bhabha, 291–322. New York: Routledge, 1990.

Brewster, Ben, and Lea Jacobs. *Theater to Cinema: Stage Pictorialism and the Early Feature Film.* New York: Oxford University Press, 1997.

Briggs, Laura. *Reproducing Empire: Race, Sex, Science and U.S. Imperialism in Puerto Rico.* Berkeley: University of California Press, 2002.

Bruno, Giuliana. *Streetwalking on a Ruined Map: Cultural Theory and the City Films of Elvira Notary*. Princeton, NJ: Princeton University Press, 1993.

Canales, Nemesio. "Querido Mr. Wilson." In *Antología de Nemesio Canales*, edited by Servando Montaña Peláez, 140. San Juan: Editorial de la Universidad de Puerto Rico, 2000.

Capino, José B. "Cinema and the Spectacle of Colonialism: American Documentary Film and (Post) Colonial Philippines, 1898–1989." PhD diss., Northwestern University, 2002.

Chasteen, John Charles. *Born in Blood and Fire: A Concise History of Latin America*. New York: W.W. Norton and Company, 2006.

Cheah, Pheng. *Spectral Nationality: Passages of Freedom from Kant to Postcolonial Literatures of Liberation*. New York: Columbia University Press, 2003.

Cherchi Usai, Paolo. "Italy: Spectacle and Melodrama." In *The Oxford History of World Cinema*, edited by Geoffrey Nowell-Smith. New York: Oxford University Press, 1996.

Christensen, Terry, and Peter J. Haas. *Projecting Politics: Political Messages in American Film*. New York: M.E. Sharpe, 2005.

Cinemovida Entertainment Inc. "Biografías." *Cinemovida*. July 2, 2011. http://www.cinemovida.net/historia_del_cine_en_puerto_rico/biografias.

Crafton, Donald. *The Talkies: American Cinema's Transition to Sound, 1926–1931*. Berkeley: University of California Press, 1999.

Curry, Ramona. "Benjamin Brodsky (1877–1960): The Transpacific American Film Entrepreneur—Part One, Making *A Trip Thru China*." *Journal of American-East Asian Relations* 18, no. 1 (2011): 58–94.

Dahlquist, Marina. "Unhooking the Hookworm: The Rockefeller Foundation and Mediated Health." *Rockefeller Archive Center Research Reports*. Sleepy Hollow, NY: Rockefeller Archive Center, 2012.

Davis, Elmer. *History of the* New York Times *1851–1921*. New York: New York Times, 1921.

de la Vega Alfaro, Eduardo. "Allá en el rancho grande." In *The Cinema of Latin America*, edited by Alberto Elena and Marina Díaz López, 25–34. New York: Columbia University Press, 2003.

Deleuze, Gilles, and Félix Guattari. *A Thousand Plateaus: Capitalism and Schizophrenia*. 1980. Minneapolis: University of Minnesota Press, 1987.

Díaz, Luis Felipe. *La na(rra)ción en la literatura puertorriqueña*. San Juan: Ediciones Huracán, 2008.

Díaz Quiñones, Arcadio. *El arte de bregar*. San Juan: Ediciones Callejón, 2000.

———. Introduction to *Luis Lloréns Torres: Antología, verso y prosa*, by Luis Lloréns Torres. San Juan: Ediciones Huracán, 1996.

———. Preface to *Luis Lloréns Torres: Antología, verso y prosa*, by Luis Lloréns Torres. San Juan: Ediciones Huracán, 1996.

Dietz, James L. *Economic History of Puerto Rico: Institutional Change and Capitalist Development*. Princeton, NJ: Princeton University Press, 1986.

Duany, Jorge. *The Puerto Rican Nation on the Move: Identities on the Island and in the United States*. Chapel Hill: University of North Carolina Press, 2002.

Eckhardt, Joseph P. *The King of the Movies: Film Pioneer Siegmund Lubin*. Cranbury, NJ: Associated University Presses, 1997.

Evered, Kyle. "Fostering Puerto Rico: Representations of Empire and Orphaned Territories during the Spanish-American War." *Historical Geography* 34 (2006): 109–135.

Fahlstedt, Kim. "Marketing Rebellion: The Chinese Revolution Reconsidered." *Film History* 26, no. 1 (2014): 80–107.
Fanon, Frantz. *Black Skin, White Masks.* New York: Grove Press, 1967.
Faust, Ernest Carroll, Charles A. Jones, and William A. Hoffman. "Studies on *Schistosomiasis mansoni* in Puerto Rico." *Puerto Rico Journal of Public Health and Tropical Medicine* 10, no. 2 (December 1934): 132–147.
Fedunkiw, Marianne P. "The Rockefeller Foundation's 1925 *Malaria* Film." Presentation, Quinnipiac/Rockefeller Archive Center Workshop, November 2003.
Fernández Valledor, Roberto. *El mito de Cofresí en la narrativa antillana.* San Juan: Editorial de la Universidad de Puerto Rico, 1978.
Fernós, Antonio. *¡Ser nosotros mismos!: La angustiosa lucha del pueblo puertorriqueño por su soberanía nacional.* San Juan: Editorial de la Universidad de Puerto Rico, 2003.
Flores, Juan. *Insularismo e ideología burguesa.* San Juan: Ediciones Huracán, 1979.
García, Osvaldo. *Fotografías para la historia de Puerto Rico 1844–1952.* San Juan: Editorial de la Universidad de Puerto Rico, 1989.
García Morales, Joaquín "Kino." *Breve historia del cine puertorriqueño.* San Juan: Cine-gráfica, 1984.
———. *Historia del Cine Puertorriqueño (1900–1999): Un siglo de cine en Puerto Rico.* San Juan: Editorial de la Universidad de Puerto Rico, 2000.
———. "Puerto Rico: Towards a National Cinema." *Sargasso* 8 (1992): 70–74.
Goldstein, Alyosha. "The Attributes of Sovereignty: The Cold War, Colonialism, and Community Education in Puerto Rico." In *Imagining Our Americas: Towards a Transnational Frame*, edited by Sandhya Shukla and Heidi Tinsman, 313–337. Durham: Duke University Press, 2007.
Gomery, Douglas. "The Rise of Hollywood." In *The Oxford History of World Cinema*, edited by Geoffrey Nowell-Smith, 43–53. New York: Oxford University Press, 1996.
González, Francisco. "La gran ilusión: la industria de cine en Puerto Rico." In *Dominio de la imagen; hacia una industria de cine en Puerto Rico*, 4–8. San Juan: Librería Editorial Ateneo, 2000.
González, José Luis. *El país de cuatro pisos y otros ensayos.* San Juan: Ediciones Huracán, 1980.
Gott, Richard. *Cuba: A New History.* New Haven, CT: Yale University Press, 2005.
Griffiths, Alison. *Wondrous Difference: Cinema, Anthropology, and Turn-of-the-Century Visual Culture.* New York: Columbia University Press, 2002.
Hall, Stuart. "Cultural Identity and Cinematic Representation," *Framework* 36 (1989): 68–81.
Hidalgo, Dionisio. "Sacrificio de una madre." *Boletín Bibliográfico Español y Extranjero* 1, no. 20–24 (1850): 317.
Higbee, Will, and Song Hwee Lim, "Concepts of Transnational Cinema: Towards a Critical Transnationalism in Film Studies," *Transnational Cinemas* 1, no. 1 (2010): 7–21.
Higson, Andrew. "The Concept of National Cinema," *Screen* 30, no. 4 (1989): 36–47.
———. "The Limiting Imagination of National Cinema." In *Cinema and Nation*, edited by Mette Hjort and Scott MacKenzie, 63–73. London: Routledge, 2000.
Hobsbawm, Eric J. *Nations and Nationalism since 1780: Programme, Myth, Reality.* New York: Cambridge University Press, 1990.
Kanellos, Nicolás. *Hispanic Firsts: 500 Years of Extraordinary Achievements.* New York: Visible Ink Press, 1997.

King, Rob. *The Fun Factory: The Keystone Film Company and the Emergence of Mass Culture*. Berkeley: University of California Press, 2008.

Koszarski, Richard. *An Evening's Entertainment: The Age of the Silent Feature Picture, 1915–1928*. Berkeley: University of California Press, 1994.

———. *Hollywood on the Hudson: Film and Television in New York from Griffith to Sarnoff*. New Brunswick, NJ: Rutgers University Press, 2010.

LaCapra, Dominick. *History and Memory after Auschwitz*. Ithaca, NY: Cornell University Press, 1998.

Lindstrom, J. A. "Where Development Has Just Begun: Nickelodeon Location, Moving Picture Audiences, and Neighborhood Development in Chicago." In *American Cinema's Transitional Era: Audiences, Institutions, Practices*, edited by Charlie Keil and Shelley Stamp, 217–238. Berkeley: University of California Press, 2004.

López, Ana M. "Are All Latins from Manhattan? Hollywood, Ethnography, and Cultural Colonialism." In *Unspeakable Images: Ethnicity and the American Cinema*, edited by Lester D. Friedman, 404–424. Urbana: University of Illinois Press, 1991.

———. "Early Cinema and Modernity in Latin America." *Cinema Journal* 40, no. 1 (2000): 48–78.

López Baralt, Luce, and Mercedes López Baralt. "La crónica del 98 de Esteban López Giménez." In *Un cambio de siglo 1898: España, Cuba, Puerto Rico, Filipinas y Estados Unidos*, edited by José Girón, 325–330. Oviedo: Universidad de Oviedo, 2008.

Maldonado, A. W. *Luis Muñoz Marín: Puerto Rico's Democratic Revolution*. San Juan: Editorial de la Universidad de Puerto Rico, 2006.

Marqués, René. *El puertorriqueño dócil y otros ensayos*. San Juan: Editorial Antillana, 1993.

Marsh, Catherine. "La negociación de la cultura en una nación sin estado: La producción cultural de la División de Educación de la Comunidad del Estado Libre Asociado de Puerto Rico (1948–1968)." PhD diss., University of California, Berkeley, 2001.

Meredith, Martin. *Diamonds, Gold and War: The British, the Boers, and the Making of South Africa*. New York: Public Affairs, 2007.

Merrill, Dennis. *Negotiating Paradise: U.S. Tourism and Empire in Twentieth-Century Latin America*. Chapel Hill: University of North Carolina Press, 2009.

Molina, Luis. "Luis Molina: Un nuevo modelo de cine educativo." In *Dominio de la imagen; hacia una industria de cine en Puerto Rico*, 33–41. San Juan: Librería Editorial Ateneo, 2000.

Montaña Peláez, Servando. Preface to *Antología de Nemesio Canales* by Nemesio Canales. San Juan: Editorial de la Universidad de Puerto Rico, 2000.

Mould, David Harley. *American Newsfilm, 1914–1919: The Unexposed War*. New York: Garland Publishing, 1983.

Musser, Charles. *Before the Nickelodeon: Edwin S. Porter and the Edison Manufacturing Company*. Berkeley: University of California Press, 1991.

———. *The Emergence of Cinema: The American Screen to 1907*. Berkeley: University of California Press, 1990.

Negroni, Héctor Andrés. *Historia militar de Puerto Rico*. Madrid: Sociedad Estatal Quinto Centenario, 1992.

Norman, Wayne. *Negotiating Nationalism: Nation-Building, Federalism, and Secession in the Multinational State*. New York: Oxford University Press, 2006.

Nowell-Smith, Geoffrey. "The Heyday of the Silents." In *The Oxford History of World Cinema*, edited by Geoffrey Nowell-Smith, 192–204. New York: Oxford University Press, 1997.

O'Regan, Tom. *Australian National Cinema*. New York: Routledge, 1996.

Pabón, Carlos. "De Albizu a Madonna: Para armar y desarmar la nacionalidad." *Bordes* 1 (1995): 22–40.

———. *Nación postmortem: Ensayos sobre los tiempos de insoportable ambigüedad*. San Juan: Ediciones Callejón, 2003.

Pedreira, Antonio Salvador. *El periodismo en Puerto Rico*. San Juan: Editorial Edil, 1982.

Perea, Juan E. "Fulfilling Manifest Destiny: Conquest, Race, and the *Insular Cases*." In *Foreign in a Domestic Sense: Puerto Rico, American Expansion, and the Constitution*, edited by Christina Duffy Burnett and Burke Marshall, 140–166. Durham, NC: Duke University Press, 2001.

Picó, Fernando. *Historia General de Puerto Rico*. San Juan: Ediciones Huracán, 1986.

Pike, Fredrick B. *The United States and Latin America: Myths and Stereotypes of Civilization and Nature*. Austin: University of Texas Press, 1992.

Pizzitola, Louis. *Hearst over Hollywood: Power, Passion, and Propaganda in the Movies*. New York: Columbia University Press, 2002.

Ramos Perea, Roberto. *Cinelibre: Historia desconocida y manifiesto por un cine puertorriqueño independiente y libre*. San Juan: Editions Le Provincial, 2008.

Recillas Enecoiz, Luis. "Atisbo al cine mudo en Toluca, 1896–1905 (Primera parte: 1896–1900)." *El ojo que piensa*. Last modified July 1, 2011. http://www.elojoquepiensa.net/elojoquepiensa/index.php/articulos/148#citas.

Ríos Ávila, Rubén. *La raza cómica del sujeto en Puerto Rico*. San Juan: Ediciones Callejón, 2002.

Rivera, Miluka. "Blanca de Castejón." In *Legado puertorriqueño en Hollywood: Famosos y olvidados*, 59–60. Burbank: Kumaras Center for the Arts & Etiquette, 2010.

Rivero Méndez, Ángel. *Crónica de la Guerra Hispanoamericana en Puerto Rico*. Madrid: Sucesores de Rivadeneyra, 1922.

Rockett, Kevin. "History, Politics and Irish Cinema." In *Cinema and Ireland*, edited by Kevin Rockett, Luke Gibbons, and John Hill. New York: Routledge, 1987.

Roosevelt, Theodore. "Puerto Rico: Our Link with Latin America." *Foreign Affairs* 12, no. 2 (1934): 271–280.

Rosario Natal, Carmelo. *Puerto Rico y la crisis de la Guerra Hispanoamericana*. San Juan: Ramallo Brothers Printing, 1975.

Rosen, Philip. "Nation and Anti-Nation: Concepts of National Cinema in the 'New' Media Era." *Diaspora* 5, no. 3 (1996): 375–402.

Ross, Steven J. *Working-Class Hollywood: Silent Film and the Shaping of Class in America*. Princeton, NJ: Princeton University Press, 1998.

Rossell, Deac. *Living Pictures: The Origins of the Movies*. Albany: State University of New York, 1998.

Sáez, José Luis. *Historia de un sueño importado: Ensayos sobre el cine en Santo Domingo*. Santo Domingo: Ediciones Siboney, 1982.

Said, Edward W. *Culture and Imperialism*. New York: Vintage Books, 1994.

Scarano, Francisco A. "The Jíbaro Masquerade and the Subaltern Politics of Creole Identity Formation in Puerto Rico, 1745–1823." *American Historical Review* 101, no. 4 (1996): 1398–1431.

———. *Puerto Rico: Cinco siglos de historia*. México D.F.: McGraw Hill, 2008.

Semonche, John E. *Censoring Sex: A Historical Journey through American Media*. Lanham, MD: Rowman and Littlefield, 2007.

Serna, Laura Isabel. "Exhibition in Mexico during the Early 1920s: Nationalist Discourses and Transnational Capital." In *Convergence Media History*, edited by Janet Staiger and Sabine Hake, 69–80. New York, Routledge, 2009.

———. *Making Cinelandia: American Films and Mexican Film Culture before the Golden Age*. Durham: Duke University Press, 2014.

———. "Translations and Transportation: Toward a Transnational History of the Intertitle." In *Silent Cinema and the Politics of Space*, edited by Jennifer M. Bean, Laura Horak, and Anupama Kapse, 121–145. Bloomington: Indiana University Press, 2014.

Serra Collazo, Soralla. *Explorando la Operación Serenidad*. San Juan: Editorial de la Fundación Luis Muñoz Marín, 2011.

Sistema Universitario Ana G. Méndez. "SUAGM celebra 100 años de cine puertorriqueño." Last modified September 12, 2011. http://www.suagm.edu/news02.asp?cnt_id=701.

Skidmore, Thomas S., and Peter H. Smith. *Modern Latin America*. New York: Oxford University Press, 2005.

Slide, Anthony. *American Racist: The Life and Films of Thomas Dixon*. Lexington: University Press of Kentucky, 2004.

———. *Silent Players: A Biographical and Autobiographical Study of 100 Silent Film Actors and Actresses*. Lexington: University Press of Kentucky, 2002.

Stewart, Jacqueline Najuma. *Migrating to the Movies: Cinema and Black Urban Modernity*. Berkeley: University of California Press, 2005.

Stoler, Ann Laura. "Making Empire Respectable: The Politics of Race and Sexual Morality in Twentieth-Century Colonial Cultures." In *Dangerous Liaisons: Gender, Nation, and Postcolonial Perspectives*, edited by Anne McClintock, Aamir Mufti, and Ella Shohat, 344–373. Minneapolis: University of Minnesota Press, 1997.

Studlar, Gaylyn. "Theda Bara: Orientalism, Sexual Anarchy, and the Jewish Star." In *Flickers of Desire: Movie Stars of the 1910s*, edited by Jennifer M. Bean, 113–136. New Brunswick, NJ: Rutgers University Press, 2011.

Swanson, Philip. "Going Down on Good Neighbors: Imagining América in Hollywood Movies of the 1930s and 1940s (*Flying Down to Rio* and *Down Argentine Way*)." *Bulletin of Latin American Research* 29, no. 1 (2010): 721–784.

Taylor, Deems. *A Pictorial History of the Movies*. New York: Simon and Schuster, 1943.

Torres, José Artemio. "Apaga Musiú: Los primeros pasos de cine puertorriqueño." In *Idilio tropical: La aventura del cine puertorriqueño*, 48–63. San Juan: Banco Popular, 1994.

Trelles Plazaola, Luis. *Ante el lente extranjero: Puerto Rico visto por cineastas de afuera*. San Juan: Editorial de la Universidad de Puerto Rico, 2000.

University of Puerto Rico Museum Exposition. *Irene y Jack Delano en Puerto Rico*. San Juan: Afirmación cultural, 1981.

Uricchio, William. "The First World War and the Crisis in Europe." In *The Oxford History of World Cinema*, edited by Geoffrey Nowell-Smith. New York: Oxford University Press, 1996.

Vallejo de Paredes, Margarita, and Lilia Portalatín Sosa. *Antología literaria dominicana: Teatro*. Santo Domingo: Instituto tecnológico de Santo Domingo, 1981.

Vasey, Ruth. *The World According to Hollywood, 1918–1939*. Madison: University of Wisconsin Press, 1997.

Vega, Bernardo. *Memoir of Bernardo Vega: A Contribution to the History of the Puerto Rican Community in New York*. New York: Monthly Review Press, 1984.
Vincendeau, Ginette. "Hollywood Babel: The Coming of Sound and the Multiple Language Version." In *The Classical Hollywood Reader*, edited by Stephen Neale, 137–146. New York: Routledge, 2012.
Waldman, Harry. *Hollywood and the Foreign Touch*. Lanham, MD: Scarecrow Press, 1996.
Warzeski, Jeanne-Maris. "Mapping the Unknown: Gendered Spaces and the Oriental Other in Travelogues of Egypt by U.S. Women, 1854–1914." *History and Anthropology* 13, no. 4 (2002): 301–317.
Williams, Linda. "Melodrama Revised." In *Refiguring American Film Genres: History and Theory*, edited by Nick Browne, 42–88. Berkeley: University of California Press, 1998.
Zurinaga, Marcos. "Marcos Zurinaga: Cine de proyección internacional." In *Dominio de la imagen; hacia una industria de cine en Puerto Rico*, 25–31. San Juan: Librería Editorial Ateneo, 2000.

Articles in Newspapers and Trade Journals, and Other Primary Sources

ANONYMOUS WORKS

"Acquires Major Product for Porto Rico Circuit." *Film Daily*. August 15, 1935, 2.
Acts and Resolutions of the Fourth and Fifth Special Sessions of the Twelfth Legislature of Puerto Rico and of the First Regular Session of the Thirteenth Legislature of Puerto Rico. San Juan: Bureau of Supplies, Printing and Transportation, 1933.
"Amor Tropical." *El mundo* (San Juan). October 25, 1921, 5.
"Amor Tropical." *El mundo* (San Juan). October 27, 1921, 3.
"Amor Tropical." *La correspondencia* (San Juan). October 25, 1921, 8.
"Anoche hizo su primera exhibición." *La correspondencia* (San Juan). May 10, 1897, 2.
"Blackton Again Heads Trade Board." *Moving Picture World*. February 26, 1916, 1275.
"Bombay Amusements." *Times of India*. December 23, 1922, 23.
"Bou v. Colorado." *Porto Rico Reports Volume 24: Cases Adjudge in the Supreme Court of Porto Rico from May 30, 1916 to March 15, 1917*. San Juan: Bureau of Supplies, Printing and Transportation, 1917.
"Brunet Promises Broader Pathé Aims." *Motion Picture News*. November 22, 1919, 3724.
"Calendar of Current Releases." *Variety*. November 6, 1934, 38.
"Calendar of Current Releases." *Variety*. September 25, 1935, 37.
"Cataño la Meca de los curiosos." *El mundo* (San Juan). October 24, 1925, 16.
"Cine Ideal." *La democracia* (San Juan). July 25, 1916, 8.
"Cine 'Las Tres Banderas.'" *Gráfico*. April 5, 1913.
"Cine 'Las Tres Banderas.'" *Gráfico*. May 17, 1913.
"Cine Puerto Rico." *La correspondencia* (San Juan). November 18, 1922, 1.
"Cine Puerto Rico." *La democracia* (San Juan). November 18, 1922, 1.
"Cinematógrafo." *Boletín Mercantil* (San Juan, Puerto Rico). July 5, 1901, 3.
"Cinematógrafo Lumier." *Boletín Mercantil*. March 4, 1898, 3.
"Cinematógrafo Lumier." *Boletín Mercantil*. March 6, 1898, 3.
"Clements on Dicker for Roulien, Par Release." *Variety*. March 23, 1936, 2.
"Cobian Planning New Cuban Theater Chain." *Film Daily*. May 16, 1946, 1.
"Cobian Signs Mexican Stars." *Film Daily*. January 27, 1939, 13.

"Cobian to Make Four 'A's' in Spanish for 20th-Fox." *Film Daily*. August 12, 1938, 2.
"Cobian to Make Spanish Pix for Para. on Coast." *Film Daily*. April 21, 1938, 2.
"Cobian to Start His Second for 20th-Fox in Three Weeks." *Film Daily*. March 9, 1939, 5.
"Cobian Will Produce for Spanish-Speaking Markets." *Film Daily*. March 4, 1938, 1–2.
"Cobian's Spanish Plans." *Film Daily*. January 13, 1938, 3.
"Cofresí, el pirata del Caribe." *Cine Mundial*. June 1921, 433.
"Coming to the Theaters." *Washington Post*. July 5, 1917, 9.
"Courtship in Porto Rico." *Washington Post*. August 28, 1899, 7.
"De Puerto Rico." *Cine Mundial*. May 1917, 245.
"Dead on Stage." *Boston Daily Globe*. May 17, 1901, 1.
"E Brunel." *New York Times*. Mar 2, 1919, 38.
"Edward A. MacManus Makes Industrial Film." *Printers' Ink*. April 3, 1919, 170.
"El aparato." *La democracia* (Ponce). August 7, 1897, 3.
"El arte cinematográfico en Puerto Rico." *Puerto Rico Ilustrado*. June 1, 1912.
"El arte de la cinematografía en Puerto Rico." *Gráfico*. August 9, 1913, 21.
"El cine en el gobierno." *Cinema*. January 21, 1923, 1.
"El cine Versalles." *La correspondencia*. May 30 1912, 8.
"El cinematógrafo." *Boletín Mercantil*. May 12, 1897, 3.
"El cinematógrafo." *Boletín Mercantil*. March 9, 1898, 4.
"El cinematógrafo de Payret." *Diario de la Marina* (Habana, Cuba). January 29, 1900, 4.
"El cinematógrafo Vargas." *Boletín Mercantil*. January 23, 1906, 1.
"El estudio cinematográfico se abrirá en breve." *El mundo* (San Juan). September 4, 1920, 1.
"El hijo del desierto." Advertisement, *El mundo* (San Juan). January 20, 1923, 9.
"El hijo del desierto." Advertisement, *La democracia* (San Juan). January 18, 1923, 8.
"El hijo del desierto." *Cinema* (San Juan). January 21, 1923.
"El hijo del desierto." *El mundo* (San Juan). January 20, 1923.
"El hijo del desierto." *La democracia* (San Juan). January 18, 1923, 8.
"Espectáculos." *El mundo* (San Juan). September 6, 1919.
"Espectáculos." *El mundo* (San Juan). June 26, 1935, 4.
"Éxito de la cinematografía." *La democracia* (San Juan). September 25, 1916, 8.
"Ex-king Kleagle of Klan in Maine Dead." *Boston Daily Globe*. March 15, 1926, A3.
"Farnsworth on Panama." *Washington Post*. January 28, 1911, 3.
"Farnsworth Travel Talks." *Washington Times*. January 8, 1911, 9.
"Farnsworth's Lectures." *New York Tribune*. March 5, 1911, C6.
"F. E. Farnsworth, Ex-Kleagle, Dies." *Boston Daily Globe*. March. 16, 1926, 11.
"Fighting the Porto Rican Microbe of Laziness." *Washington Times*. August 7, 1904, 7.
"The Foreign Service." *New York Times*. March 31, 1935, N10.
"Forty Thousand Babies Die Daily." *El Paso Herald*. September 25, 1912, 7.
"Four New Fox Films are Now Announced." *Baltimore Sun*. August 11, 1918, CA11.
"Fox Scoops Newsreels on Hurricane Pictures." *Exhibitors Daily Review*. September 19, 1928, 2.
"Frank Z. Clemente." In *1940–41 International Motion Picture Almanac*, edited by Terry Ramsaye and Ernest A. Rovelstad, 110. New York: Quigley Publishing Company, 1941.
"Frank Z. Clemente." Advertisement. In *The 1936 Film Daily Yearbook*, edited by Jack Alicoate, 232. New York: The Film Daily, 1936.
"Free Exhibition of War Pictures." *Trenton State Gazette*. December 15, 1898, 5.

"Fresh from the Busy Film Mart." *Los Angeles Times*. December 20, 1925, I3.
"Gabriel Tejel." *Juan Bobo*. March 3, 1917, 25.
"Gilda Departs." *Los Angeles Times*. October 11, 1925, 27.
"Gilda Gray Film Feature at Palace." *Washington Post*. November 14, 1926, F1.
"Heart and Soul." *Variety*. May 25, 1917, 22.
"Heat in Porto Rico Nearly Ruins Films for Photoplay." *Boston Daily Globe*. July 22, 1923, 54.
"Hoy llegará el productor portorriqueño Ramos Cobián." *El mundo* (San Juan). September 4, 1939, 6.
"In the Wake of the Camera." *Los Angeles Times*. November 15, 1925, J4.
"Industria que beneficiará grandemente a Puerto Rico." *El mundo* (San Juan). October 11, 1919, 3.
"Inside Stuff- Pictures." *Variety*. February 15, 1950, 16. "King Kleagle of Maine Quits." *Boston Daily Globe*. April 25, 1924, 14.
"La casa 'Pathé' ha hecho proposiciones a la 'Photoplays.'" *El mundo* (San Juan). October 28, 1921, 6.
"La empresa del cine." *La correspondencia*. May 29, 1912.
"La industria del cine en Puerto Rico." *Cinema*. February 25, 1923, 1–2.
"La nueva producción de Ramos Cobián estrenará aquí." *El mundo* (San Juan). September 2, 1939, 7.
"La Porto Rico Photoplays, Inc." *Cine Mundial*. January 1921, 8.
"La premier de 'Mis dos amores' en el teatro Paramount." *El mundo* (San Juan). October 6, 1938, 6.
"La semana." *Juan Bobo*. December 16, 1916.
"Las tres banderas." *La correspondencia*. May 25, 1912.
"Las tres banderas." *La correspondencia*. May 28, 1912.
"Last Night's Openings at Local Theaters." *Washington Post*. February 6, 1923, 9.
"Lazy Bug Gets Porto Ricans." *Detroit Free Press*. March 7, 1920, C5.
"Learn Photography." *New York Times*. October 10, 1915, 113.
"Letter List." *Mexican Herald* (Mexico City). February 12, 1896, 7.
"The Liar." *Variety*. September 13, 1918, 44.
"Los artistas cinematográficos que llegaron ayer en el 'Puerto Rico' a filmar una película." *La correspondencia* (San Juan). October 14, 1925, 2.
"Los cuadros que exhibió anoche." *La correspondencia* (San Juan). May 14, 1897, 3.
"Los hijos mandan." *El heraldo de Brownsville* (Texas). November 3, 1939, 2.
"Marines in Haiti in Film." *New York Times*. April 26, 1916, 11.
"May Allison Comes to the America in Latest Film Play." *Colorado Springs Gazette*. December 31, 1922, 31.
"Mis dos amores." *Mensajero Paramount*. July 1938, 9.
"Mis dos amores." *Puerto Rico ilustrado*. October 8, 1938, 49.
"'Mis dos amores' se estrena hoy en el teatro Paramount." *El mundo* (San Juan). October 4, 1938, 6.
"Monte Carlo y Real." *La correspondencia* (San Juan). November 7, 1922.
"New Export Firm Will Produce in Puerto Rico." *Billboard*. March 27, 1954, 7.
"New Theda Bara Drama Four Days at Strand." *Atlanta Constitution*. May 20, 1917, C6.
"The New York Theater." *New York Daily Tribune*. July 12, 1854, 5.
"Northwestern District." *Baltimore Sun*. January 21, 1923, MA10.
"Of Local Origin." *New York Times*. January 14, 1938, 20.

"Para esta noche." *La correspondencia*. May 9, 1897, 3.
"Paramount Signs Cobian." *Motion Picture Daily*. April 21, 1938, 7.
"Película cómica." *Juan Bobo*. March 3, 1917, 27.
"Photography That Is Perilous." *Atlanta Constitution*. August 13, 1899, A4.
"Photoplays." *Indianapolis Star*. November 5, 1917, 8.
"Por esos mundos." *La correspondencia* (Madrid). July 2, 1921, 3.
"Por la hembra y por el gallo." *La correspondencia*. September 20, 1916, 7.
"Porto Rican Films." *Film Daily*. April 15, 1922, 1
"Porto Rico Bidding." *Variety*. July 12, 1923, 22.
"Porto Rico Future Movie Studio Home." *Bisbee Daily Review* (Ariz.). June 1, 1919, 6.
"Porto Rico Is Ideal for Movie Studios." *Washington Herald*. June 1, 1919, 7.
"Puerto Rico ofrece un gran campo para el cinematógrafo." *El mundo* (San Juan). September 8, 1919, 3.
"Quince portorriqueñas trabajaran con Gilda Gray." *El mundo* (San Juan). October 13, 1925, 2.
"R. Cobian to Coast Today to Start Spanish Picture." *Film Daily*. April 25, 1938, 2.
"Ramos Cobian." In *The 1929 Film Daily Yearbook*, edited by Jack Alicoate, 1040. New York: The Film Daily, 1929.
"Rare Art Treasure Used in Film Made in Porto Rico." *Washington Post*. February 4, 1923, 60.
"Rasgo jíbaro." *Juan Bobo*. March 3, 1917, 25.
"Reviews of the New Films: Foreign." *Film Daily*. October 16, 1934, 9.
"Rialto." *La Correspondencia* (San Juan). January 27, 1923, 1.
"Romance Tropical." In *The 1935 Film Daily Yearbook of Motion Pictures*, edited by Jack Alicoate, 185. New York: The Film Daily, 1935.
"Romance Tropical at Campoamor." *Film Daily*. October 12, 1934, 2.
"Roulien to Aid Spanish Revival." *Los Angeles Times*. March 19, 1936, 11.
"Ruth Clifford Demanda." *Cine mundo*. August 1921, 572.
"Sails Columbus Route." *New York Times*. August 4, 1930, 4.
"San Juan y la isla." *La democracia* (San Juan). May 28, 1912, 1.
"Shadows on the Screen." *New York Tribune*. April 23, 1922, 4.
"Sheiks Again Busy in 'Tents of Allah.'" *Los Angeles Times*. April 3, 1923, II11.
"Tells of Canal Zone." *Boston Daily Globe*. February 18, 1911, 4.
"'Tents of Allah' Made in Tropics." *Los Angeles Times*. March 29, 1923, I17.
"Theater Man Candidate." *Film Daily*. September 11, 1936, 14.
"Trees Rain Cocoanuts." *Washington Post*. November 14, 1926, F5.
"Tropical Love." *Bisbee Daily Review* (Ariz.). July 23, 1922, 6.
"Tropical Love." *Coconino Sun* (Ariz.). January 13, 1922, 2.
"Tropical Love." *Pullman Herald* (Wash. State). March 24, 1922, 2.
"Tropical Love at the Elko Theater Saturday." *Bemidji Daily Pioneer* (Minn.). September 8, 1922, 4.
"20-Fox Latin-Amer, Expansion Policy." *Film Daily*. April 20, 1939, 1 and 6.
"Un empresario inglés." *La democracia* (Ponce). August 6, 1897, 3.
"Un gran acontecimiento." *La correspondencia* (San Juan). December 8, 1916, 2.
"Un grupo de notables artistas de la pantalla se encuentra aquí para hacer una admirable producción cinematográfica." *La democracia* (San Juan). October 14, 1925, 1.
"Uncle Sam Planning Movie Campaign for Recruiting Marines." *Salt Lake Telegram*. August 26, 1916, 9.

"Virginia Pearson Tonight." *Bemidji Daily Pioneer* (Minn.). August 24, 1918, 3.
"Willing Slave to the Men Are Our Puerto Rican Sisters." *Cincinnati Enquirer*. August 13, 1899, 25.

AUTHORED WORKS

Amadeo, Jesús M. "La cinematografía en Puerto Rico, el patriotismo y el dólar: Asunto de dignidad." *El mundo* (San Juan). October 10, 1919, 10.
Amencio, Lys. "Lloréns Torres y Paloma del monte." *Juan Bobo*. February 10, 1917, 14.
———. "Notas cinematográficas." *Juan Bobo*. February 24, 1917, 29.
Arreche, Cándido. "Mis dos amores." *El mundo* (San Juan). October 1, 1938, 6.
Asenjo, Conrado. *Quién es quién en Puerto Rico*. 2nd ed. San Juan: Real Hermanos, 1936.
Bermejo, Fernando. "Juan Emilio Viguié." *El mundo* (San Juan). August 16, 1935, 4, 10.
Blanco, Mary Louise. "Cobian Out of Cuban Circuit." *Film Daily*. November 5, 1945, 1.
Borgia, César. "El secretario y los cines." *Juan Bobo*. April 1, 1916.
Brown, Harry D. "The Importance of the Studio Electrician." *The American Cinematographer*. August 1922. 7.
Carpenter, Frank G. "Pretty Porto Girls." *St. Paul Globe* (Minn.). July 30, 1899, 24.
Carreras, Carlos. "Una película portorriqueña, Romance Tropical." *El mundo* (San Juan). March 14, 1935, 4.
Casiano, Tello. "¡Pan pan . . . Vino vino!" *El curioso* (Brooklyn). March 16, 1935, 2.
Cine Luna. Advertisement. *La democracia* (San Juan). August 24, 1916, 8.
———. Advertisement. *La democracia* (San Juan). December 7, 1916, 8.
Cine Puerto Rico. Advertisement. *Gráfico* (San Juan). July 14, 1912.
Cinematógrafo Hervet. Advertisement. *Boletín Mercantil*. July 5, 1901, 1.
Coll, Edna. "Los hijos mandan." *Puerto Rico ilustrado.* September 2, 1939, 11 and 56.
Colorado, Rafael. "Nostalgia . . . de tiempos viejos." *El Mundo* (San Juan). February 21, 1959, SS2.
Colorado, Rafael Jr. "Impresiones." *Gráfico*. September 20, 1913.
Crane, Stephen. "Burial at Ponce." *Boston Daily Globe*. August 15, 1898, 3.
Cronista. "Hoy llegará el productor portorriqueño Ramos Cobián." *El mundo* (San Juan). September 4, 1939, 6.
Danilo, Conde. "La 'premier' de 'Mis dos amores' constituyó un acontecimiento social." *La correspondencia* (San Juan). October 8, 1938, 3.
———. "La premier de Mis dos amores en el Paramount." *La democracia* (San Juan). October 8, 1938, 6.
———. "La premier de 'Mis dos amores' en el teatro Paramount." *El mundo* (San Juan). October 6, 1938, 6.
de la Torre Muñiz, José. "De Puerto Rico." *Cine Mundial*. November, 1916, 477.
de Lázaro, Obdulia C. "Amor Tropical." *La correspondencia* (San Juan). October 24, 1921, 1.
Don Panchito. "La estética en el cine." *Juan Bobo*. July 8, 1916, 5.
Empresa E. Hervet. Advertisement. *Estado de São Paulo* (Brazil). April 11, 1905, 4.
Escalante, Emilio. "La película: Los hijos mandan." *La prensa* (San Antonio). April 9, 1939, 11.
Eureka. Advertisement. *El mundo*. April 23, 1935, 5.
Fox News. Advertisement. *Exhibitors Daily Review*. September 19, 1928. 4.
Fox-Delicias (Ponce). Advertisement. *El mundo* (San Juan). April 4, 1935, 4.

Gran establecimiento fotográfico de Rafael Colorado. Advertisement. *Gráfico*. November 10, 1912.
Gregory, Carl Louis. "Camera Study in the Movies." *New York Times*. October 24, 1926, X6.
Haggar, J. Ridder. *Jess*. N.P: n.p., 1887. *Project Gutenberg*. June 10, 2013. http://www.gutenberg.org/files/5898/5898-h/5898-h.htm.
Hall, Mordaunt. "Farce-Comedy Serves as Antidote to Adroitly Directed Melodrama." *New York Times*. May 23, 1926, X2.
Hogg, B. Yorkton. "General Wood's Future." *New York Tribune*. July 11, 1920, II.8.
Hopper, Hedda. "Hedda Hopper's Hollywood." *Los Angeles Times*. August 17, 1938, 12.
H.T.S. "Film from Puerto Rico." *New York Times*. October 15, 1934, 20.
Hugo. "Cine Ideal." *La correspondencia*. July 28, 1916, 8.
Hunt, William H. *Third Annual Report of the Governor of Porto Rico*. Washington, DC: Government Printing Office, 1903.
J. B. Vandegrift and Company. *Handbook of the United States Tariff Containing the Tariff Act of 1909*. New York: J. B. Vandegrift and Company, 1909.
Johnston, Julanne. "Flashes." *Los Angeles Times*. December 5, 1925, 7.
Kameneff, Igor. "Los últimos estrenos: *Romance tropical*." *El mundo* (San Juan). March 19, 1935, 4.
L. M. Martin's Cineograph. Advertisement. *Omaha World Herald*. April 14, 1900, 3.
Leffingwell, W. H. *Making the Office Pay*. New York: A. W. Shaw Company, 1918.
M. Roman. Advertisement. *Juan Bobo*. July 1, 1916, 15.
McLeary, James H. *First Annual Register of Porto Rico*. San Juan: Press of the San Juan News, 1901.
Navarro, Gabriel. "Habla Tito Guizar sobre las películas en español que se hacen en Hollywood." *La prensa* (San Antonio). July 31, 1938, 2.
———. "La embajada artística de México en Hollywood." *La prensa* (San Antonio). January 29, 1939, 9.
———. "Mal principio lleva la película *Mis dos amores*, con Tito Guizar de estrella." *La prensa* (San Antonio). June 19, 1938, 10.
New York State Archives. *Los hijos mandan* Motion Picture Case File. File-Box# 37430-733.
———. *Mis dos amores* Motion Picture Case File. File-Box # 39915-851.
———. *Picturesque Porto Rico* Motion Picture Case File. File-Box# 11266-2742.
———. *Romance Tropical* Motion Picture Case File. File-Box#: 28117-324.
———. *The Tent of Allah* Motion Picture Case File. File-Box# 15788-2816.
———. *Tropical Love* Motion Picture Case File. File-Box# 16897-2839.
Ordóñez, María E. "La ciudad y los cines." *Cinema*. January 7, 1923, 1.
Ortiz Jiménez, Juan. "40 años de cinematografía puertorriqueña: Primera Parte." *Puerto Rico ilustrado*. February 16, 1952, 38–51.
———. "40 años de cinematografía puertorriqueña: Segunda Parte." *Puerto Rico ilustrado*. February 23, 1952, 34–38.
Paramount. Advertisement. *El mundo* (San Juan). March 15, 1935, 4
Pego. "Mis dos amores." *Cine mundial*. October 1938, 512.
Puerto Rico Supreme Court case *Miriam J. Ramírez de Ferrer v. Juan Mari Brás* (1997) ratified in *Miriam J. Ramírez de Ferrer v. Juan Mari Brás II* (2006).
Ramos Cobián, Rafael. "Nosotros no somos monopolizadores del negocio." *El mundo*. March 15, 1935, 5.

Rex (Cataño). Advertisement. *El mundo*. March 27, 1935, 5.
Rialto Theater. Advertisement. *El mundo*. March 20, 1935, 4.
S. Lubin Manufacturing Optician. Advertisement. *New York Clipper*. January 21, 1899, 802.
Sánchez Longo, Luis Pío. Phone interview by author. Providence, December 4, 2012.
Scheuer, Philip K. "Producers Turning to Latin Countries." *Los Angeles Times*. August 21, 1938, C3.
Sherwood, R. E. "Aloma of the South Seas." *Life*. June 3, 1926, 26.
———. "The Silent Drama." *Life*. June 3, 1926, 26.
Simpler. Advertisement. *Gráfico*. September 6, 1913.
S.I.S. "El cinema portorriqueño: Lo que dice el 'Times' de 'Romance Tropical.'" *El mundo* (San Juan). March 23, 1935, 6.Teatro Oliver (Arecibo). Advertisement. *El mundo* (San Juan). April 3, 1935, 4.
The Superior Board of Health. *Report of the Military Governor of Porto Rico from October 18, 1898, to April 30, 1900*. Washington, DC: Government Printing Office, 1901.
Teatro Paramount. Advertisement. *El mundo* (San Juan). September 4, 1939, 6.
Tinée, Mae. "Where Rodolf Loses Some of His Laurels." *Chicago Daily Tribune*. July 14, 1923, 19.
Tropical Film Company. Advertisement. *Juan Bobo*. December 23, 1916, 28.
———. Advertisement. *Juan Bobo*. February 10, 1917.
United States Democratic Party. *Official Report of the Proceedings of the Democratic National Convention, Chicago, Illinois August 13 through August 17, 1956*. Boston: Beacon Press, 1956.
U.S. Marine Corps. "'Reel' Recruiting." *Recruiter's Bulletin*. November, 1916, 12.
Variedades (Bayamón). Advertisement. *El mundo* (San Juan). May 4, 1935, 4.
Wear. "Mis dos amores." *Variety*. August 17, 1938, 23.

Index

About the Author

NAIDA GARCÍA-CRESPO is an assistant professor of English at the U.S. Naval Academy.